I0104363

THE PLAGUE OF MODELS

How Computer Modeling Corrupted Environmental, Health, and Safety Regulations

THE PLAGUE OF MODELS

How Computer Modeling Corrupted Environmental, Health, and Safety Regulations

by

Kenneth P. Green, D.Env.

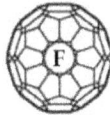

Fullerene Publishing Inc.

The Plague of Models: How Computer Modeling Corrupted Environmental, Health, and Safety Regulations
by Kenneth P. Green

Copyright © 2023 Fullerene Publishing Inc. All rights reserved.

No part of this publication may be reproduced, stored in a retrieval system or transmitted in any form or by any means, without the prior written permission of the publisher, nor to be otherwise circulated in any form of binding or cover other than that in which it is published and without a similar condition being imposed on the subsequent owner.

ISBN 978-1-7780413-0-3 (print version)
ISBN 978-1-7780413-1-0 (electronic version)

1 2 3 4 5 6 7 8 9 10

The author of this book has worked independently, and the opinions expressed are therefore their own and do not necessarily reflect the opinions of Fullerene Publishing Inc. Any errors or omissions and the accuracy and completeness of this book remain the responsibility of the author.

Fullerene Publishing Inc.
308 1st Avenue SE, Langdon, Alberta, Canada T0J 1X1.
Email: administration@fullerenepublishing.ca

Dedication

I dedicate this book to my wife of more than 25 years, Patricia Green, who has been my best friend, my steadfast companion, my most ardent (and unswerving) supporter, and my fellow adventurer as we've moved around North America chasing the guiding-star of my career in public policy research. I couldn't have written this book, nor done much that went before, without her by my side.

Acknowledgements

I have many people to acknowledge for their assistance and support leading up to the production of this book, and my development of the ideas within. A very partial list would include:

- My mother who gifted me with many books in my childhood, and always encouraged me to read at the highest levels, and to the broadest extent I could. 'Twas she that gave me Ayn Rand's classic *Atlas Shrugged* to read at the tender age of 14, and Carl Sagan's Pulitzer prize-winning *Dragons of Eden* to read when I was 16.

- The many excellent teachers I had, from kindergarten through my doctoral studies, a fair number of whom were "old school" educators devoted first and foremost to imparting objective knowledge, and teaching how to think, without trying to tell me what to think.

- My employers and mentors in the Land of Think Tanks. In the US, I was supported by great folks at the Reason Foundation, in California, the American Enterprise Institute in Washington DC, The Georgia Public Policy Foundation, the Texas Public Policy Foundation, and the Pacific Research Institute. In Canada, I was supported and welcomed into my second nationality by the good people at the Fraser Institute, and the Frontier Centre for Public Policy Research. I won't name (or shame!) them individually, but I am grateful to them all, and they know who they are. I would particularly like to call out the Frontier Centre and the Pacific Research Institute for their support in the development and production of this book. Their help was indispensable, and it came at a critical time in my life. I am deeply thankful.

- Finally, I need to thank (yes, by name) a few of my career mentors who, gently (or *ungently* when needed), helped me navigate the strange pathway I chose in a career of public policy research. Thus, I am grateful to Martin Wachs, my doctoral advisor who led me to the think-tank world; Robert Poole and Patricia "Lynn" Scarlett at Reason Foundation; Christopher DeMuth and Steven F. Hayward at the American Enterprise Institute; and my Canadian mentors at the Fraser Institute and the staff of Frontier Center.

My deepest thanks to them all.

It goes without saying however, that all errors of fact, judgement, grammar, logic, common sense, or good taste that may have found their way onto the pages of this book are solely, 100 per cent the responsibility of the author.

Forward

Back in the good old days, liars lied with statistics. Damn liars lied with statistics. Don't get me started about statisticians, and similarly for many, many bureaucrats, public officials, academics, journalists, public policy analysts, and indeed virtually anyone with an axe to grind. Ditto for Uncle Bob explaining why his empty lot overgrown with weeds three feet high does not differ as a matter of statistical significance from the manicured lawns across the street, in particular if one uses a statistical test with a "confidence interval" sufficiently generous.

OK, maybe they didn't "lie"—that is such a distasteful word—as much as find creative ways to use statistics—data—in support of their preferred conclusions. Well, fortunate readers of this wonderful book, that was then. And this is now: We've come a long way, baby, in that there no longer is any need to use actual data, however creatively and mendaciously, in pursuit of support for preconceived conclusions.

Instead, welcome to modern times, in which models have replaced data. For those seeking a specific conclusion, a model is a marvel. It necessarily incorporates assumptions about what variables are relevant, which means that variables inconsistent with the preferred narrative tend to be (not so) curiously absent. And then once the preferred variables are chosen, the values of those variables must be incorporated, and to say that the values can be manipulated is one of those realities for which the phrase "vast understatement" is profoundly inadequate.

You believe that I am exaggerating for effect? Uh, no, as a brief review of, say, the climate "debate" reveals. The mainstream climate narrative, ostensibly "scientific" in the most rigorous sense, is nothing of the kind, as Ken Green explains beautifully; but allow me to add a few words.

The actual data on climate phenomena do not support the "crisis" narrative ubiquitous in the public discussion. There is little trend in the number of "hot" days for 1895–2017, and most such days occurred before 1960. The U.S. Climate Reference Network—137 meticulously maintained temperature stations across America—shows no trend over the available 2005–2020 reporting period. An official reconstruction of global temperatures over the past one million years, from ice sheet formations, shows nothing unusual about the current period.

Since satellite measurements began in 1992, global sea level has been increasing at about 3.3 mm per year, or about thirteen inches over a century. A "crisis" that is not. The arctic sea ice has been declining, while the Antarctic Sea ice has been stable or growing. U.S. tornado activity shows a slight downward trend since 1954. The number and intensity of tropical cyclones shows no trend since satellite measurements began in the early 1970s. The number of U.S. wildfires shows no trend since 1985, and global acreage burned has declined over past decades. The Palmer Drought Severity index shows no trend since 1895, and there has been no global change in drought conditions in 120 years or more. U.S. flooding over the past century is uncorrelated with greenhouse gas concentrations. The data do not support assertions about the dire impacts of declining pH levels in the oceans.

And so on and so forth. What is a climate alarmist to do? After all, foundation grants, publication in the peer-reviewed journals, promotions, paid junkets to five-star resorts, and invitations to all the right cocktail parties are on the line.

Not to worry. We'll ignore the data and use models to predict a climate problem emergency crisis catastrophe existential threat. The models have been created by the smartest people in the world! The models are the most sophisticated ever invented! And they say that because of fossil fuels and modern living, atmospheric temperatures must have increased by 0.44 degrees Celsius per decade since 1979. And if we fail to do take radical action, worsening climate trends will wreak havoc no later than 2000 2005 2010 2015 2020 2025 sometime soon. Just you wait!

Alas, the actual data from the satellites show temperature increases of 0.17 degrees Celsius since 1979. Oops. And so, the climate alarmists have been reduced to arguing—no, I am not kidding—that their models are correct, and the data are wrong. Wow!

Every silver lining has its cloud, and one subtle effect of the huge increase in computing power has been a proportionate decline in the need for many analysts to engage in actual thinking. When computations had to be done by hand, or when computing power was far more primitive, analysts were forced to think their models through—the variables and their values— because running the models required enormous time and effort. Now that only a few keystrokes are needed, no such care is needed. If the model spits out nonsense, no problem! We'll change a few assumptions and see what pops out.

Combine that with an imperative to derive conclusions favored politically, and it is not difficult to see that the world of modeling has become a plague, as Ken Green puts it so aptly. This book is destined to become a classic, and need I remind anyone that it is never too early to begin planning for the holiday gift-giving season? Read it—Learn it—Live it. And don't let your kids grow up to be modelers.

Benjamin Zycher

*Benjamin Zycher is a senior fellow at the American Enterprise Institute. He is a former Intelligence Associate in the Office of Economic Analysis, Bureau of Intelligence and Research, US Department of State; a former senior fellow at the Manhattan Institute; a former senior economist at the RAND Corporation; a former adjunct professor of economics at the University of California, Los Angeles; and a former senior economist at the Jet Propulsion Laboratory, California Institute of Technology. He served as a senior staff economist for the President's Council of Economic Advisers, with responsibility for energy and environmental policy issues.

Table of Contents

1

Plague? What Plague?

Welcome fearless reader! I am honored that you'd devote some of your scarce and all-too-limited time to reading these humble musings! I hope, that after the nightmare years of 2020-2022, many people will find the thesis of this book conforms to their own personal experiences, of having their lives, livelihood, health, and home lives whipsawed half to death based on speculative computer models taken by policymakers as the veritable Word of God. Or, in modern parlance, The Science!

As the title suggests, this book is about a plague that has infected and corrupted the world's largest, most prosperous, most technologically advanced, most liberal democracies, leading to a massive expansion (and I would say corruption) of the regulatory state, especially in areas of environment, health, and safety (EHS).

The plague of models is not a biological plague, though it certainly involves biological plagues. It is not viral, bacterial, fungal, protozoal, parasitic, nor prionic. It is not COVID-19, and it wasn't Polio, or Tuberculosis, Ebola, Herpes, Mononucleosis, E. coli, or Salmonella, Measles, Mad Cow Disease (BSE), or any of those very real, very observable, and often life-threatening diseases. Though, as we will explore, the plague of models has indeed infected and tainted the public policies intended to manage these problems.

Nor is the plague of models a plague of space aliens, illegal aliens, Critical Race Theory, high-fashion models, low-fashion models, or horribly bad direct-to-Streaming movies, though, the latter category is somewhat related.

No, this is a plague that strikes fear in the hearts of men[1], inducing panic: literally! A plague of abstract, computerized models has corrupted

---

[1] Pronoun alert: If you're looking for some pattern in how I use pronouns for males, females, persons, or whatever, you're unlikely to find one. Personally, I find the straightjacket of style guides with regard to such things rather uncomfortable,

how we, as humans, distinguish large threats from small threats; distinguish true threats from false threats; differentiate acute threats from chronic threats, perceive imminent threats versus distal threats, and so on. This is a plague that leads people to *confuse actual, tangible, measurable, empirical reality with imaginary computer constructs.*

The plague of models drives policymakers and the voting public to bounce from one proclaimed threat to another, like a frenetically bouncing pachinko ball in an infinitely tall pachinko-machine from hell, issuing a clanging, jingling, bell ringing audiovisual fountain of regulations that have tied Western societies into giant red-tape sticky-balls of nearly omnipresent regulations.

"But wait," you may be thinking, "that's a bit extreme. Don't we need regulations?" And "don't we need computer models to understand complicated things?" The answer to both questions is "yes." Yes, a functioning society based on certain principles such as the rights to life, liberty, property, and the pursuit of happiness definitely needs some governance, and some regulation to ensure those principles are preserved and protected. But that required quantity of regulation is neither zero, nor is it infinite.

To shamelessly steal an analogy, I picked up in years of think-tankery with some very smart people: we absolutely need both computer models and regulations. Both are vital to our society and its social contract. But we need them in much the way we need fire. Fire, and the use of fire is also vital to our society and our lives. Especially, in my opinion, barbecue, without which life is meaningless. But fire is only helpful when it's tightly controlled and applied in a careful and controlled way so that it does not spill out of the hearth or off the stovetop and spread to the carpet and the drapes, at which point, it is the essence of *not good*." Regulations and the models used to shape them are like fire: necessary, but they must be rigidly controlled, and their dangers must be clearly understood.

But, right off the bat, as Richard Nixon might have said (and Rich Little most certainly did), "I want to make one thing perfectly clear." Well, several things.

---

and I'd prefer not to write (or think!) while wrapped in one. However, if you are offended by such things, I suggest you implement an "auto-replace" in your biological reading-software that substitutes the term of your choice on the fly to replace pronouns as you wish. I do that all the time with regard to the typos and grammatical horrors that are now routinely found in our popular media, so I'm sure that you've conditioned yourself to do so as well!

1.1   This Is Not about Denial, Which Is Not a River in Egypt

Nothing in this book should be interpreted in any way as suggesting that I disagree with any of the fundamental laws of the universe as best we understand them through the lens of the hard (not "social") sciences: physics, chemistry, biology, etc. I spent quite a few years studying each of those branches of science at a fair bit of depth in the pursuit of a doctorate in environmental science and engineering, and I totally believe that the hard sciences have given human beings the greatest insight into what the universe is, and how the universe functions of any other "ways of knowing." Science to me is akin to "revealed truth" for the religious: I think it is the closest we will ever get to seeing reality for what it is.

So, gravity? I'm normally down with that (literally). Cause and Effect? Yes. Reaction and opposite reaction? Definitely. The earth is round? Well, an oblate spheroid, at least. Are there atoms, and sub-atomic particles, and all that stuff that we can't see directly with the naked eye but can still kill us as dead as last week's newspaper headlines? Yes indeed.

Can chemical, biological, radiological, meteorological, hydrodynamical, or a zillion other aspects of our biological existence cause real harm to real people, and have we identified a bunch of those things beyond any actual shadow of doubt? Yes, we have.

And let's shoot straight for the hottest of hot buttons (literally): is climate change a real thing? Yes, absolutely. Can human beings alter the Earth's radiative balance by changing the composition of the atmosphere? Plausibly, yes. Are changes in the climate reflected in climate physics, climate chemistry, climate biology, and are they partly due to human activities on Earth? All, in my opinion, established fact. Could all that be a bad thing? Yes. Or a good thing? Or a mix of bad and good? Yes, all that is possible.

Now, can we also misinterpret those things? "Yes, we can!" Does our knowledge continue to evolve? Always: that's the nature of knowledge, it is all and always contingent. Can we react intelligently to things we find in nature? Yes. Can we react foolishly and to our own detriment, absolutely. As Einstein reputedly (but probably never said), "Two things are infinite: the universe and human stupidity."

One last word, and we'll climb out of De Nile: people who throw the "denial" word around in disputes about public policies or things that have nothing to do with science (like, projections of the future, or *what we should* **do** about some proposed problem), are basically lousy human beings. They are trying to impugn the motivations of anyone they disagree by tying them to the motivations that led to the Holocaust. If I believed in Hell, I'd believe there was a special place waiting just for people who throw the word "denier" around in contexts other than the actual Holocaust.

1.2   No Conspiracies Need Apply, nor Motivations Ascribed

This is also not a book about good guys and bad guys, though there are, of course, plenty of both involved in the development of today's plague of models. This is not a book about conspiracy theories, nor about hoaxes, rent-seeking, market manipulation, or politics, though, of course, such things are part and parcel of virtually all aspects of society to one extent or another. If you're hoping for validation of conspiracy theories, or the declaration that this or that thing is a massive hoax, perpetrated by any one of a myriad of theorized malign forces or organizations, this is not the book for you, because, I really don't think conspiracy-thinking has much relevance to the nature of the plague of models, nor pretty much any of the other social afflictions that occupy our time and minds.

Now I know some people are going to scoff at that disavowal of motivations, conspiracies, and the like, so I should elaborate a bit. It's not that I do not believe that some people might *want* to do things like orchestrate, say, a panic over climate change, or conspire to drive internal combustion cars out of the market, or conspire to fatten people up with chemical sweeteners, or conspire to fool people about aliens, bigfoot, or the existence of perpetual motion machines (always a perennial favorite!). I'm very sure that there are such people. A vast number of them, in fact. It's just that I don't think it's possible to actually do.

And it's not that I don't believe that some people might like to perpetuate a cover up over some dangerous additive in vaccines, or your breakfast cereal, nor about that non-biodegradable cheeseburger that I read about on the interwebz. I'm sure some people do.

And I certainly won't dispute the idea that there are people who would have *dearly* loved to be part of a great conspiracy to: elect/impeach/elect for a third term/or defenestrate Joe Biden, Donald Trump, Hilary Clinton, George W. Bush, Bill Clinton, Ronald Reagan, Jimmy Carter, and every President back to George Washington, all of whom, I'm quite sure were avatars of Cthulhu.

But I don't believe in conspiracy theories for several pragmatic reasons. First, I simply don't believe that people are smart enough to propagate such grandiose conspiracies successfully. I know, that's conceited. Still, think about today's tech oligarchs, the people everyone routinely assumes are in fact secretly conspiring to take over the galaxy. Yes, they're super-rich. They have big houses, fly around in private jets, pop up to the edge of the atmosphere now and then, and are generally surrounded by wealth, opulence, and all the other trappings we'd associate with having successfully carried out their grand plans of domination. But take a closer look at them. Do these people look like super-genius arch-villains to you? Several of them don't seem to have mastered personal grooming yet. It is unclear to me that one of them (name starts with a "z") is actually a human being. At least one of them seems to strive diligently to look like a homeless person. *And they step on their own tongues, and trip on their own feet all the time.* Remember Windows ME? Facebook's blatant data grabs? Apple's Newton (though Siri just snickered on my ipad about that one), Apple's IIvx (okay, that's a pet-peeve of mine, got screwed on that one), Amazon's flying drone idea (they wound up going with human drones instead)?, getting caught up in politics (Twitter, anyone)?, Marrying women without pre-nuptials? Gaming search results for political purposes...the blunder-list goes on ad infinitum. So, call that rule-of-thumb number one: don't presume malice as a motivation for something when simple cupidity or stupidity might be more explanatory.

Rule number two would be that there is no honor among thieves, and I believe in the economic principle that "people respond to incentives." So, the more profitable a conspiracy might be, the more profitable it would be to rat your co-conspirators out, walk away with a bundle, and leave your fellow rats languishing in prison, where they won't hang themselves, unless, well, you know. What, you think that Ponzi tier one people are going to actually care about the Ponzi tier two people any more than the Ponzi tier threes who are going to lose their shirt? Do you think there's much honor flowing the other direction either? Anyway, given the right incentives, someone will rat out the conspiracy. It's just a statistical likelihood.

My third anti-conspiratorial rule-of-thumb comes into play when people ask *"Okay, wise guy, then how do you explain all of these events happening in just this way? It had to have been planned!"* And my answer to that is, "it does not take a conspiracy to get the lemmings off the cliff, the herd of buffalo to stampede, the pod of whales to beach itself, fish to school, birds to flock, bees to swarm, termites to build mounds, sharks to join a feeding frenzy, slime-molds to congeal into a fruiting body, or an astonishing number of idiots to take the Tide Pod Challenge or lick a toilet seat to show their defiance of COVID-19 on TikTok. It just takes a lot of individual decisions driven by instinct, emotion, and common incentives rather than by rational thought." Finally, conspiracies also fail the test of Occam's razor – they are neither a necessary nor sufficient explanation for just about anything we see in the universe, so let's not waste any further time with those, shall we?

Lastly, is this book is not about science fraud. So, I'm also not picking on *Science*, *Nature*, or the other journals of the time that published the various studies we will discuss, nor the researchers who conducted such research. Having worked with people who do that kind of research over the years, I'm assuming that all of the people involved were fine, upstanding people of good character, genuinely dedicated to the pursuit of knowledge.

And, before my critics start howling, yes, I studied Thomas Kuhn, as well as Karl Popper, not to mention a good bit of economic materials on Public Choice theory, and rather a lot of evolutionary and game theory, and I'm aware that pretty much everything humans do is biased, consciously and unconsciously, primarily to serve their own advancement relative to other human beings, a phenomenon that applies to the institution of Science throughout. So, there's that.

Now, let us carve into the meatus of the subject, the fundus of the foundations, and the corpus of the conversation!

1.3 Patient Zero in the Plague of Models

In the context of western history, Patient Zero in the plague of models may have been Thomas Robert Malthus, who created a mathematical model of human starvation, and whose name became synonymous with "OMG, we're all going to die!"

The Malthusian model was very simple, though it did, in fact, rely on both computerization (slide-rules, and the logarithm look-up tables that lets them work) are types of semi-automated computing and graphic representation of the model. Based on observations from the past, and using established biological growth principles of the time, Malthus *predicted* (another word to note as we go on) that uncontrolled human populations would grow exponentially, while agricultural productivity would only grow arithmetically.

> If the subsistence for man that the earth affords was to be
> increased every twenty-five years by a quantity equal to what the
> whole world at present produces, this would allow the power of
> production in the earth to be absolutely unlimited, and its ratio
> of increase much greater than we can conceive that any possible

exertions of mankind could make it ... yet still the power of population being a power of a superior order, the increase of the human species can only be kept commensurate to the increase of the means of subsistence by the constant operation of the strong law of necessity acting as a check upon the greater power.

Malthus T. R. 1798
An Essay on the Principle of Population. Chapter 2, p. 81

The result of this most simple of abstract models of risk, illustrated below, was that within a predictable period, human population growth would outstrip the ability of agriculture to feed them, resulting in mass starvation. Too many mouths and too little food would lead to mass hunger and death. This argument (made about starvation in Ireland) later led Jonathan Swift to satirically propose "A Modest Solution," that basically came down to, "So let's eat all the babies."

Of course, Malthus was wrong on both assumptions: human populations don't grow exponentially indefinitely (nor do any living things, for that matter), and agriculture was quite capable of matching or exceeding the human population's demand for food. Fortunately, Swift was also wrong, and there was no need to eat the babies.

Figure 1. Malthusian Catastrophe

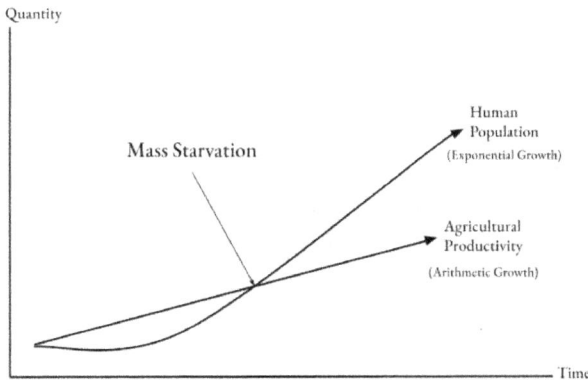

Source: Gerard A. Lucyshyn

Even though Malthusian thinking has been disproven more often than sightings of UFOs and Bigfoot, you probably still see variations on Malthusian models nearly every time you open a web browser, or watch a news program, or do research on everything from property values to the price of Corinthian leather or Italian marble bath tiles. If there's anything that we're not either running out of, or going to be overwhelmed by, you generally won't read about it in the popular press.

This is the world we now inhabit, a world of endless fears driven by utterly opaque abstract, computerized threat-models that an ever more authoritarian "science" invokes to tell us what we must do. Usually that's to take some urgent action we'd rather not take, with everything we have, all at once, to forestall a predicted Armageddon. If we don't do this, or stop doing that, or fail to do this other thing, at this precise rate in this precise place, in this exact way, well, we're all going to sicken/die/lose things we love/be judged badly by our gods, ancestors, descendants, posterity or our nosy neighbor. Houston! We have a *Crisis!* And 2020/21, dear readers, could have been reasonably named the Year of the Crises.

So, what fears has the plague of models brought us? The list of fears is very long, but in broad categories, we're now afraid of:

- chemicals in the air we breathe;
- chemicals in the water we drink and the food we eat;
- chemicals in the soil, the oceans, the clouds (yes, the clouds);
- too much sunlight;
- too little sunlight;
- the wrong kind of light (radiation);
- running out of stuff;
- drowning in wasted stuff;
- killing off animal species;
- being overrun by animal species;
- causing mutations to animal species;
- Not finding animals where they've historically lived;
- Having animals fetching up in places they have NOT historically lived; and, of course...
- diseases of a zillion sorts, with viruses top-of-mind at present.

As of this writing, for example, a Google "news" search for "We're running out of" brought in approximately 261 million results. Apparently, we are running out of: Lithium (for batteries), seafood, landfills (a perennial!), TV (we could only wish), ambulances, salmon, and antibiotics (another perennial!), bees, and, of course, there is this:

> Global Warming is Driving Polar Bears Towards Extinction, Researchers Say

But, as the saying goes, "It's all in good fun when the glaciers are retreating away from the village. It's not so good when they're expanding toward the village." (Okay, I'll admit it, I made up that saying.) Because, of course, there are worse things out there than running out of things, even cuddly Coca-Cola polar bears:

> Memes hit Twitter as 'murder hornet' invasion continues a rough 2020.

And while we're in the mutant invasion column, send in the "Spotted and Oddly Striped Zebras." And don't forget the mutant wolves of Chernobyl, cougars with deformed tails, deformed sea urchins, deformed frogs, mutant bugs and birds, two-headed sharks, and deformed fish with tumors. And lest we forget, the dreaded alligators of Lake Apopka, with their deformed genitals. (And wouldn't' you like to be the person who measures that little variable, hmm?) There is hope, though, because:

> Surprise! Beer cans are less polluting than glass bottles

1.4   So, Let's Talk about Models

To avoid misunderstanding, let's first talk about the kind of models that we will **not** be discussing in this book (though arguably, they could well make for a more stimulating book). So, we will not be talking about fashion models:

Image 1. Fashion Models

Source: Pexels.com

We will also not be talking about representative physical models of things that exist in the real world:

Image 2. Model Trains and Fire Truck

Source: Pexels.com

And we won't even be talking much about models that we speculate may have been concrete things in our shared world of empirical reality once upon a time, based upon bits and pieces of bones, stones, drawings, folk tales, and the like:

Image 3. Australopithecus

Source: Pexels.com

Finally, we won't even be talking about models of imaginary things, no matter how stunningly cool they might be, and regardless of the number of them I have wanted to own in my life.

Image 4. Star Trek Classic Phaser

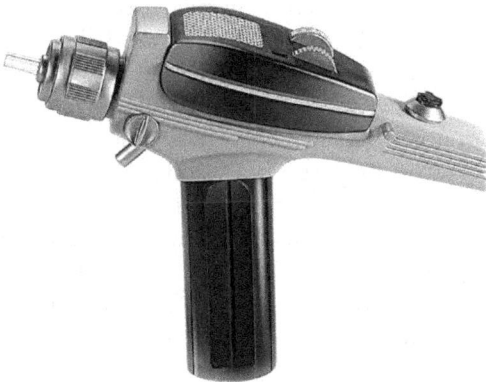

Source: Pexels.com

What we will be talking about are *intangible* models: they are representations of things that we cannot directly see, describe, or point to in our shared empirical reality. They are most often models of events predicted to transpire in the future. The kind of models we're going to talk about look like this:

We're running out of lithium for batteries – can we use salt instead?
Lithium-ion batteries power the world, but with lithium running low, we desperately need a viable alternative. Here's why common salt may be our best bet.
Katharine Sanderson, New Scientist, 2021

And of course, a (literally!) perennial favorite of mine…

Polar Bears Heading for Extinction by 2100 - Study.
A new study has predicted that most polar bears in the Arctic will become extinct by 2100 if greenhouse gas emissions remain on their current trajectory. Further, polar bears are likely to experience reproductive failure by 2040, reducing the number of offspring needed for population maintenance.
Carol Konyn, Earth.Org, 2021

What's wrong with these kinds of models, aside from the fact that they're neither particularly aesthetically pleasing, and you can't play Godzilla vs. King Kong with them?

Well, one problem with models like the ones mentioned in the headlines above is that they are generally used less to inform, than to motivate: there is an implied threat that you're being told about because someone thinks you might want to do something to avoid them. To buy something, or not to buy something. To eat something, or not to eat it. To go somewhere, or not to go somewhere, to ban something from the market or not, to pass a law or not pass a law…and so on.

But the biggest problem with models such as the ones mentioned above (and more that we will discuss) is that they are inherently, and by intent misleading: models do not add information that lets us understand reality, they rely on discarding most actual information representing reality to let us get a highly generalized understanding of what seems to be happening.

Models are an abstraction, and approximation of what we understand to be reality, and that could be about the reality of the past, present, or (completely unpredictable) future. We'll have to unpack this a bit, but first…

Author Context Box 1

This is probably a good time to add a bit of personal context in the broader scheme of things. You'll find more author-contextualization insertions like this as we go along. I'm including these just to let the reader know, in a broader philosophical scheme of things, "where the author is coming from." I sometimes find that can be easy to lose track of in a wide-ranging discussion like the one we'll be having, hence, a shiny new innovation, *Author Context Boxes*. Collect the whole set. Or ignore them completely. Your choice. Trigger Warning: these boxes will be in first person, and may (probably will) contain snark, and might be considered politically incorrect. Reader discretion is advised.

But before we get into the details of what's wrong with using computer models in the formation of public policy, we need some framing. Because although the content of this book will go moderately deeply into computer modeling, that's not really what the book is about. The book is about the influence of computer risk-modeling on public policy, specifically, the giant gushing fountain of EHS regulations that have poured forth since the 1970s.

So, what is "public policy," anyway? Merriam-Webster (and it all starts with Webster), defines public policy as "government policies that affect the whole population." That's helpful, if rather terse. But a good place to start. Our friends at the Canadian Encyclopedia are a bit more verbose, defining it thus:

> Public Policy generally denotes both the general purpose of government action and the views on the best or preferred means of carrying it out; more specifically it refers to government actions designed to achieve one or more objectives. "Policy" can have at least 2 distinct meanings: it can refer both to how something is done (rules and procedures), which may be called administrative policy, or to what is being done, e.g., substantive programs.

Across the pond, Britannica defines it as "Public policy generally consists of the set of actions—plans, laws, and behaviours (sic)—adopted by a government." Even more officially, the Legal Dictionary defines it this way:

> The term "public policy" refers to a set of actions the government takes to address issues within society. For example, public policy addresses problems over the long-term, such as issues with healthcare or gun control, and as such, it can take years to develop. Public policy addresses issues that affect a wider swath of society, rather than those pertaining to smaller groups.

And Wikipedia, that unimpeachable fountain of knowledge, defines it thus:

> Public policy is a course of action created and/or enacted, typically by a government, in response to public, real-world problems. Beyond this broad definition, public policy has been conceptualized in a variety of ways.

A popular way of understanding and engaging in public policy is through a series of stages known as "the policy cycle". The characterization of particular stages can vary, but a basic sequence is agenda setting – formulation – legitimation – implementation – evaluation.

Definitions of public policy are relatively consistent across political perspectives. The "Climate Reality Project," a climate policy advocacy group defines public policy (in its government 101), as: "...actions taken by any branch of the government, which includes laws, rules, regulations, executive orders, and legal precedents."

For a more protracted definition, I recommend Anderson, J. E. (2003). Public policymaking: An introduction. Boston: Houghton Mifflin Company, pp. 1–34. To save you some time, Anderson puts some flesh on the bones of what is meant by "public policy," starting from "whatever governments choose to do or not to do," and traveling all the way out to actions by public officials that "enact statutes, issue executive orders or edicts, promulgate administrative rules, or make judicial interpretations of laws."

My own definition of public policy is in line with those above, expansive, but I believe what is left out of the previous definitions is an important factor: *public policy ultimately involves governmental coercion*: it imposes mandates upon individuals (even if that mandate is only that their tax moneys are to be used in conducting a "public awareness" program) at the behest of some aspect of government.

This point is salient to our discussion because we will be discussing whether or not abstract, assumption-laden, deeply speculative computerized models of risk are reasonable justifications for the promulgation of public policy, specifically in the form of coercive regulations. In other words, we'll be asking whether abstract models of risk, either prospective or forecasted, are adequate justification for governments to use their most central, and most easily abused power: the power to override the rights of the individual and mandate certain behaviors against the will of that individual.

Put more colloquially, I generally would not want such abstract models used as evidence in a court of law, either for me, or against me, because the uncertainties and assumptions involved in computer modeling, and imagery of modeled outputs, no matter how many "adjustment factors" are incorporated into the modeling, can never be unambiguously eliminated. At the end of the day, models are speculation, they are not statements of physical law. And models don't produce data, or evidence, or even estimates, they produce guesstimates. I'm betting that you wouldn't want them used against you if you ever stood accused of doing something harmful to others in a court of law either.

> What I consider a plague on society is the way that models are portrayed as reality, and are used, and abused in our society to justify inflicting some people's mere preferences on other people. Because models, as we will discuss at length, are *abstractions* from reality, and *guesstimations* about reality. They are **not** reality.

Now that we have that out of the way, what is the problem with using models for assessing and regulating health risk? Quite a lot really, but we only have space for a few big-ticket problems here to give one the flavor of the problem. To go beyond that, well, that's what college is for. Or that's what it used to be before it was for what it is for now. And, who knows what that is.

Author Context Box 2

I have nothing against models. Any of them, really, from the supermodels I mentioned earlier, to the most recent COVID-19 models that are coming out of some epidemiologist's computer. In fact, I think models are very useful, even awesome things. I have spent tens of thousands of hours entertaining myself with models: verbal models, logic models, plastic models, clay models, wood models, photographic models, paper models, video models, chemistry models, biochemical models, physics models, electronic models, landscaping models, combat models, architectural models, drafting models, 3-D CGI models…and more. Supermodels, fashion models, and beauty models, not so much. As I flipped past them to read the articles. Really!

Anyway…the biggest problem is this: as mentioned above, models are not reality. Computer models[2] are *abstractions* of reality, and while they have some value in research settings of comparing "what-if" scenarios, they are of extremely limited utility for making decisions about everyday life. Computer models are not about "what is," they a nested shell of what if X," wrapped around "if we assume Y." What if we focus on this aspect or that aspect of something? What if we make this or that assumption about something? What if we predict something will happen in the future? So, what are abstractions? As our friends at Britannica explain succinctly:

Abstraction, the cognitive process of isolating, or 'abstracting,' a common feature or relationship observed in a number of things, or the product of such a process. The property of electrical conductivity, for example, is abstracted from observations of bodies that allow electricity to flow through them; similarly, observations of pairs of lines in which one line is longer than the other can yield the relation of being longer than. What is abstracted—i.e., the abstraction or abstractum—is sometimes

---

[2] I'm going to use "computer modeling," and variations on that theme as shorthand for "speculative models that ultimately find their expression through the use of computers, rather than anything more tangible, such as a drawing, a sculpture, a scale-replica. I intend nothing pejorative toward computers in this (indeed, I welcome our robot overlords!), it's simply easier to say "computer models," "computer guesstimates," "computer graphic representations," than it is to say "the outputs of vast mathematical models, laden with assumptions, using heavily massaged data, model non-linear processes using iterative mathematical-approximation modeling, with output values usually mis-represented as point or range values of artificial precision and accuracy, and turned into visually-compelling charts and graphs that create an impression of empiricism which is not actually present."

taken to be a concept (or 'abstract idea') rather than a property or relation.

They elaborate that "Abstract as an adjective is contrasted with concrete in that, whereas the latter refers to a particular thing, the former refers to a kind, or general character, under which the particular thing—i.e., the "instance"—falls.

Thus, war is abstract, but World War I is concrete; circularity is abstract, but coins, dinner plates, and other particular circular objects are concrete. *The term abstract is sometimes used to refer to things that are not located in space or time; in this sense, numbers, properties, sets, propositions, and even facts can be said to be abstract, whereas individual physical objects and events are concrete* [emphasis added]. The capacity for making and employing abstractions is considered to be essential to higher cognitive functions, such as forming judgments, learning from experience, and making inferences." The folks at the New World Encyclopedia have a similarly helpful definition:

> Abstraction is the process of generalization by reducing the information content of a concept or an observable phenomenon, typically in order to retain only information which is relevant for a particular purpose. For example, abstracting a black-and-white leather soccer ball to a ball retains only the information on general attributes and behavior of a ball. Similarly, abstracting "happiness" to an "emotional state" reduces the amount of information conveyed about the emotional state. Abstraction typically results in the reduction of a complex idea to a simpler concept or a general domain, which allows the understanding of a variety of specific scenarios in terms of certain basic ideas. Abstract things are sometimes defined as those things that do not exist in reality or exist only as sensory experience, but there is a difficulty in deciding which things 'exist'. It is difficult to reach agreement on whether concepts like God, the number three, and goodness are real, abstract, or both.

For a good backgrounder in how abstraction plays out in computer modeling, the interested reader should check out Chapter 10, (2005) Abstraction and Modeling, in: Beginning Java Objects, by Jacquie Barker:

> Take a moment to look around the room in which you're reading this book. At first, you may think that there really aren't that

many things to observe: some furniture, light fixtures, perhaps some plants, artwork, even some other people or pets. Maybe there is a window to gaze out of that opens up the outside world to observation. Now look again. For each thing that you see, there are myriad details to observe: its size, its color, its intended purpose, the components from which it's assembled (the legs on a table, the lightbulbs in a lamp), etc. In addition, each one of these components in turn has details associated with it: the type of material used to make the legs of the table (wood or metal), the wattage of the lightbulbs, etc. Now factor in your other senses: the sound of someone snoring (hopefully not while reading this book!), the smell of popcorn coming from the microwave oven down the hall, and so forth. Finally, think about all of the unseen details of these objects: who manufactured them, or what their chemical, molecular, or genetic composition is. It's clear that the amount of information to be processed by our brains is truly overwhelming! For the vast majority of people, this doesn't pose a problem, however, because we're innately skilled at abstraction, a process that involves recognizing and focusing on the important characteristics of a situation or object and filtering out or ignoring all of the unessential details.

Ms. Barker also offers up two more graphic examples:

One familiar example of an abstraction is a road map. As an abstraction, a road map represents those features of a given geographic area relevant to someone trying to navigate with the map, perhaps by car: major roads and places of interest, obstacles such as large bodies of water, etc. Of necessity, a road map can't include every building, tree, street sign, billboard, traffic light, fast-food restaurant, etc. that physically exists in the real world. If it did, then it would be so cluttered as to be virtually unusable; none of the important features would stand out. Compare a road map with a topographical map, a climatological map, and a population density map of the same region: each abstracts out different features of the real world—namely, those relevant to the intended user of the map in question. As another example, consider a landscape. An artist may look at the landscape from the perspective of colors, textures, and shapes as a prospective subject for a painting. A homebuilder may look at the same landscape from the perspective of where the best building site may be on the property, assessing how many trees will need to be cleared to make way for a construction project. An ecologist may closely study the individual species of trees and other plant/animal life for their biodiversity, with an eye toward preserving and protecting them, whereas a child may simply be looking at all of the trees in search of the best site for a tree house! Some elements are common to all four observers abstractions of the landscape—the types, sizes, and locations of trees, for example—while others aren't relevant to all of the abstractions.

So, contrary to popular belief, models do not add information to our understanding of actual data or evidence we may have gathered and be examining. In fact, models *strip most of that knowledge away* to derive something that we think might represent reality in some useful way. Call this the–law of subtraction–behind the idea of abstraction. When it comes to models, less is more.

In our particular context of the plague of models, I would have you consider the abstraction involved in using rodents as a "model" of human vulnerability to chemical exposures, amazingly enough, despite it being the 21st century, our discussions will return to rodents regularly as we progress.

Consider the mouse in image 5, it's a cute little bugger, isn't it? In a very simple way, the picture of the mouse is a *model* of the mouse. It's an *abstraction* of the aspects of a mouse that would register in your vision if you were there to look at that mouse (in that particular time, place, lighting, etc.) directly. But of course, the picture is not a mouse. And while it might be immediately identifiable, that mouse-model tells you remarkably little about the actual nature of mice. More importantly, that picture of a mouse excludes virtually all of the information you'd actually have access to were you holding a real mouse in your real hand, and having a chance to see its real life, real behaviors, its health trajectory, its role in the ecosystem, the inside of its organs, tissues, cells, biochemical processes, DNA, its inclination to urinate or defecate on you if you pick it up (yes, they do that) and so on *ad reductio*.

Image 5. Lab Mouse

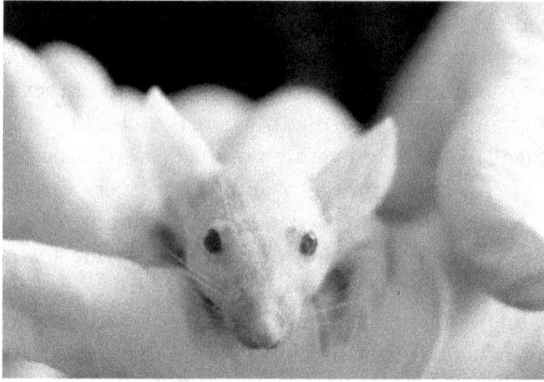

Source: Pexels.com

Consider this: You showed your picture of a mouse to someone who had been raised, say, in a rodent-free universe (perhaps on a space-station somewhere), and asked them to tell you about the picture. Let's assume, for the moment, that the being you're talking to is capable of processing the information in a photograph, which is probably not all that good of an assumption, for future xenosociologists, or, in an age of deep fakes, for readers of the daily newspapers or watchers of video, for that matter.

What, if anything at all, could the picture–the model of the mouse–tell them about the reality of what a mouse is, what it does, how it fits into the biological kingdom, what its role is in the ecosystems it inhabits, whether or not if you gave the mouse a cookie, he would either eat it, or be able to ask you for a glass of milk? The answer to the question is, "almost nothing." The model of the mouse brings almost no information to you in and of itself. It simply evokes a body of knowledge that you already have about a mouse, some of which are probably accurate, and some of which is decidedly not. The picture mouse-model is less a body of knowledge of a mouse, than it is an array of symbols that trigger your thoughts about mice, as you've experienced them. And that's with a "model" that was actually generated by light rays bouncing off of an object, and thence being recorded and captured by another object. Abstractions grow much larger the farther away we move from such empiricism.

Mickey Mouse, for example, is yet another abstraction of a mouse. When you see the line-drawing of Mickey, you see a mouse, but in fact, Mickey tells you far less still than your photograph of an actual mouse.

Were you to actually believe that the things you see Mickey Mouse do are representative of the things that a real mouse does; or were you to believe that real mice are as smart as Mickey, as resilient to physical assault as Mickey, as immune to the laws of physics as Mickey, you would have been led about as far astray by the mouse-model that Mickey Mouse represents as it is possible to be, with regard to actually understanding a real, honest-to-goodness, mouse.

As the great astrophysicist George O. Abell explained in my early science education, to truly model something as simple as a mouse, you would *need to have the knowledge to create the mouse outright*, and humanity is far from doing that even for as small a thing as a virus (we still are, and that was 40 years ago now).

Or consider a sculpture. To quote Michelangelo, "The sculpture is already complete within the marble block, before I start my work. It is already there; I just have to chisel away the superfluous material." This is essentially what a model does with the full body of knowledge that constitutes reality. Again, it is an *abstraction* of meaning (in this case one possible meaning) from the infinite possible number of meanings that reside in any body of information, or in Michelangelo's case, any block of stone.

Since I'm not all about stone, let's consider a wood carving, instead, like this one, a carving really, taken from a single piece of a tree.

Image 6. Wooden Owl

Source: Pexels.com

This happens to be a model of an owl. In order to get this identifiable model of an owl, the carver did not *add* information to the block of wood she started with. In fact, she subtracted a vast amount of information about the block of wood in carving the model.

If you had the original block of wood that the sculptor started from, you could have learned a lot more about the wood that the model is made of. You might be able to look at it and recognize it as "hickory wood," but what you can no longer know, because the artist carved all of that information away, was how large was the original tree? How old? Where did it grow? How fast? What was the climate like when it grew? (Yes, scientists actually try to estimate this sort of thing from looking at tree rings in both live and petrified wood.) Furthermore, you would not know what part of the tree she carved to create the owl, nor if the tree was healthy, or dying, or already dead when she found the wood. Was the tree the last of its kind, in a barren field burned out by a forest fire, or was it only one that happened to have been thrown into a dumpster after someone else was done with it in its original form? Did she kill a tree herself in order to make the model of the owl? We will never know.

The point here, is that a sculpture, like a photograph is a model. It is an abstraction of a few bits of information from what is invariably vastly more complex than the model—any model—can faithfully represent.

Author Context Box 3

Models are useful ways of understanding the world because human senses are limited. Without models - mathematical, logical, physical, biological and the rest, we can't hope to understand things that are outside of the range of our direct senses. And most things are far outside the range of our direct senses. One could make a good case for the idea that humanity's ability to model things we can't directly sense might be a distinguishing characteristic of our ability to reason. Even to a 4-year-old, a leaf on a stream is a model of a boat on a river, or a ship on the ocean. And who wouldn't marvel at something like that.

So, let's put the whole "I hate models" thing down hard: I love models, respect the people who make them, and have paid significant sums of money over the course of my life to play with models, and to do things only possible through the use of models.

I currently have a somewhat absurd amount of computer power grinding away in my house doing little more than generating a bazillion models of reality, both mathematical and graphical.

But that said, I do not make the mistake of believing that most of myriad models around me are particularly accurate or reliable representations of empirical reality. I would not, in "real life," assume that the type of combat strategies that I employ in a video game would work in the real world. I do not assume that a 3-d generated image of a mountain actually represents the empirical characteristics I'd see if I got up close and personal with one. I would also hope that anyone seeing a computer-generated model of myself, say, through the popular "memojis" we can now use with various types of internet messaging programs, understand that they are not particularly solid depictions of the empirical reality that is my very "not-like-my-avatar" self.

That is, in fact, the very reason why we model: to bring something understandable—or at least, that *we think* is understandable, out of a mass of information that would otherwise be impossible to characterize.

But to hammer (and chisel) home the point: when you see a model, you are not seeing reality. You are seeing a tiny, tiny hint of what reality might be, as abstracted from it for your elucidation by another human being, with all of that person's biases and interests baked into the cake. Or the mouse, or owl, in this case.

As I mentioned earlier, we're not going to go into the motivations behind *why* people who create and utilize risk models want to make them, we want you to know about them, or why they want you to act in a certain way on account of those models. For one thing, we can't know those motivations, and for another thing, they're probably all over the map, from utterly altruistic, to utterly self-serving.

Instead, we're going to focus on the use of models, specifically computer models, to generate guesstimates of risks in the arenas of environment, health, and safety, and that are used to justify public policies: specifically, the rules, regulations, authoritative guidelines and guidance's, laws, mandatory actions and mandated illegal actions of a million sorts that drive and constrain our behavior in myriad ways, literally from cradle to grave.

2

Models That Ate Our Lunch

The 1970s will be damned by historians for many gifts to mankind: the Vietnam War, inflation, stagflation, Olympic massacres, Watergate, 8-track tape players, polyester leisure suits, Jimmy Carter's "Malaise," blacklight posters, mood rings, shag carpeting, "Whip Inflation Now" buttons, Barry AuH2O, drug culture, head shops, pet rocks, disco, spandex, pull-tabs and oh, so much more. Oh, and Valley Talk. I grew up as it evolved in the San Fernando Valley, and I attended the opening of the Sherman Oaks Galleria. I still have the scars.

Image 7. Radio and Record Player 1970s

Source: Pexels.com

But on top of all that, the 1970s also brought us a new social plague, the plague of models–specifically speculative computer models used to assess whether a given (not visible or directly measurable) thing was "bad for us" and would henceforth be "regulated," or banned from our existence. This would start out innocently enough, with the hunt for chemicals or radiation that might cause cancer, but it would quickly expand far beyond those major causes of human misery and mortality and expand throughout the entire sphere of human activity.

The plague of models would eventually turn entire generations of Americans into germo-, chemo-, nutri-phobics who would eventually wind up strapping layers of porous, unsterilized (often not even laundered!) layers of randomly selected cloth over their lower face to ward off a virus that, being far smaller than the pores in the masks, could easily pass right on through, or, given that most people's eyes were completely uncovered, could easily enter your body through your unprotected eyeballs, with all their juicy mucus membranes and secretory ducts right there for the world to see, as any number of infections can and do.

But let's not get started on the mask thing yet, our story of the plague of models has a long, long way to go before we reach the insane gyrations of the COVID-19 pandemic.

At any rate, in the 1970s, the ever-present ascetic scolds of the Western World found a new scolding super-power when an explosion of new technologies, and particularly the advent of increased computing power entered the life sciences. These new technologies gave the scolds of the world vast powers to persuade people to believe their claims that any given thing they dislike is "bad for your health," and that banning or regulating such things would be "for your own good."

And with the zeal of, well, zealots, the scolds launched their attack on three of the great mainstays of human pleasure, the pursuit of sweetness, the love of saltiness, and the satisfaction of the savory. And their weapons were speculative models, in this case, animal experimentation models.

Humans have always loved sweet, salty, and savory foods, and for a very good reason: sweet and fatty (savory) foods are high in caloric content, and contain vital nutrients that humans need to grow and thrive. Salt is also a vital biochemical necessity, frequently in short supply, (away from oceans, of course). And sweet foods and animal fats are not usually toxic. Sweetness in fruit, in fact, is nature's way of getting animals to eat it, and spread the plant's seeds around. In an evolutionary sense, plants need animals to eat their fruit, transport, and fertilize their seeds, and filling them with sugar is an incentive to animals to eat them. It was probably not an accident of authorship that humanity's first sin was to take a bite of an apple–possibly one of the oldest symbols of sweetness known to man. (Yes, I know, the whole Garden of Eden thing is apocryphal, and it could have been an orange. Or possibly a fig or a date. It could have been a bacon-wrapped shrimp, for all I know, though the gustatory inclinations of the author's descendants would suggest otherwise.)

2.1 Let's Start with The Sweet

In the 1970s, the leading causes of death in the United States were, according to the U.S. Centers for Disease Control, heart disease, cancer, and stroke, much as they are today (with a brief, but painful detour into COVID-19). Accidents, influenza, and infant mortality came in fourth, fifth, and sixth, with diabetes a solid seventh, killing about 19 in 100,000 Americans. With food being a major causal factor in all but influenza and accidents, the importance of chemicals that might mitigate some of that risk was highly significant. One suspected contributor to all that heart disease and stroke was the consumption of sugar, and carbohydrates in general. (Yes, the low-carb dietary concept long pre-dated the current fad).

And Americans loved them some sugar. As the table below shows, Americans make the rest of the world look like sourpusses when it comes to taking in the sweet stuff.

Table 1. Top Sugar Loving Nations in the World

Rank	Country	Avg. Consumption (grams/individual)
1	United States	126.40
2	Germany	102.90
3	Netherlands	102.50
4	Ireland	96.70
5	Australia	95.60
6	Belgium	95.00
7	United Kingdom	93.20
8	Mexico	92.50
9	Finland	91.50
10	Canada	89.10

Source: World Atlas

And of course, it's not just Americans who love the sweet stuff. Figure 2 below shows consumption of sucrose (in England) from 1815 to 1970. As you can see, outside of the rationing *whoop-de-do* of two world wars, the trend is a quite clear increase over time. Sucrose, by the way, is table sugar: it's actually a two-sugar molecule composed of one molecule of glucose and one molecule of fructose. Sucrose is produced naturally by plants such as beets, and sugarcane. Other common sugars include lactose (found in milk), and maltose (found in well, malt).

Figure 2. Sucrose Consumption (England) 1815-1970

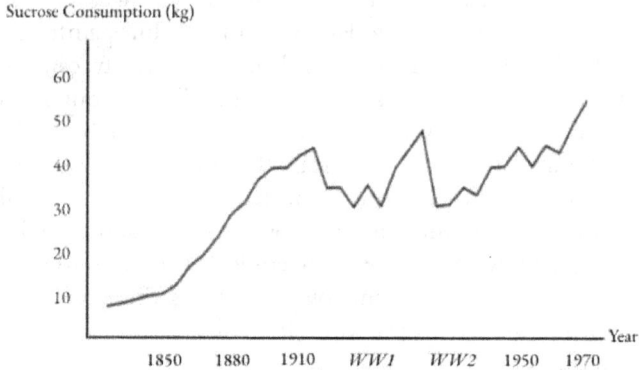

Source: Adapted from Cordain 2005.

The figure below shows consumption of all commercial sweeteners in the United States from 1970 to 2000. Like our English cousins, we also like the sweet stuff, and the trend of consumption of natural sweeteners showed a steady increase through the end of the millennium. The discerning observer might note that over the decades since the 1970s, refined sugar consumption has shifted from simple sucrose to high-fructose corn syrup and glucose. Some will also note that obesity in the population has also grown significantly over that period of time. That is probably not a complete coincidence.

And, as many a bank account can attest, there are significant expenditures on sweets in the American household budget. One suspects that the ratio of these expenditures will look very different in 2019 and 2020, once the population has sobered up, and lost enough COVID-weight to get off the sofa and gather up the data. I'm thinking that bar number one in Figure 4 would stretch across several pages at this scale.

Figure 3. Per Capita Consumption of Refined Sugars (US) 1970-2000

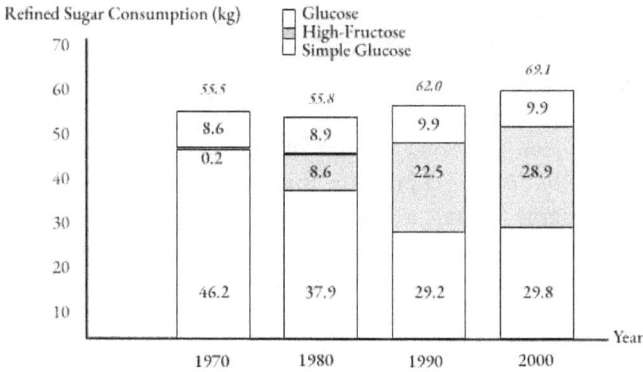

Source: Adapted from Cordain 2005.

Figure 4. Annual Expenditure on Sweets (US) 2016

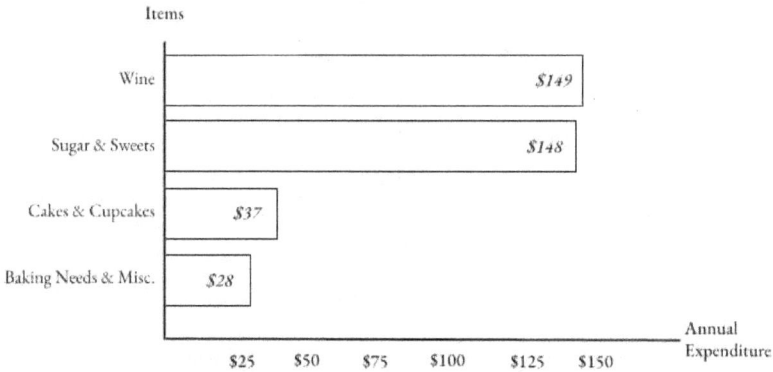

Source: Adapted from Bureau of Labor.

A First Taste of Sweetness

Saccharin is the common name of the chemical o-Benzoic sulfimide, which has, according to PubChem, a chemical formula $C_7H_5NO_3S$. I tell you that not because it's likely to mean anything to you, but because chemical formulas are inherently impressive, and they make for great computer passwords that empower you to pretend to have knowledge of chemistry.

Chemical nomenclature might have been the prototype of the new rules for password creation that rule our everyday lives. One wrong keystroke is the difference between carbon dioxide, which is harmless, and carbon monoxide, which will kill you. Chemistry. It's a gift that keeps on giving.

In case you're writing a police procedural, "saccharin, sodium salt, appears as odorless white crystals or crystalline powder. Aqueous solution is neutral or alkaline to litmus, but not alkaline to phenolphthalein [fee-noll-thale-een] [sic] Effloresces in dry air. Intensely sweet taste." "Saccharin is a 1,2-benzisothiazole having a keto-group at the 3-position and two oxo substituents at the 1-position. It is used as an artificial sweetening agent. It has a role as a sweetening agent, a xenobiotic, and an environmental contaminant. It is a 1,2-benzisothiazole and a N-sulfonyl carboxamide." For the graphically inclined, a graphic molecular model of saccharine looks like this:

Image 8. Saccharin 2D Structure

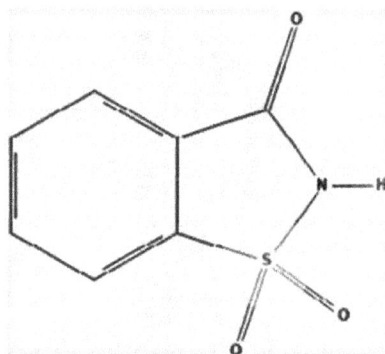

Source: PubChem. https://pubchem.ncbi.nlm.nih.gov

Like many great chemical discoveries, saccharin's discovery as a sweetener was something of an accident. The actual creator of the chemical was a fellow named Ira Remsen, a chemist at Johns Hopkins University in 1878. A couple of years later, a colleague of Remsen's named Constantin Fahlberg who unknowingly brought some saccharin home with him on his fingertips, used his fingers to shove a roll into his face, and voila! The sweetness of saccharin was discovered.

To give you an idea about just how eager people were to discover new sweeteners back in the day, according to an article by author Jesse Hicks in the Science History Institute, after Fahlberg's fortuitous finger finding he "ran back to Remsen's laboratory, where he tasted everything on his worktable—all the vials, beakers, and dishes he used for his experiments." Yes, you read that right, he "tasted everything on his worktable."

Now, I don't know about you, but I wouldn't do that test on my own kitchen counter, much less my laboratory (or someone else's laboratory) worktables, but those were different times, when heroic scientists often tested their own creations on themselves. In fact, Fahlberg would go on to test the safety of saccharin by eating 10 mg of the stuff himself, determining that almost all of it passed through his body unchanged (we won't discuss how he determined that), and was therefore probably metabolically inert in humans, or, in other words, safe to eat.

Quickly after its discovery, Saccharin was a hit, and people began consuming the stuff in pills, powders, and food additives, while physicians were prescribing it for obesity, headaches, nausea, and more. And just about as quickly, the scolds hated the stuff. Saccharin seemed to give pleasure without paying a stiff price, which is something that ascetics dislike instinctively. And so, the regulatory world (in the West) would launch a war on Saccharin. But they would not stop there.

2.2 They Also Came for the Salty and Savory

Along with all the horrors mentioned above, the 1970s were also the beginning of worries over the growing consumption of Chinese food–not because of the whole "bat soup" thing, but because Chinese cuisine (and other Asian cuisines) often featured a flavor enhancing chemical named monosodium glutamate (or MSG).

MSG gives food a savory quality, while simultaneously enhancing the flavor of saltiness at the same time. The discovery of MSG led to the designation of a unique flavor called "umami," the Japanese word for "savory." As with seemingly anything people might take pleasure in, the popularity of saccharin and MSG sparked the inevitable reaction of the scolds: If people were enjoying the stuff, then, it must be bad, (and, to paraphrase from the prophetic Sylvester Stallone movie *Demolition Man*, if something is bad, it should probably be illegal). So, every year, a parade of scolds shows up to warn us why we should not eat sweet, salty, or savory foods, scare us to death with stories of what will happen to us if we do, and noisily lobby lawmakers for bans, labeling laws, state lawsuits, shaming campaigns, and of course, more money for research and "outreach" to vulnerable consumers. As the consumption data shows, all of that scolding wasn't really doing that much good prior to the 1970s.

So, enter monosodium glutamate, whose "real name is" $C_5H_8NNaO_4$. According to PubChem, it is a monosodium salt of L-glutamic acid, which is one of our non-essential amino acids (meaning, we can produce it ourselves biochemically, and are not biochemically obligated to ingest it from outside the body, even though we do.) MSG is a "white or off-white crystalline powder with a slight peptone-like odor," and it is used to impart a meat-like flavor. In case you're deeply into chemistry trivia, this is what an atomic structure model of MSG looks like:

Image 9. Monosodium Glutamate (MSG) 2D Structure

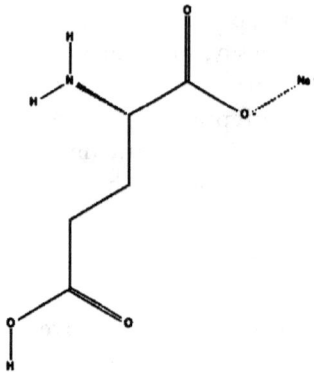

Source: PubChem. https://pubchem.ncbi.nlm.nih.gov

MSG was discovered by a Japanese Chemist at the University of Tokyo, Professor Kikunae Ikeda, and entered the global market in 1909. The Japanese had long used (and still use) Kombu, a type of seaweed, that makes for particularly flavorful foods. The good professor narrowed down the causal agent of that flavor enhancement to the amino acid, glutamic acid (or glutamate), mentioned above. He named the particular flavor that glutamate brings to food "umami," a Japanese word that means "meaty" or "savory." This follows a long tradition in the sciences of naming things in different languages that mean the same thing. MSG was originally difficult to produce. As Glutamate.com (who else?) explains:

A slow and costly extraction process was used to produce MSG until 1956, when the Japanese succeeded in producing glutamic acid by means of fermentation; large-scale production of MSG began – the American ideal of Chinese Food was changed forever. The substance caught on rapidly in the U.S. By the 1960s, Accent, a leading brand of MSG had become a household name. [Today, the chemical firm that makes MSG produces 1.5 million tons of the stuff annually.]

It took a whole two years after MSG's large-scale production began for someone to start raising concerns about its consumption. Again, our friends at Glutamate.com explain,

> MSG was first condemned in 1968, when a physician, Robert Ho Man Kwok, contacted the New England Journal of Medicine with a letter describing Chinese Restaurant Syndrome. "[It usually begins 15 to 20 minutes after I have eaten the first dish, and lasts for about two hours," noted Kwok. "The most prominent symptoms are numbness at the back of the neck, gradually radiating to both arms and the back, general weakness, and palpitations."

The Regulatory War on Sweet and Savory Started Much Earlier than the 1970s

What set the stage for the saccharin/MSG wars of the 1970s, however, goes quite a way back, all the way back, in fact, to the food scares of the early 1900s, which led to the *Pure Food and Drug Act* (or *Pure*) of 1906, and which touched off, among many other jihads on chemicals, the long war on artificial sweeteners. *Pure* was signed by President Theodore Roosevelt on the same day as the *Federal Meat Inspection Act*. Both acts were, according to various sources, reactions to the hysteria over food contamination raised by Upton Sinclair (with graphic descriptions) in his book, *The Jungle*.

Pure was a far-reaching act "for preventing the manufacture, sale, or transportation of adulterated or misbranded or poisonous or deleterious foods, drugs, medicines, and liquors, and for regulating traffic therein, and for other purposes." As the legislation defines its scope:

> That the term 'drug,' as used in this Act, shall include all medicines and preparations recognized in the United States Pharmacopoeia or National Formulary for internal or external use, and any substance or mixture of substances intended to be

used for the cure, mitigation, or prevention of disease of either man or other animals. The term 'food,' as used herein, shall include all articles used for food, drink, confectionery, or condiment by man or other animals, whether simple, mixed, or compound.

The act also had significantly sharp teeth, even by today's standards:

That it shall be unlawful for any person to manufacture within any Territory or the District of Columbia any article of food or drug which is adulterated or misbranded, within the meaning of this Act; and any person who shall violate any of the provisions of this section *shall be guilty of a misdemeanor, and for each offense shall, upon conviction thereof, be fined not to exceed five hundred dollars, or shall be sentenced to one year imprisonment, for each subsequent offense and conviction thereof shall be fined not less than one thousand dollars or sentenced to one year imprisonment, or both such fine and imprisonment, in the discretion of the court* [emphasis added].

Just for reference, $500 in 1906 would be equivalent to about $15,000 at the time of this writing–that's nothing to sneeze at, no matter what someone might have put in your snuff box. Simply transporting and delivering materials deemed adulterated or misbranded under *Pure* carried serious consequences as well:

...and any person who shall ship or deliver for shipment from any State or Territory or the District of Columbia to any other State or Territory or the District of Columbia, or to a foreign country, or who shall receive in any State or Territory or the District of Columbia, or foreign country, and having so received, shall deliver, in original unbroken packages, for pay or otherwise, or offer to deliver to any other person, any such article so adulterated or misbranded within the meaning of this Act, or any person who shall sell or offer for sale in the District of Columbia or the Territories of the United States any such adulterated or misbranded foods or drugs, or export or offer to export the same to any foreign country, *shall be guilty of a misdemeanor, and for such offense be fined not exceeding two hundred dollars for the first offense, and upon conviction for each subsequent offense not exceeding three hundred dollars or be imprisoned not exceeding one year, or both, in the discretion of the court* [emphasis added]; Provided, That no article shall be deemed misbranded or adulterated within the provisions of this Act when intended for export to any foreign country and prepared or packed according to the specifications or directions of the foreign purchaser when no substance is used in the preparation or packing thereof in conflict with the laws of the foreign country to which said article is intended to be shipped; but if said article shall be in fact sold or offered for sale for domestic use or consumption, then this proviso shall not exempt said article from the operation of any of the other provisions of this Act.

In plain English, *Pure* says, "don't sell or ship anything deemed 'adulterated,' or 'misbranded' in the United States, if you know what's good for you." I'm pretty sure you can get away with less punishment for interstate shipping of crack cocaine, these days. But you probably shouldn't test out that hypothesis. And don't blame me if you do.

Pure also brought us a regime of testing for foods, drugs, and other ingestible substances, by the Bureau of Chemistry in the Department of Agriculture. This seems rather self-evidently necessary, but as will be seen, the institution of chemical testing as an element of regulation, the determination of guilt in violating that regulation, and estimating the consequences of that regulatory violation would come to dominate how we think about risk management today.

Pure was followed by the Delaney Clause, (Delaney) inserted into the *Federal Food, Drug, and Cosmetics Act* (FD&C Act) in 1958, "to ban food additives which are found to cause or induce cancer in humans or animals as indicated by testing." The core precept of Delany was that no substance, in any amount, may be intentionally added to food if it has been shown to cause cancer. Note that this is at once a focusing in on a specific type of chemical adulterant, and a broadening of the definition of harm, because cancer is not an immediately manifest illness; it takes years to decades to develop after exposure to a potentially carcinogenic substance, and even then, does not affect any population uniformly in susceptibility, time of development, severity, or consequences of cancer development. According to law professor Richard A. Merrill, writing in the *Yale Journal on Regulation*, Delaney was actually:

> ...three parallel provisions applicable to three classes of food constituents: (1) food additives, the subject of language adopted

in 1958…(2) color additives, the subject of an almost identical prohibition adopted in 1960…and (3) animal drug residues, the product of fine-tuning amendments to the FD&C Act in 1968.

The text of Delaney (section 4009c) read as follows:

> No such regulation shall issue if a fair evaluation of the data before the Secretary fails to establish that the proposed use of the food additive, under the conditions of use to be specified in the regulation, will be safe: Provided, that *no additive shall be deemed to be safe if it is found to induce cancer when ingested by man or animal, or if it is found, after tests which are appropriate for the evaluation of the safety of food additives, to induce cancer in man and animal* [emphasis added]. Except that this proviso shall not apply with respect to the use of a substance as an ingredient of feed for animals which are raised for food production, if the Secretary finds (i) that, under the conditions of use and feeding specified in proposed labeling and reasonably certain to be followed in practice, such additive will not adversely affect the animals for which such feed is intended, and (ii) that no residue of the additive will be found (by methods of examination prescribed or approved by the Secretary by regulations, which regulations shall not be subject to subsections (f) and (g) of this section) in any edible portion of such animal after slaughter or in any food yielded by or derived from the living animal.

As Merrill observes, "Implementation of this policy might have engendered little controversy if the universe of 'food additives' had remained well-defined, if few compounds had displayed the capacity to 'induce cancer' in laboratory animals, and if no food constituents shown to cause cancer had gained popularity among consumers or producers." But of course, this was not at all the case, because, as Merrill later observes, "Improvements in analytic chemistry have enlarged the universe of compounds that FDA regulates as food (and color) additives. *More extensive testing of chemicals and more sensitive protocols have enhanced toxicologists' ability to identify substances capable of producing tumors, including several substances adopted for food use years ago. Some of these substances gained market acceptance long before their carcinogenicity was discovered* [emphasis added]."

Shortly after the passage of Delaney, avid scientists decided to test whether or not saccharin and MSG (along with other chemicals) might be harmful to humans by…dosing animals with it at completely unrealistic exposure pathways and at levels of consumptions over time periods vastly unlike any real-world potential human exposure. To be fair, they had to do this, as it's how a lot of animal testing works. To detect responses to various toxins, using a small population of animals, researchers must keep the dosing at a high enough level to generate measurable (and detectable) harm. From that exposure level, scientists then—model—the effect similar exposures would have on humans.

In those days, for some reason, rats and mice were thought to closely resemble human beings all the way down to the biochemical and genetic level (to the extent that genetics was understood then, which is to say, not all that much). A cynical observer might speculate that the reason rodents were so popular as a research vector and so critical to the development of the plague of models is because they were cheap, easy (and relatively genteel) to maintain and work with, and nobody gives (well, gave) much of a rat's behind if you experimented thousands of them to death every year, which, of course, scientific researchers have done with great abandon.

Yes, the plague of models infected humanity via rodent transmission: lab rats and mice. Or more accurately, the plague of models was born when politicians (somewhat akin to rats and mice) realized that abstract and inherently unreliable model-based risk estimations can be used in a regulatory context of public health protection to compel people's behavior.

Best of all, it was for your own good. And if that mentality doesn't ring a bell by the time you're reading this book, you have not been paying attention to life after COVID-19.

Author Context Box 4

Now, it's probably time for a bit more context. Anyway, I have nothing against the use of animals as test subjects to evaluate the potential harms of substances, activities, insults, or whatever else might pose a hazard to humankind, providing (and this is a *big* caveat) that it is done as compassionately as possible. While animals are highly imperfect as a model for human beings (especially but not exclusively at very tiny concentrations of particular chemicals), I do believe that they are certainly useful for studying higher level insults of a variety of kinds that would directly relate to comparable human insults, whether physical, chemical, radiological, or so on.

38 | The Plague of Models

> In fact, I believe that untold millions of lives have been saved (and yes, perhaps destroyed) by the knowledge gained from animal research.
>
> As I value human life above animal life, I think it's morally acceptable to use animals as test subjects to gain some understanding of what a particular physical, chemical, or mechanical agent might do to a human being. In my years studying biology and working in biology and biochemistry labs, I did quite a bit of research on chickens, rats, mice, frogs, and a veritable ocean of bacteria, and I will fully bear the karmic debt that research produced (should you believe in such debts). Of course, that will be lost in the general karmic noise of all that I've eaten in my life, so there's that.
>
> Otherwise, I will leave this discussion to the self-appointed "bioethicists," who, love them or hate them, enjoy exploring the metaphysical nuances of this position more than I do.

2.3 What Was the Evidence That Justified the War on Flavor Enhancers?

In 1970, *Science Magazine* published *Bladder Tumors in Rats Fed Cyclohexylamine or High Doses of a Mixture of Cyclamate and Saccharin* by J. M. Price, C. G. Biava, B. L. Oser, E. E. Vogin, J. Steinfeld and H. L. Ley, which summarizes the scientific study data that led the Secretary of Health, Education, and Welfare to remove cyclamates from the list of substances "Generally Recognized as Safe" (GRAS) under the regulations of the day:

Abstract. Papillary transitional cell tumors were found in the urinary bladders in 8 rats out of 80 that received 2600 milligrams per kilogram of body weight per day of a mixture of sodium cyclamate and sodium saccharin (10:1) for up to 105 weeks. From week 79 on, several of these rats received cyclohexylamine hydrochloride (125 milligrams per kilogram per day, the molecular equivalent of the conversion of about 10 percent of the cyclamate dosage to cyclohexylamine) in addition to the sodium cyclamate and sodium saccharin. In another study in which 50 rats were fed daily 15 milligrams of cyclohexylamine sulfate per kilogram of body weight for 2 years, eight males and nine females survived. One of the eight males had a tumor of the urinary bladder. In neither study were bladder tumors found in the control rats or in rats treated with lower doses of the compounds. [Yes, I know, that seems somewhat impenetrable to those fortunate enough to have limited their exposure to biological journals, so let's break that out a bit.]

In the first study discussed in the Price et al. abstract, rats were fed 1600 milligrams of saccharin per kilogram of body weight, every day. How much is that? Well, if the average laboratory rat weighs about 400 grams (which is about average for a male rat) a dose of 1600 milligrams per day would be 1600 x 0.4, or about 640 milligrams per day. Every day, for up to 105 weeks. That would be 640 x 7 milligrams over the 105 weeks, which is 470,000 milligrams of saccharin, or 470 grams. That's about half a kilo of saccharin. That is a lot of saccharin, even spread out over the equivalent human life span.

Remember, the average rat weighed about 400 grams, so over the course of two years, the rats would have eaten more than their own body weight in saccharin. So, your 150-pound cousin Joey (a sweet freak) would have had to eat about 75 pounds of saccharin per year for two years to match that performance. That's rather a lot of saccharin.

Even at that level, of the eighty rats fed that amount of saccharin, only eight of them had "transitional" cell tumors in their bladders which were assumed, all things being equal, to have been caused by the ingestion of saccharin. Not a lot to hang a scare on but it was enough.

Another sweetener of interest during the sweetener wars of the 1970s was colloquially referred to as "cyclamates." Cyclamates are known better to most as the active ingredient in Sweet-and-Low, or as we used to call it, "the pink packet." Back in olden days, sugar served at mass-market restaurants was offered in small single-serving packets of white paper, usually found in a cup at the table. Saccharin was packaged in small pink paper packets so that people would not mistakenly confuse it with sugar. This unique innovation would lead to a veritable rainbow of sweetener packet colors, with white for sugar, pink for saccharin, blue for aspartame, yellow for Splenda (or sucralose, something I won't discuss further), and recently, green for Stevia, a plant-based sweetener made from a South African shrub which, as with Splenda, has largely been uncontroversial.

Cyclamates, according to the *New York Times*, was another accidental finding: "a chemical isolated in 1937 when a student, working with a fever-reducing drug, flicked some tobacco off his lips and wondered why his fingers tasted so sweet." (For younger readers, people used to smoke tobacco without filters, sometimes resulting in a bit of tobacco leaf sticking to the lips or tongues of tobacco smokers. Odd, I know.

At any rate, in the second saccharin study described in Price et al. abstract, fifty rats were fed 15 milligrams of cyclohexylamine sulfate daily (a type of cyclamate) per kilogram of body weight per day for two years. That's 4,368 mg, or about 4 grams. Not quite as dramatic as in the previous study, and of this benighted rodent cohort, eight males and nine females survived. (Well, they survived before the dissection. Afterward, not so much.)

One of the eight males had a tumor of the urinary bladder. That's one rat in a population of 50, over the lifetime of the rats. If you think feeding the rats by, say, feeding them through a tube into their stomachs might have been traumatic, and might have contributed to their overall stress levels having some impact on their overall probability of developing cancer, well, you'd be right, but that would have been nothing compared to one of the earlier studies on saccharin:

> Allen et al. reported in 1957 that surgical implantation of pellets containing 4 parts of cholesterol and 1 part of saccharin into the urinary bladder of mice induced one papilloma and three carcinomas of the bladder among 13 animals that survived 40 to 52 weeks.

Ah, the exciting life of the toxicologist! Surgical implantation of fatty, sweet, pellets of "might be poison" directly into the urinary bladder of an animal. And only one rat out of thirteen developed cancer. So, the moral of the story could be, don't shove diet candies directly into rat bladders. It's bad for them. Of course, that was not necessarily the story that made it out into the mainstream media of the time.

To be fair, some exculpatory data existed even at this time when saccharin and cyclamates came in for their days of disapprobation, but apparently, it was not sufficient to exonerate the suspect. As Price et. al. reported:

> Studies looking at lower, potentially more plausible doses with saccharin or cyclamates produced no effects at the lower dose and no distinct toxic effects at the high dose. Toxicological studies in rats fed diets containing 1 and 2 percent sodium

cyclamate for periods up to 11 months indicated no significant adverse effects of this compound.

Price et al. concluded their article by observing:

> The development of bladder neoplasms had not been reported in other species or in other strains of rats fed cyclamate or saccharin. There is no evidence that the use of cyclamate or saccharin has caused cancer in man, malformations in children, or any other abnormality in humans other than a rare skin hypersensitivity. *However, in view of the requirements of the Delaney clause of the Food Additives Amendment, the removal of cyclamates from the classification of substances generally recognized as safe resulted in the prohibition of their use in general purpose food products* (Emphasis mine).

And as we now know, despite being taken off the "safe" list, your saccharine and MSG were likely safe after all, and, judging from the fact that we're back to consuming them in massive quantities and have not all dropped dead, they probably were never that dangerous to begin with.

The "finger-licking good" story of sweeteners didn't end with saccharin or cyclamates, however. From the *New York Times* again, "while developing a new ulcer drug, a research chemist for G. D. Searle & Company licks his fingers and discovers aspartame, an amino-acid compound 180 times sweeter than sugar." Yes, again with the finger-licking. Aspartame was marketed as NutraSweet, and sold in little blue paper packets, completing the rainbow of sweetness in the formerly designated "sugar bowls" of America.

Naturally, the first thing to do with the new entrant to the sweetener wars was…you guessed it, to feed it to rats and mice in unnatural ways, at unnatural doses. The initial battle over Aspartame played out in the European media and was ultimately an internecine war between two factions of ancient Roman haruspices (yes, that's a word). Strike that, it was a dispute between research groups headed by Italian toxicologists. Some would say that is a distinction which makes no difference.

The Aspartame battle kicked off with a study by a group of Italian researchers working with the European Ramazzini Foundation (as Dave Barry might say, "no, I am not making this up"). The Ramazzini findings were, admittedly, troubling:

The CRC/ERF study was conducted on 1800 rats (900 males, 900 females) of the colony used for over 30 years by the Foundation. In order to simulate daily human intake, aspartame was added to the standard rat diet in quantities of 5000, 2500, 100, 500, 20, 4, and 0 mg/kg of body weight. Treatment of the animals began at 8 weeks of age and continued until spontaneous death. A complete necropsy and histopathological evaluation of tissues and organs was then performed on each deceased animal, for a total of over 30,000 slides examined by microscope. The first results of the experiment show: (1) a dose-related statistically significant increase of lymphomas and leukemias in female rats. This statistically significant increase was also observed at a dose level of 20 mg/kg of body weight, a dose inferior to the accepted daily intake permitted by current regulations (50-40 mg/kg of body weight); (2) that the addition of aspartame to the diet induces a dose-related reduction in food consumption, without however causing a difference in body weight between treated and untreated animals. The above results demonstrate for the first time that aspartame is a carcinogenic agent, capable of inducing lymphomas and leukemias in female rats, including when administered at dose levels very close to the acceptable daily intake for humans. In addition, the data demonstrate that the integration of aspartame into the diet did not affect the body weight of treated animals compared with untreated animals.

Put simply, the Ramazzini study found that Aspartame caused cancer in female rats at doses comparable to humans, and adding insult to injury, the poor rodents didn't even lose weight on the stuff.

But before you purge all the Aspartame in your house, you can take a deep breath, because other Italian researchers punctured the Ramazzini hypothesis in a review of the evidence by the European Food Safety Authority. The review study was long (44 pages), and it's fascinating reading if you're keenly interested in rat biology, but I'll just excerpt/summarize the findings here, since several of the points are critical to the understanding of why taking models at face value is problematic:

In the view of the Panel the study does not provide evidence of a relationship between administration of aspartame and induction or enhancement of the development of lymphomas/leukaemias in rats.

This conclusion is based on: the absence of a dose-response relationship for the tumour incidences, which is remarkable given the width of the dose range; the fact that the incidence of lymphomas/leukaemias in both female and male treated groups fell within the respective historical control range provided by ERF for each sex; and '...the aggregation of the haemolymphoreticular tumour types for statistical purposes, involving a combination of tumours of different cellular origin which is not justified in the view of the Panel.'

In other words, wherever those tumors came from, it did not seem to have much to do with aspartame.

As mentioned above, scientists raised questions about MSG early on as well. A 2019 review of "the alleged" *Health Hazards of Monosodium Glutamate*, a meta-analysis of research data by Zanfirescu et al., runs down the list of suspected ailments proposed as a risk of MSG based on human and rodent studies conducted back to the 1990s.

In humans, the risks of MSG centered around the previously named the Chinese Restaurant Syndrome, a label which has been challenged as being racialized (but what hasn't been challenged as being racialist?). The Chinese Restaurant Syndrome alluded to claims that people eating large quantities of Chinese food seasoned with MSG experienced headaches, including "that Won Ton Soup Headache."

But Zanfirescu et al., (hereafter referred to as simply Zanfirescu, with apologies to the co-authors) observed that six reviews of the literature regarding Chinese Restaurant Syndrome (CRS), and MSG consumption were largely negative. In addition to five reviews concluding that not only was MSG not causing headaches or other central nervous system problems, Zanfirescu reported one survey of the risk literature as concluding that:

There is no evidence that dietary MSG of a typical western diet induces symptoms of the CRS. There are not enough data to associate MSG consumption with rhinitis. The overall quality of the evidence supporting a relationship between MSG consumption and for urticaria and angioedema is low.

2.4   The Biology Behind the Fear

The literature on pre-clinical, mostly rodent studies was also reviewed. Zanfirescu conducted extensive searches on PUBMED, which "comprises more than 32 million citations for biomedical literature from MEDLINE, life science journals, and online books." After combing through search term hits going back to the 1990s, the authors found 40 studies that met their stringent cross-checking and eligibility analysis for inclusion in their review. The studies (of rats and mice) looked for health impacts of dietary MSG on the cardiovascular system; liver function; central nervous system function; fertility and fetal development; the promotion of tumors caused by "MSG-induced obesity," and impacts of MSG consumption on the immune system.

Heart Problems

Four studies were examined that looked for potential cardiovascular damage in dietary feeding of MSG to rats and mice. The four studies that met inclusion guidelines in Zanfirescu did find evidence of cardiotoxicity in the rats and mice, but, as Zanfirescu concludes:

> However, when analyzing whether these studies could indicate a threat to human health one must consider the high doses and routes of administration used. The subcutaneous, intraperitoneal, or intravenous administrations of doses that are a few-folds higher than the dietary intake of humans, have little, if any, relevance for human exposure to MSG, as these routes overcome the normal metabolic pathway of ingested glutamate.

In other words, if you feed rodents doses higher than humans might consume, via introductory pathways (such as injection under the skin, into the stomach cavity, or intravenous), your findings are not very likely to mimic the way that MSG would be processed by the human body ingested in the usual fashion (by mouth) in the usual doses, over the usual time intervals.

Liver Problems

Zanfirescu found seven studies eligible for inclusion in their meta-analysis which suggested potential liver problems associated with MSG ingestion in rats and mice. Specifically, cellular shape-changes; damages to venous tissues; changes to the shape of several cellular organelles (mitochondria, endoplasmic reticulum); and changes in a variety of liver metabolites, enzymes, proteins, and blood components were observed in rats, as well as the development of fatty liver in mice when fed MSG at a range of doses, schedules, and administration pathways. In at least one of the studies showing liver problems, other organs were seen to be impacted as well, including the kidneys and brain, though that particular study had the MSG injected into the peritoneal cavity (the belly) of the rats, which would not be a common pathway of exposure in the wild. But again, as with the cardiovascular studies (internal references omitted):

> The seven studies included in this analysis indicated alterations in hepatic morphology and antioxidant defense, observed for different doses and routes of administration. Only one report of increased oxidative stress, following oral administration of doses that approach human dietary intake, seems substantial. The high dosing and routes of administration that fail to mimic the normal metabolic pathway of orally ingested glutamate make it difficult to extrapolate to plausible hepatotoxic effects associated with chronic dietary intake of MSG.

Central Nervous System Problems

In their mega-review of MSG damages, Zanfirescu also found studies that observed damages to the central nervous systems of rats and mice, including damaged and killed brain neurons; changes in brain enzymes and metabolic products and normal activity markers; and more esoteric activities. One of the studies listed led to increased obesity smaller bodies, and reproductive organs in mice; while another led to decreased "spontaneous locomotor activity" (i.e., walking around) in rats.

Again though, in most of these studies, there were issues that rendered them unsuitable to comparing with humans. For one thing, five of the six studies identified as causing central nervous system problems had the MSG introduced parenterally (injected, basically), which is not how most humans would consume it. Or at least, it's not how I hope that most humans would consume it.

Furthermore, newborn and infant mice were used which have developmental features that differed from those of dogs, primates, or people, aside from an inability to inject themselves. For example:

> "...infant mice are not equipped with enzymes necessary to metabolize MSG and that doses of 2 mg/g, administered to infant mice, were comparable to about 6 g in human infants."

Zanfirescu concludes, "it remains to be proven that diet-added MSG could induce behavioral, biochemical, and morphological changes in structures such as cerebrum, hippocampus, and cerebellum of adult mammals."

Fertility and Fetal Development

Rather than go through the specific findings in the eight studies of concern regarding reproductive health found in the Zanfirescu review, I'll skip straight to their evaluation:

> With respect to MSG's effects on fertility and fetal development, six of the eight studies included in the analysis used exceedingly high doses, with little relevance for human dietary intake, and/or parenteral routes of administration.

Similar conclusions were reached when evaluating studies of tumor development:

> Thus, MSG was shown to contribute to tumor progression in a preclinical setting. However, these experimental conditions do not mimic human dietary consumption of MSG and have little relevance for human tumorigenesis.

And for effects on the immune system:

> Although we do not contest the results of the studies presented above, we cannot conclude that MSG exerts detrimental effects on the immune system in humans, as their design is inappropriate for extrapolation to human dietary exposure.

Finally, for the question we all really care about, "will this make my butt look big?" Zanfirescu looked at several studies in humans, with mixed results:

> Data on MSG effects on energy intake are contradictory. Some clinical studies showed no significant differences in hunger ratings or subsequent energy intake. Other studies, undertaken in nursing homes and institutions for the elderly, reported a similar dietary intake of foods with and without MSG.

With much human exposure to MSG encountered in the nursing homes by way of broth, and soup, and other largely soft and mushy foods, one must respect the generosity of the trial participants, and their determination to advance human knowledge. It gives the concept of "soup nazi" a particular salience in this case.

2.5   How Is This about The Plague of Models?

So, what's the big deal, you might ask? Some people invented some chemical sweeteners, and flavor enhancers, others were concerned that they might have hidden risks to human health that should be understood and set out to kill a bunch of rodents to find out what those risks were, and regulators were trying to protect the public health, and all that.

Well, the main problem with animal-experimentation models is that animals are not, mostly, "like people." Getting back to the concrete world for a few minutes, let's get back to the issue of saccharine, MSG, and the consumption thereof by rodents.

We could spend a very, very long time talking about the nearly infinite ways that people are mostly not rats or mice, or wooden owls for that matter, but alas, we do not really have the kind of time we'd need for that, especially since rodent models were only the opening act of the plague of models, but later acts are even more interesting. Instead, I'll limit the discussion to two fairly obvious ways that pertain to the concept of "dosing" with regard to studying toxicity in rodents, then extrapolating that risk out to human beings: body mass, and digestive systems.

2.6   People Are Not Rodents

First off, most people are not rodents. Yes, some have rodent-like characteristics at some superficial level, and we sometime attribute rodent-like behavior to people, such as calling a nasty person a rat, a timid person a mouse, an inquisitive person a ferret, and so on. Most people, deep down, actually understand that people are not that much like rodents, and rodents are not all that much like people, but, since it's morally wrong to experiment on humans by poisoning them to death, early toxicologists decided that animals made an *adequate model* for toxicological research.

I'm sure that even they understood that really, using a rodent to simulate what would happen to a human when exposed to plant-extract or chemical, or element, (or effluvium, vapor, heat, cold, or weapons impact) was probably a very weak simulation in many thousands of ways. But they had a lot of rodents, they were cheap, and nobody thought they were cute, much less potential pets back then, so they were deemed better than nothing.

Unfortunately, over time, people have lost sight about just how different rodents are from people (I blame Hollywood, especially Disney), and when we hear that "agent X caused cancer in rats at dose Y," we're automatically inclined to assume that there is some significance in that observation with regard to what agent X might do to ourselves.

Let's start with the most meaningful word in that sentence, which is, "dose, and the further assumption embedded in that sentence, suggesting that you can scale the impacts of a particular substance simply by the mass of the animals involved, and retain some kind of meaningful relationship between the animals.

In studies like the ones discussed with saccharin, you'll notice a certain metric, of "mg/kg." That stands for "milligrams per kilogram," and is shorthand for "milligrams per kilogram of body weight," which is usually paired with some kind of time-metric, such as mg/kg-dy, which is milligrams of something consumed, per kilogram of the consuming organism, within what is defined as a day, usually 24 hours.

On the surface, this is an intuitive metric. If I just said, "I gave a rat 5 milligrams of crack cocaine and he sprouted wings," you would have many questions, other than "do you have any more crack?" Or "and how much did you give yourself?" You might ask, "how big was the rat?" If that was a New York rat, weighing in at a kilogram (1 million milligrams), that wouldn't seem like much crack. If it was an average male lab rat, weighing in at 400 grams, it might seem like more. It probably would to the rat. But the fun just begins there, because, again, a rat is not a person. Let's compare Rat v. Human:

Table 2. Normative Values for Rats

Lifespan	2.5-3.5 years
Adult weight	Males 300-500g, Females 250-300g
Birth weight	5-6g
Heart rate	330-480 beats per minute
Respiratory rate	85 breaths per minute
Body temperature	35.9-37.5°C
Blood volume	50-70 ml/kg
Urine volume	3.3 ml/100g bwt/day
Allergens	Dander, urinary protein

Source: John Hopkins University

Table 3. Normative Values for Humans

Lifespan	71-76 years (m/f)
Adult weight	Males 61-70kg, (m/f)
Birth weight	2.5-4.5kg
Heart rate	70-82 beats per minute
Respiratory rate	12-18 breaths per minute
Body temperature	36-37°C
Blood volume	65-75 ml/kg
Urine volume	1.2-3.6 ml/100g bwt/day
Allergens	Many! (especially me)

Source: (data tabulated by author from various sources)

Now, I could make the observation that there is no such thing as an average rat, nor an average human for that matter, because, again, the very concept of an "average," or a mean, is an abstraction of information about the central tendency of a body of information. The average human after all has nearly one testicle, and one ovary. There might be such a person, but then again, there might not. The "average" of a range of values does not have to land on a precise data point that happens to be within your sample. Again, the very concept of "average" is an abstraction of the central tendency of a set of data, as one of my statistics professors explained at some length, actually triggering me to study more statistics, but I'm getting off track, since we could follow the spiral of abstraction downward, well, pretty much forever.

So, back to the dose makes the poison—that's the first law of toxicology by the way, a concept observed by the great alchemist Paracelsus, who recorded it for posterity in the 1500s, in Latin naturally, as *dosis sola facit venenum*. This just shows that anything sounds more authoritative if you say it in Latin, or Greek, as every physician is taught from the first day of medical school. (Don't get me started on this…I went to a physician once, with a patch of inflamed skin. The doctor looked at it and told me that I had "*dermatitis.*" I said, "Well yes, I have an inflammation of my skin. I know that. Does putting it in Latin make it somehow worth more money?" the doctor was not amused. I recommend not to do this).

Back to milligrams/kilograms, and why people are not like rats. Notice anything different in those average-value biometric tables above that might make the simple mg/kg equivalency a bit iffy? Like, say, almost everything? The total gross body mass of human vs. rodent is accounted for, but what about the metabolic rate? No. Respiration rate? No. Body temperature? No. Whether the rat is male or female, and has ovaries vs. testicles? No. Is this a lean, Arnold Schwarzenegger-like, rat compared to a not-so-lean, Tom Arnold-like, rat? Mg/kg-dy doesn't tell you any of that. In fact, like the statuette of the wooden owl, or mickey mouse, the idea of a mg/kg equivalency is an extreme abstraction from the reality of whether or not a dose of cyanide given to a mouse is in any meaningful way likely to have the equivalent impacts when given to a human.

2.7   Digestion: Where Exposure Happens

Another way that humans are unlike rodents is because they might look vaguely similar in some matters, but behind the skin and fur, things are rather markedly different. Rodents and humans don't even share the same internal organs, and the ones they do are not necessarily doing the same jobs.

If this topic interests you, by the way, you could do worse than to pull up this article and give it a read: *Comparison of the gastrointestinal anatomy, physiology, and biochemistry of humans and commonly used laboratory animals,* by Tugrul T. Kararli, published in the journal *Biopharmaceutics and Drug Disposition.* The article, from 1995, may be somewhat dated by now but it probably offers up more information than most people would need or want in one somewhat digestible (sorry no pun intended) article. And, really, animals haven't changed all that much in 20 years. Well, there's Gen Z, but I think that's a different subject. Anyway, the level of detail in that article should also be comprehensible (in my perhaps biased opinion) to the interested reader that has mastered introductory level biology and chemistry.

Let's start on our digestive tour, as Professor Kararli did, with the stomach, since this is the point, for food related studies at least, where lab animals meet up with what may be their last meals. It's also a good place to start because there is a nice picture that probably won't upset too many readers, as it's not overly sanguinary.

Image 10. Variations in the Type and Distribution of Gastric Mucosa

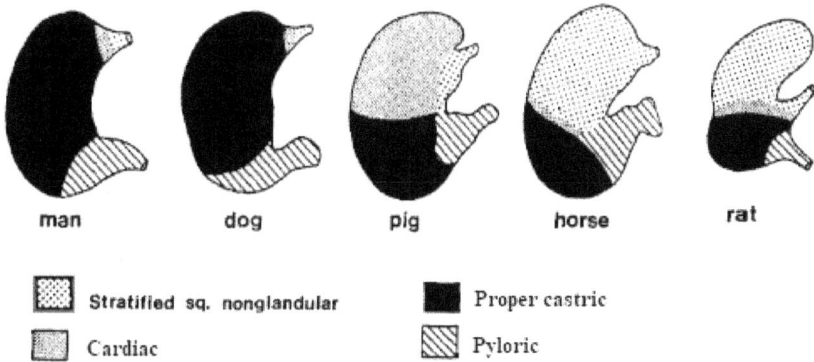

| man | dog | pig | horse | rat |

Stratified sq. nonglandular   Proper gastric

Cardiac   Pyloric

Source: Adaption from Kararli, T.T. (1995)

As one can see, while a donut is a donut, all the world round (sort of), a stomach is not a stomach all around the animal kingdom. Setting aside matters of sheer external morphology and size, as the figure shows, animal stomachs vary widely in the extent and distribution of various tissue types that are involved in the digestion process, again, the first step in which an introduced experimental substance will encounter an animal's digestive system. Note in particular that the rat stomach (first stomach, second row) is wildly different than that of a dog or a pig (two popular experimental animals) in terms of metabolically active and less active tissues:

> In the human, pig, dog, and monkey, the stomach is of glandular type and is lined with cardiac, gastric, and pyloric mucosa (Image 10). The pig stomach is two to three times larger and the cardiac mucosa occupies a greater portion of the stomach compared to the human stomach. Both gastric and pyloric mucosa contain parietal and chief cells. The cardiac cells secrete mainly mucus. The occurrence and distribution of the cells in the gastric glands differs considerably among the mouse, rat, hamster, guinea pig, gerbil, and rabbit. In mice, rats, hamsters, and gerbils, the lower one-third of the glandular lamina propria is occupied by a varying proportion of parietal and chief cells. In rabbits, the predominant

chief cells are distributed in the lower three-quarters of the glands intermingling with parietal cells, but in guinea pigs the chief cells are not discernable. In hamsters there is, however, a gradual increase of chief cells from the junction between non-glandular and glandular stomach toward the pyloric region. In all these species, the parietal cells are the dominant cell type in the upper one-third of the gastric glands, often extending up to the neck of the gland interspersing between mucus neck cells and occasionally chief cells.

Does that all sound super comparable to you? Well, but you say, that's only the stomach. Surely the rest of the digestive system is comparable, after all, we've all mammals, right?

Image 11. Variations in Gross Anatomy of the G.I. Tract of Different Animals

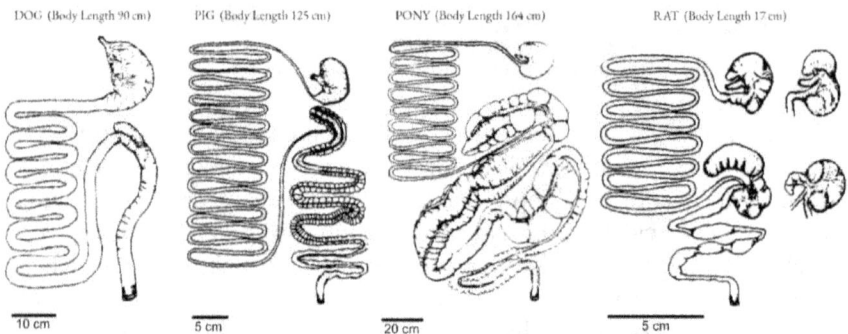

DOG (Body Length 90 cm)   PIG (Body Length 125 cm)   PONY (Body Length 164 cm)   RAT (Body Length 17 cm)

10 cm   5 cm   20 cm   5 cm

Source: Adaption from Kararli, T.T. (1995)

As can be seen from the figure above (supplemented with other data from Kararli), we all may have guts, but not all guts are alike. Consider just the length of the small intestine, the place where your body digests most of your food and absorbs most of your nutrients. The small intestine is the major site for the absorption of nutrients and drugs. That's because the inside of your intestines is all folded up itself and has lots of little finger-like (or sometimes tongue-shaped) protrusions that create still more surface area for the absorption of various chemicals from one's food.

This table gives you an example of how sharply different that animal digestive systems can be from one another. For reference, a human, as Professor Kararli describes in the text of the article, has about three meters of small intestine (when uncoiled, postmortem hopefully), with a "lumen," (that's the center space in the tube) of about five centimeters. Given that the average human adult is about 1.6 meters tall, that's a ratio of about 1:2.

Table 4. Lengths of Parts of the Intestine

Animal	Part of Intestine	Relative length (%)	Average absolute length (m)	Ratio of body length to intestine
PIG	Small intestine	78	18.29	1:14
	Cecum	1	0.23	
	Colon	21	4.99	
	Total	100	23.51	
DOG	Small intestine	85	4.14	1:6
	Cecum	2	0.08	
	Colon	13	0.60	
	Total	100	4.82	
HORSE	Small intestine	75	22.44	1:12
	Cecum	4	1.00	
	Large colon	11	3.39	
	Small colon	10	3.08	
	Total	100	29.91	

Source: Kararli, T.T. (1995)

But focusing simply on the length of the small intestine we can see how different humans are from an assortment of other animals, such as, pig, horse, dog, and mouse just in this one abstracted value from all the others.

Humans 1:2   Horse 1:12
Pig 1:14   Dog 1:6
Mouse 1:4 (my calculation: 10cm / 40cm)

As you can see, mammals vary tremendously in this one ratio alone. An astute observer might ask the question as to why animals that eat primarily vegetation require such insanely long intestines, compared to carnivores and omnivores. I will leave that question as a topic for conversation over dinner, or the next time you debate a vegetarian.

Beyond gross measurements, a host of digestive variables differ between species, such as the ratio of the different functional elements of the intestines to each other, and the density of nutrient-absorbing cells and structures that line the inside of the intestine. Acidity (pH) varies between species as well, as does the volume, concentration, and transit rates of food through the digestive system. There's also a vast difference in the way in which foods and test substances are introduced into laboratory animals, compared with how humans ingest food. For many rodent studies, foods (or chemical compounds) are introduced into the stomach by intubation (called *gavage*), dissolved in pure water (lavage), or injection into the peritoneal cavity (to enter intestines and interstitial liquids by absorption, called "intraperitoneal" injection. None of these methods are directly comparable to a normal human ingestion pathway, skipping past, or involving ancillary systems that might usually be involved in the digestion or biological assimilation of a test material. Oh, and there's this from the Interwebz: Rats can't vomit.

> Rats can't vomit. They can't burp either, and they don't experience heartburn. Rats can't vomit for several related reasons: (1) Rats have a powerful barrier between the stomach and the esophagus. They don't have the esophageal muscle strength to overcome and open this barrier by force, which is necessary for vomiting. (2) Vomiting requires that the two muscles of the diaphragm contract independently, but rats give no evidence of being able to dissociate the activity of these two muscles. (3) Rats don't have the complex neural connections within the brain stem and between brain stem and viscera that coordinate the many muscles involved in vomiting.

Of course, rats are not so foolish as to need to be able to vomit much, such as after a long Friday night of partying. Another way that they are not "just like humans:"

> One of the main functions of vomiting is to purge the body of toxic substances. Rats can't vomit, but they do have other strategies to defend themselves against toxins. One strategy is super-sensitive food-avoidance learning. When rats discover a new food, they taste a little of it, and if it makes them sick, they scrupulously avoid that food in the future, using their acute senses of smell and taste. Another strategy is pica, the consumption of non-food materials (particularly clay), in response to nausea. Clay binds some toxins in the stomach, which helps dilute the toxin's effect on the rat's body.

So, if you're worshipping at the porcelain altar after drinking too much or eating poisonous things and failing to ingest your daily ration of clay, you might have been stupid, but you probably were not a rat last night, at least.

2.8   The Plague of Models Wants Your Sweet-And-Sour Pork

At this point, I'm going to state my opinion of the validity of the critical question: Did modeled health risks from the consumption of artificial sweeteners and savory-building food additives constitute sufficient evidence to warrant having the government coerce people (in a myriad of ways described above) to change their behavior such as to mitigate that harm for the net benefit of themselves, and the greater society in which we dwell. Did the reliance on models justify the resulting regulatory bloat in the market for food additives?

To my way of thinking, when it comes to regulating the marketing and/or consumption of artificial sweeteners such as: saccharin, aspartame, Sucralose, or the consumption of savory-flavor enhancers such as MSG, the answer to that question is No! The evidence of harm was based far too little on empirical and mechanistic understandings of risk, and far too much on models of reality that contain unverifiable assumptions, circumstantial evidence, and to an extent, hearsay (which is what health surveys are, really). Over time, a lack of demonstrable harms from artificial sweeteners and MSG, along with public sentiment seem to have come down on that same side of the question, and today, we have access to a vast range of food and beverage enhancers that make like more pleasant and less caloric.

Of course, your mileage may vary, and you may disagree, perhaps even vehemently. Great! Perhaps if you face a trial someday about whether or not you can be forbidden to do something (or be held responsible for doing something) that is non-injurious to others, such as, collecting seashells, you'd accept the kind of evidence we saw above as a reasonable grounds for the government to forbid you from collecting seashells, or maybe even mandate that you do some other thing, like collecting government savings bonds (or who knows, even taking an experimental vaccine). That is something we all must decide as rational human beings. Or so one hopes.

As we will explore in succeeding chapters, in the 1970s, the plague of models went into full swing, fueled in part by the computerization of the sciences. The ability to quantify, qualify, identify, and detect ever more chemicals in ever lower quantities grew sharply in the decades after the invention of the microprocessor. Data analysis also grew in sophistication and would ultimately evolve into sophisticated mathematical modeling that would create the impression that we could not only understand and quantify risks from the distant past, but also to predict such risks into the distant future with sufficient certainty as to warrant using the power of regulation and law to institute controls over people's exposures to risk, and the responses to such exposures.

And the social incentives in the 1970s were all aligned to serve as an attractive host for the plague of models: an ever-hungry regulatory state, ever-more access to "if it bleeds it leads" news coverage and the incipient advent of 24/7 news coverage, the expansion of activist government, the passage of tax law (and legal bounty-hunting laws) that enabled non-profit advocacy groups to endlessly sound the alarms of panic, a legal system ever more consumed with lawfare, and legalistic rent-seeking, and the ever-present desire for politicians to be seen as "acting in your own good," were a perfect storm of incentives.

Eventually, risk-models would dominate consideration of managing risks from the tiniest of the tiny (radioactive exposures) to the Earth as a whole (climate); and in its subsectors and subdomains down to the smallest chemical exposures to some of the smallest living things on Earth.

The modern plague of models began with the innocent pursuit of the sensual pleasures of sweet, salty, and savory, and spread through our society on the backs of rodents and the people who studied them. But the pursuit of more threats to worry about quickly transcended those limited to direct chemical exposures or infectious risks to human beings and expanded quickly to indirect exposures to toxic and infectious agents in the ambient environment. It would then expand outward still, to look for threats to non-human life forms, then entire ecosystems, and then the planet itself. At the same time, the means of assessing those threats changed from direct measurement to the use of abstract, complex, assumption-laden, and often impenetrable (or proprietary) computer models.

This two-way expansion of the quest for threats, from direct to indirect, and from the concrete to the abstract, from the proximal in time and space, to the distal were the critical elements that fueled the plague of models.

3

Models That Take My Breath Away (Literally!)

In Chapter One, we explored how the plague of models infected American public policy (as well as the public policy of other countries with similar democratic-legal-regulatory systems), when, after several decades of generic societal angst about food purity had festered, findings from *models of human health risk* (in this case, animal feeding studies) escaped the laboratory and entered America's legal, regulatory, social, governance and media ecosystems in the 1970s.

While the plague of models outbreak in the 1970s manifested in the simplest, most direct exposures to potentially harmful things (poisons taken in with food basically), the focus on threats quickly shifted from looking *inward* at ingested chemical or internal biological exposures to human beings, to looking *outward* to exposures to toxic and infectious agents in the ambient environment, then to the remote ambient environment, and then to the theoretically "might someday happen" ambient environment.

But it was not just a matter of internal to external threat exposure. It was, simultaneously, a change of focus from high exposures to low exposures; from long exposures to short exposures; from fast-acting harms to harms remote in time; from threats to all people; to threats to specific subsets of people; and even to harms suspected of posing secondary or tertiary impacts on still other perceived threats.

The expansion of the plague of models was a full-on 1000x zoom outward from asking the simple question of whether, say, licking your finger after working in the chemistry lab all day might be a health hazard (um, duh?) to asking whether something, somewhere in the entire concept of licking your fingertip could cause some kind of harm.

In short, the focus on defining threats moved from the mainly measurable to the mostly modellable. This began the exponential growth phase of the plague of models.

In this chapter, we will look at a major feature of that exponential growth phase – by looking at the evolution of air pollution policy. Air pollution was the first "genuinely environmental" issue to gain the undivided attention of society and government from top to bottom in what was then called the "Developed World."

Prior to the world's focus on air pollution, most conflicts over pollutants were local issues, that were generally produced by discrete, identifiable activities. There wasn't all that much guessing about it, people could generally track say, water pollution or soil pollution back to a source by following the gravity gradient of water or wind flow through the ecosystem. These were local problems, generally more about one person harming another with an action transmitted through the environment from point A to point B.

Pollution problems of that sort had a long history but were generally addressed piecemeal and primarily as a matter of property infringement and legal nuisance. The most iconic example of tracking down such pollution in the developed/western world was the story of how John Snow, later called the father of epidemiology, tracked down the source of a Cholera epidemic in London in 1858 to well water contaminated by waste flowing from apartments nearby, destroying the previously-held belief that Cholera spread by air, in a "maisma."

Another legendary example was the tracking down (in the 1950s) of the cause of a continuing problem with cadmium poisoning afflicting the Toyama Prefecture in Japan since 1910. Cadmium poisoning causes a disease named "itai-itai," Japanese for "it hurts, it hurts," which, given the nature of the disease is not a joke in any way.

Still another iconic public health example was tracking down of the cause of Minamata Disease to bioaccumulated mercury in fish consumed by fishing communities in Minamata Bay, Japan, in 1956. That disease was later renamed Chisso-Minamata Disease, after the name of the company that was dumping methylmercury into the Bay.

Another thing that distinguishes air pollution as the first "genuinely environmental" pollution problem in that it was not the product of a discrete source, but rather, broad or even universal activities (such as fossil fuel combustion); it was not apparently causing a specific ailment; it had no known (at the time) causal mechanistic connection to particular health outcomes; and it was not readily traceable to a source or agent. For that matter, even in the 1950s, air pollution was not all that well-defined chemically. Yes, there were plenty of belching smokestacks to point at, but air pollution was a much larger class of chemicals than only those released by localized sources. It was generated from a vast array of human–and natural–biochemical activities that mixed freely in the atmosphere and generated secondary and tertiary chemicals that could not be traced back to particular sources for easy remediation. Farming, (amazingly enough) is one such activity that leads to increased air pollution.

Thus, unlike earlier environmental problems, air pollutants had to be addressed systemically, first at the level of airsheds (the equivalent of watersheds, but for the atmosphere), and then, as understanding of regional movement of air pollutants improved, via pollution control measures from local, to national, to global scales. It was the first truly trans-boundary environmental challenge.

And it still is such a challenge, California still faces considerable difficulty in controlling air quality because of ambient pollution that drifts in from emissions released in Asia. Greenhouse gas emissions are "freely mixed" in the global atmosphere, as are ozone-depleting chemicals, and even fine particulate matter, though, to a limited extent.

3.1 The Great Smogs of the Twentieth Century

We're not going to give a detailed history of air pollution because most people are at least somewhat familiar with the tale, and it's an extremely long tale, but some readers might want some background.

For as long as we've had recorded history (and most likely, as long as humanity has had control over fire and engaged in agriculture), it has been known that concentrated populations of people emit a variety of chemicals into the air, which depending on terrain and climate conditions, can be concentrated into an unsightly, noisome, noxious, or toxic miasma. The written story of air pollution (in the western world, at least) started all the way back Roman times, when the noxious air of Rome was mentioned in a variety of writings (along with noise pollution, sewage pollution, pest populations, and worse).

But in the mid-1900s, two galvanizing events made it crystal clear that air pollution was indeed a direct threat to human health and could be a quite severe one. Here are two of the crystalizing events in the history of air pollution that presaged the plague of models.

Great Smog of Pennsylvania (1948)

In October of 1948, just prior to Halloween, the steel town of Donora, Pennsylvania, was besieged by a toxic cloud of air pollution, that had been the product of decades of uncontrolled industrial pollution, and which was concentrated to lethal proportions by (as is often the case in events such as these) an atmospheric inversion layer that increased the concentration of pollutants over the city, creating a lethal brew of toxic air. As the New York Times explained:

> Sulfur dioxide emissions from U.S. Steel's Donora Zinc Works and its American Steel & Wire plant were frequent occurrences in Donora. What made the 1948 event more severe was a temperature inversion, in which a mass of warm, stagnant air was trapped in the valley. The pollutants in the air mixed with fog to form a thick, yellowish, acrid smog that inhibited the normal process where the sun would burn off the fog. This smog hung over Donora for five days. The sulfuric acid, nitrogen dioxide, fluorine and other poisonous gases that usually dispersed into the atmosphere were caught in the inversion and continued to accumulate until rain ended the weather pattern.

Image 12. The Donora Smog 1948

Source: Smithsonian Magazine, The Deadly Donora Smog of 1948.

Over the course of three days, hundreds of people became ill, and twenty-six died from inhaling the poisonous "Smog," a term coined to encapsulate the combination of smoke, fog, and toxins seen in events such as Donora.

Lorraine Boissoneault, writing in *Smithsonian Magazine*, describes the 1948 Donora smog as the worst air pollution disaster in United States history, and suggests that it, "jumpstarted the fields of environmental and public health, drew attention to the need for industrial regulation, and launched a national conversation about the effects of pollution."

Boissoneault further observes that the Donora event led President Harry S. Truman to convene the first national air pollution conference in 1950.

Great Smog of London (1952)

The Great Smog of London, according to our friends across the pond at (who else?) *Brittanica*, covered the city of London for five long days in early December 1952, caused by (as will sound eerily familiar), a combination of industrial pollution and high-pressure weather conditions:

> The Great Smog of 1952 was a peasouper of unprecedented severity, induced by both weather and pollution. On the whole, during the 20th century, the fogs of London had become more infrequent, as factories began to migrate outside the city. However, on December 5, an anticyclone settled over London, a high-pressure weather system that caused an inversion whereby cold air was trapped below warm air higher up. Consequently, the emissions of factories and domestic fires could not be released into the atmosphere and remained trapped near ground level. The result was the worst pollution-based fog in the city's history.

Image 13. Police Officer Directing Traffic 1952

Source: Encyclopedia Britannica, Great Smog of London

The near-term death toll was estimated at 4,000 dead, with later estimates that included delayed deaths up to 12,000. As with the United States, the

Great Smog of 1952 was a galvanizing event in Great Britain, leading to the passage of the *British Clean Air Act* in 1956.

Author Context Box 5.

My family moved from New Jersey to the San Fernando Valley of California, from the Garden to the Golden State in 1969, when my lungs and I were at the tender age of 9 years old. Life in the garden state had not, in any way, helped to condition my lungs to be accustomed to the toxic air of Los Angeles. For those who somehow managed to grow up without ever having watched television, the San Fernando Valley was California's worst polluted region, due to a high concentration of people, industry, cars, sunlight, and yes, Ronald Reagan's infamous pollution-causing trees (more on this in a bit), all trapped in a geographical basin that cooked down pollution on stagnant summer days into an eye-watering, lung-searing toxic disaster.

This was not your abstract air pollution most people experience today, this was air pollution you could see with the naked eye (if they weren't watering too badly), smell with your own nose, and see imprinted as soot on your clothing at the end of a summer day. In other words, it was extremely gross, and extremely unhealthy for, as we said in posters of the day, "People and Other Living Things." As Johnny Carson, another relic from television history would joke, he never trusted the air when he left Los Angeles, because you couldn't see it.

Image 14. California Smog

Source: UCLA Library Special Collections

For me, the wakeup year for air pollution was around 1975, when I was sent to run the 600 (yards, not meters) in high school physical education class. This was in the San Fernando Valley of California (Woodland Hills, in fact, one of the nascent homes of Valley Talk, and more recently, the new stomping ground of BLM's Patrice Cullors), in the pollen and air-polluted Spring, if my memories can be relied upon after all this time.

About ¾ of the way around the track, my lungs seized up, and I could not breath. My breathing sounded like a train whistle in my ears, and I collapsed on the track gasping like the proverbial fish out of water. On asphalt. At around 90 degrees Fahrenheit.

I was taken off to the nurse's office to recover, after which I was quickly diagnosed as asthmatic, handed an inhaler I was warned "not to use too much," (asthma inhalers were somewhat dangerous in and of themselves at the time) and consigned to the high-school-hell that they called "Corrective Physical Education," which basically consisted of throwing all the kids who could not do the standard activities in PE classes into an unused room somewhere near the gymnasium with the games used to entertain the latch-kid keys that had to stay after school until their parents could pick them up.

I tell that story not to elicit pity (though, if it leads you to want to shower me with fame and glory out of pity, that's okay), but to point out that I am acutely aware that environmental problems are real, and they can be deadly and debilitating. I suffered from it, and my asthmatic mother suffered (and probably died early because of it). My experience with Los Angeles air led me to study biology (general and molecular), and then to obtain a doctorate in environmental science and engineering from UCLA (1994).

3.2   The Clean Air Act

This brings us to the United States *Clean Air Act* (CAA), passed by Richard
Nixon in 1963, and more specifically to the creation of the United States
Environmental Protection Agency (EPA) in 1970 (also at the behest of
Richard Nixon), when the shift in focus on air pollution made the leap from
the local, primarily transportation-focused efforts at state and local levels,
into the zoomed out, big picture focus on ambient pollution, and its
relationship to human health. As with the *Pure* Act and the Delaney Clause
discussed in Chapter One, The *Clean Air Act* was the first critical movement
of the plague of models out of the abstract laboratories of chemical
exposure testing (which were then primarily related to occupational
exposures) and into the much broader domain of public policy.

As the EPA recalls "...the president sent to Congress a plan to
consolidate many environmental responsibilities of the federal government
under one agency, a new Environmental Protection Agency. This
reorganization would permit response to environmental problems in a
manner beyond the previous capability of government pollution control
programs." According to EPA's accounting, under the new plan
(reformatted):

- The EPA would have the capacity to do research on
  important pollutants irrespective of the media in which they
  appear, and on the impact of these pollutants on the total
  environment;
- Both by itself and together with other agencies, the EPA
  would monitor the condition of the environment--
  biological as well as physical;
- With these data, the EPA would be able to establish
  quantitative "environment baselines"–critical for efforts to
  measure adequately the success or failure of pollution
  abatement efforts;
- The EPA would be able–in concert with the states–to set
  and enforce standards for air and water quality and for
  individual pollutants;
- Industries seeking to minimize the adverse impact of their
  activities on the environment would be assured of
  consistent standards covering the full range of their waste
  disposal problems; and

- As states developed and expanded their own pollution control programs, they would be able to look to one agency to support their efforts with financial and technical assistance and training.

This is what we in the then-nascent field of Public Policy Analysis might have called a "big deal." Less politely, depending on which side of the equation you fell, either the regulators, or the regulatees.

The *Clean Air Act*, created in 1970, further evolved via amendments in 1977 and 1990, requires EPA to "establish national ambient air quality standards [NAAQS] for certain common and widespread pollutants based on the latest science."

EPA has set air quality standards for six common "criteria pollutants": particulate matter, ozone, sulfur dioxide, nitrogen dioxide, carbon monoxide, and lead. Of course, the *Clean Air Act* goes well beyond this focus, also covering such environmental problems as: air toxics, acid rain, ozone-depleting chemicals, regional haze, and automobile emissions, all of which are important, and all of which, to one extent or another were strongly influenced by the growing importance of threat-modeling, but none of which we'll have the time to explore here.

Now, at this point, you might be saying, "well, enough with the history and atmospheric chemistry lessons, what's the problem? How did this worsen the plague of models you've been talking about?" That, I can answer in a few key (but not short) points.

First, the *Clean Air Act* of 1970 enshrined the concept of zero-risk as the goal of air pollution control. As the EPA explains "The 1970 amendments carrie[d] the promise that ambient air in all parts of the country shall *have no adverse effects upon any American's health.* [emphasis added]" 116 Cong. Rec. 42381 (December 18, 1970).

Second, the Clean Air Act of 1970 leaves it up to the entirely subjective assessment of the EPA as to which pollutants threaten such adverse effects. Again, according to the EPA:

The first step in establishing a NAAQS involves identifying those pollutants "emission of which, *in* [EPA's] *judgment* [emphasis added], cause or contribute to air pollution which may reasonably be anticipated to endanger public health or welfare," and "the presence of which in the ambient air results from numerous or diverse mobile or stationary sources. . ." 40 U.S.C. §7408(a)(1)(A)(B).

And third, the *Clean Air Act* of 1970 tethered the entire enterprise of air pollution control to the nascent field of air pollution risk-assessment modeling.

> Once EPA identifies a pollutant, it must select a NAAQS that is based on air quality criteria reflecting *"the latest scientific knowledge useful in indicating the kind and extent of all identifiable effects on public health or welfare which may be expected from the presence of such pollutant in the ambient air* [emphasis added] … " Id. § 7408(a)(2).

In sum, EPA made the assumption that if their early experiments did not suggest some level of exposure to air pollution was neutral with regard to health, that it was all harmful, down to the last molecule. Second, they decided that even in a world of absolute impurity, the acceptable threshold for human risk was zero. And finally, they vested all decision-making power over how to implement those two utterly impossible goals in the growing field of risk assessment, which was deeply embedded in a research community with incentives to find ever-more risks that had to be extinguished. That set society on an unattainable quest for purity that to this day, consumes billions of dollars every year. To me, that is the very definition of a plague.

Finally, the *Clean Air Act* unleashed the novel idea that in the pursuit of perfect health protection with an "adequate margin of safety," cost is literally no object. This idea, while subsequently upheld by major court decisions as representing the will of Congress when the legislation was written, has been shown repeatedly to be false. As we've seen with COVID-19, consequences, such as lockdowns, economic shutdowns, massive spending sprees, and crazy, ever-changing "guidelines" from government agencies have major impacts on the overall question of "Is this activity doing more good than harm?" A "cost is no object" approach may well reflect the ideas of the founding legislators, but then, as Mr. Bumble observes in Dickens' *Oliver Twist*, "'If the supposes that,' said Mr. Bumble, squeezing his hat emphatically in both hands, 'the law is an ass—an idiot.'"

The development of the *Clean Air Act* thus leaves us with the perfect nexus of the plague of models—this excerpt is long, but important because I would not want to be accused of mis-representing reality. As the EPA itself said:

Thus, any standards that EPA promulgates under these provisions must be adequate to (1) protect public health and (2) provide an adequate margin of safety, and (3) to prevent any known or anticipated non health-related effects from polluted air. Further, the statute makes clear that there are significant limitations on the discretion granted to EPA in selecting a level for the NAAQS. In exercising its judgment, EPA (1) must err on the side of protecting public health, (2) must base decisions on the latest scientific knowledge giving due deference to the recommendations of the Clean Air Science Advisory Committee, and (3) may not consider cost or feasibility in connection with establishing the numerical NAAQS or other important elements of the standard (e.g., form of the standard, averaging time, etc.). In short, "based on these comprehensive [air quality] criteria and taking account of the 'preventative' and 'precautionary' nature of the act, *the Administrator must then decide what margin of safety will protect the public health from the pollutant's adverse effects – not just known adverse effects, but those of scientific uncertainty or that 'research has not yet uncovered.' Then, and without reference to cost or technological feasibility, the Administrator must promulgate national standards that limit emissions sufficiently to establish that margin of safety* [emphasis added].

Perhaps the two pollutants to catch the most attention in the exponential growth phase of the plague of models would be *ozone pollution* (colloquially called smog) and *particulate matter pollution* (colloquially called soot), primarily, because both are detectable by people's innate senses of sight and smell. We'll spend some time on these in a bit.

3.3   Ozone

Ozone is a gaseous chemical consisting of three atoms of Oxygen, abbreviated as O3. Ozone a pale blue gas, is the product of a chemical reaction involving two other groups of chemicals. (No, it's not the reason that the sky is blue. That's different.)

Ozone does have a distinct odor, one that we associate with lightning storms, which generate significant amounts of ozone. Some people also associate it with the operation of various electrical devices such as old-fashioned video displays. Still others, such as myself, identify it as the smell of home, the San Fernando Valley of California. Go Taft.

One of those "ozone precursor" chemical classes are called Volatile Organic Compounds (VOCs). Without getting too deep into the chemistry of it, organic compounds are just molecules that include atoms of hydrogen and carbon bonded together. So yes, hydrocarbons are organic compounds. What makes VOCs interesting is the "Volatile," part, which refers to the fact that they evaporate into air easily, and preferentially (compared to say, staying dissolved in water). That means that VOCs easily partition into and circulates in air where people (and animals) can readily inhale them. There are a near-infinite number of VOCs, by the way. As one of my chemistry professors generalized, if you can smell something, it's most likely a VOC. And yes, that means your perfume, the scent of an orange blossom, the smell of your sweat, the musk of your paramour, and the delicate fragrance of the La Brea Tar Pits and the bouquet of the Great Salt Lake…all VOCs.

Speaking of Ronald Reagan, or as my friend Steven Hayward calls him, *Ronaldus Magnus*, Reagan was rather severely ridiculed for his observation that some of the air pollution in Los Angeles is produced by trees. He was given an early taste of the full-on "Chevy Chase does Gerald Ford Falling Over Everything" treatment. Even the left-wing Guardian admits it:

> Yes, just as President Ronald Reagan said in 1981. "Trees cause more pollution than automobiles do," he opined. A little later, environmental scientists ruefully confirmed he was partially right. In hot weather, trees release volatile organic hydrocarbons including terpenes and isoprenes–two molecules linked to photochemical smog. In very hot weather, the production of these begins to accelerate. America's Great Smoky Mountains are supposed to take their name from the photochemical smog released by millions of hectares of hardwoods. [So put that in your pipe, or vaping device, and smoke it, Reagan-haters!]

But Ozone isn't just the product of VOCs, it's the product of VOCs and another group of chemicals which are oxides of Nitrogen (abbreviated NOx, presaging the formulation of "Latinx," but that's a different story). In the presence of sunlight, and at sufficient atmospheric concentrations and proper atmospheric conditions:

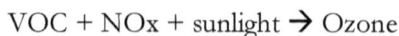

$$VOC + NOx + sunlight \rightarrow Ozone$$

Yes, this is the very short-hand, very simplified version of very complicated, very not-simple atmospheric chemistry that I had to study at rather unpleasant length. And the NOx part of this equation does not only (or even mostly) come from trees, but it is mostly a by-product of high-temperature combustion, mostly produced by, power plants, industrial furnaces and boilers, and motor vehicles.

As an aside, the recipe described above (VOC + NOx + sunlight → Ozone) is actually a model, and, like all models, it is considerably more complex than it seems on the surface (just look at Halle Berry for example). Because while the plus signs are clear in what they mean in that model ("combined with"), the arrow symbol is not clear at all–in fact, it subsumes a very long list of assumptions about the conditions under which the chemical reaction of VOCs and oxides of nitrogen will yield ozone.

Usually, the universal default assumptions in models like this are that the chemical reaction is happening at "standard," conditions of temperature, pressure, uniform chemical concentration, the absence of external disruptors, the absence of feedback pressures that might prevent the reaction...the list of "default" assumptions embedded in that little arrow is really quite long. A better way to express that formula would probably be VOC + NOx + sunlight [if and only if] conditions A-Z hold to be true then Ozone.

So, while 2+2=4 is a mathematical representation of a physical reality that is (I hope) beyond dispute, reflective of physical law, one needs to understand that A+B→C is a model, that requires a lot of other factors to exist for it to actually take reflect what will happen in physical reality.

Ozone, besides being useful to sterilize water and as a bleaching chemical, is a respiratory irritant: it irritates the tissues in the respiratory tract, causing all kinds of unpleasant effects from the overt (difficulty breathing) to the subtle (unnoticeable but measurable reduced lung efficiency). It also irritates previously existing physiological disorders such as asthma. Like most things, however, Ozone can be both good for you and bad for you, depending on where it's found. In your lungs, it's mainly bad for you. But in the air over your head, it screens out radiation that could cause skin cancer, and up higher in the atmosphere, it stops a massive flux of radioactive particles that bombard the planet that most certainly would Kill Us All™ if the ozone wasn't there. (That would be the environmental threat posed by the ozone hole, which we won't discuss here, but will discuss later in the book, but which is not so much a hole as a seasonal, climate–and orbital–dynamic thinning of a thin layer of ozone at the top of the atmosphere, but that's another story).

In 1971, the EPA promoted four National Ambient Air Quality Standards (NAAQS) for ozone pollution. EPA has two kinds of standards, one for *Primary:* pollutants that "provide public health protection, including protecting the health of 'sensitive' populations such as asthmatics, children, and the elderly," and those that are *Secondary:* meaning that they protect human welfare, including "protection against decreased visibility and damage to animals, crops, vegetation, and buildings." So, for example, decreased visibility can reduce a property's value, while acids and other chemicals in the particulate soup can stain or degrade building surfaces (or the surfaces of cherished statues, and natural monuments, for that matter). If particulate matter sickens herds or crops, then they are considered a– secondary impact–on human health. We won't spend much time discussing the secondary standards. Our focus here is on human health impacts and regulations.

The 1971 standards set the *Primary* and *Secondary* NAAQS for ozone pollution at: 0.08 parts per million (ppm), measuring only "Total photochemical oxidants." In 1979 the standards were redefined as just measuring ozone and were set at a 0.12 ppm (measured over one hour) recorded more than once per year. This was tightened to 0.08 ppm in 1997, then 0.075 in 2008, and finally down to 0.07 ppm in 2015. As with particulate matter, which we'll talk about in a moment, the technical arcana of exactly what constituted a violation of the standards evolved over time.

The Evolution of the Basis for Setting the NAAQS Illustrates the Evolution of the Plague of Models

Let's look at the EPA's ultimate rationale, as published in the *Federal Register,* for Ozone standards over the years. We'll do this for particulate matter also, in a little while.

There are several reasons for using EPA's publications in the *Federal Register* as a touchstone to evaluate EPA's rationale in setting the Ozone and Particulate Matter ambient air quality standards.

Again, this book is primarily about the nexus of risk and regulation, and in the United States at least, the *Federal Register* is where the rubber truly meets the road when it comes to promulgating national public policy. This is where, ultimately, EPA, for example not only announces what it is about to do but explains its rationale. The *Federal Register* also has several characteristics that make it a useful lens into the most critical thought that went into regulations passed at the time, and it is historically immutable. Further, it's written in language that is meant to be accessible to the public - that is, non-experts. Admittedly, the *Federal Register* entries that discussed here are quite complex, scientifically, but they should require only a decent introductory (perhaps intermediate) level classes in biology, chemistry, physics, and mathematics to comprehend them. Which, for the record, you should, as that is where unelected regulators using the delegated powers of elected government bind you to the law.

Another reason for using the *Federal Register* as a touchstone in these discussions is that over time, the exponentially multiplying literature used to justify promulgating regulations became utterly immune to rational analysis by normal humans. Thousands of scientific studies were summarized, processed, normalized, adjusted, compared, and otherwise thrown into the hopper of the analytical blender that would product the final judgements recorded in the *Federal Register*. Those studies in turn (mostly incomprehensible to anyone without a specialized degree in the life sciences) were folded into insanely long "summary" documents by successive layers of agency staff, while still the layers of staff went on to prepare summaries of the summaries, and so on, ad infinitum. There is, therefore, no way to analyze the actual evidence used to determine the EPA's National Ambient Air Quality Standards (NAAQS) in a comprehensive way, even if you had the training and made that your full-time job. And even if you could, ultimately, your own expression of the analysis would have to be too long to be assimilated by anyone, and then, at the end of the day, someone's going to start nit-picking and say, "you're cherry picking the evidence!" "That's not what study X *actually* said! You should have discussed *this* study, which was published too late for inclusion in that review, but still existed at the time, because it showed why you're wrong!

And quite frankly, those critics would be absolutely correct. That's why I am not analyzing (or criticizing!) the science of safety, health, or environmental issues, so much as I am analyzing *how aspects of that knowledge were used in the creation of public policy*–most specifically, the regulations that now enfold nearly every action in our lives.

1971 Standard for Ozone

The 1971 standard for ozone was largely based on measurement, with a soupçon of caution thrown in for good measure. As then-EPA Administrator William Ruckelshaus described in the *Federal Register* (April 30, 1971):

National standards for photochemical oxidants have also been revised. The revised national primary standard of 160 ug/m3

> (0.08 ppm) is based on evidence of increased frequency of asthma attacks in some asthmatic subjects on days when estimated hourly average concentrations of photochemical oxidant reached 200 ug/m3 (0.10 ppm).

I can most certainly attest to that one, as I mentioned earlier. Even then, however, there were still questions. According to Ruckelshaus, "A number of comments raised serious questions about the validity of data used to suggest impairment of athletic performance at lower oxidant concentrations."

I personally would have had choice words for the people who suggest that ambient ozone wasn't a problem in comments at the time, but that's neither here nor there: cautionary empiricism prevailed in 1971 in setting the nation's first ozone air quality standard: "It is the Administrator's judgement that a primary standard of 160 ug/m3 as a 1-hour average will provide an adequate safety margin for protection of public health and will protect against *known and anticipated adverse effects* [emphasis added] on public welfare."

Notice here the very pragmatic nature of this first standard: it was looking to prevent known and anticipated adverse effects, not any potential or speculative effect, but "known and anticipated."

1979 Revision to the Ozone Standard

The 1979 revision to the ozone standard are interesting for several reasons. First, the revised air quality standard narrowed the suspected harmful component of Total Photochemical Oxidants specifically to Ozone. That seems straightforward enough, and a step toward greater understanding of which components of "smog," were capable of causing harm.

But unlike the justification for the 1971 standards, the overwhelming majority of the evidence for harm was not from standard measurement studies: physical, toxicological, and medical. In fact, EPA acknowledges in 1979 that "no studies have conclusively linked exposure to ozone or photochemical oxidants with an increase in human mortality."

The 1979 revisions of the NAAQS took a significant step toward the abstract conception of harm under its "Summary of General Findings from Air Quality Criteria for Ozone and Photochemical Oxidants," with the introduction of a newly emerged "threshold" concept. Again, this is long, but important:

Although the concept of an adverse health effect threshold has utility in setting ambient air quality standards, the adverse health effect threshold concentrations cannot be identified with certainty. The lowest concentrations which cause measured health effects in a scientific experiment depends on the particular subjects who have been studied because sensitivity to pollutants varies among different members of the population. Only limited studies can be performed on groups of unusually sensitive persons. Most experimental studies of human subjects are performed on small numbers of relatively healthy persons who do not fully reflect the range of human sensitivity.... Thus, adverse health effect thresholds for sensitive persons are difficult or impossible to determine experimentally, while the threshold for healthy persons or animals is not likely to be predictive of the response of more sensitive groups.

And here's where that logic leads:

In this notice of rulemaking, EPA uses the terminology "probable effects level" to refer to the level that in its best judgment is most likely to be the adverse health effect threshold concentration. It is the fact that the adverse health effect threshold concentration is actually unknown that necessitates the margin of safety required by the Act.

Given that science will never be able to absolutely identify the negative—the no-adverse effect level—accurately, this was a declaration that "adequate margin of safety" equals zero risk.

2008 Revision to the Ozone Standard

Looking a bit deeper into the *Federal Register* publication of the revised 2008 ozone standard, we find that EPA cites as evidence only two studies (by the same research team - cited merely as Adams, 2002/2006) that is categorized "Evidence from Controlled Human Studies."

Even in 2008, almost 30 years after the passage of the first NAAQS standards there was significant uncertainty raised by those assigned to the class of commenters label as "industry," primary among them, that the decrease in *forced expiratory volume* [forced exhalation] measures in Adams was "small, less than 3%, which is within the 3 to 5% range of normal measurement variability for an individual" EPA stipulated that this was correct, however, observed that this concern was offset by a finding of the study that 7 percent of subjects exposed to ozone at 0.04 and 0.06 ppm concentrations of ozone in air experienced reduced exhalation volumes of 10 percent. However, EPA asserted that a finding that 7 percent of 30 test subjects, (which would be 2.5 of them) was representative of what would be observed by the US population as a whole.

The entire discussion of this "Evidence from Controlled Human Studies" published in the *Federal Register* document that justified the implementation of a new air pollution concentration standard which would affect the entire American population's health, and yes, their economy, was 1.5 pages long.

The discussion of epidemiological studies showing risks from ozone exposure, however, was vastly more fulsome, as were the number of studies considered. As EPA explains near the beginning of the document:

> The decision in the last review focused primarily on evidence from short-term (e.g., 1 to 3 hours) and prolonged (6 to 8 hours) controlled-exposure studies reporting lung function decrements, respiratory symptoms, and respiratory inflammation in humans, as well as epidemiology studies reporting excess hospital admissions and emergency department visits for respiratory causes. The Criteria Document prepared for this review emphasizes a large number of epidemiological studies published since the last review with these and additional health endpoints, including the effects of acute (short-term and prolonged) and chronic exposures to O3 on lung function decrements and enhanced respiratory symptoms in asthmatic individuals, school absences, and premature mortality. It also emphasizes important new information from toxicology, dosimetry, and controlled human exposure studies.

But the *Federal Register* entry containing EPA's responses to various challenges about their determination of how harmful ozone was, and what air concentrations should not be exceeded shows how many of the decisions that underpinned setting the standard were based on opinion and interpretation of studies that EPA itself admits were flawed and of limited utility.

There are three short discussions in this *Federal Register* entry that bear reading, in light of the thesis of this book, which is that assumptions, fed into the broader conceptual model of health-risk from indirect exposures to ambient chemicals in the air, set the stage for an explosive growth of regulation in years to come.

In response to comments suggesting that "EPA has proposed a standard with an inappropriate margin of safety. The margin of safety was criticized as being either inadequate or too great," the agency clarifies that the ultimate arbiter of what is safe is both permanently open-ended, and based on agency judgement, rather than empirical data. Here's EPA's response:

> The *Clean Air Act* requires that EPA set air quality standards that are requisite to protect the public health, allowing an adequate margin of safety. As stated in the legislative history of the *Clean Air Act*, the standard must protect against hazards that research has not yet identified. EPA feels that the decision regarding an adequate margin of safety is a judgment which must be made by the Administrator after weighing all the medical evidence bearing on ozone. The factors to be taken into account include inconclusive evidence as well as findings from studies that are considered definitive and not subject to challenge.

A follow-on comment suggesting that EPA's risk assessment method was incomplete, led the agency to this admission:

> As noted in the draft EPA document explaining the risk assessment method, there are complex technical problems that must be dealt with in responsibly developing information of this type suitable for use in setting National Ambient Air Quality Standards. EPA is presently developing the capability to generate this type of information and will only consider its risk assessment method complete when the method includes this capability.

Still another follow-on question in this section is particularly illuminating and shows that people were rightly concerned about the thesis of this book even in 1979, that actual empirical data was being replaced with abstract mathematical models of risk. A commenter observes that "the main problem with the risk assessment method stems from its purpose. Instead of estimating health damages, EPA provides a table of risk numbers without providing an estimate of their health significance; these numbers serve no function." EPA's response is telling, and foreshadows things to come:

> EPA agrees that the risk estimates provided do not serve the function of estimating health damage, but the Agency does not agree that the estimates are without value. The function of these estimates is to indicate the varying risk (or probability) that some sensitive people would suffer health effects in a given period of time if alternative ozone standards were just met. For each health effect category, the response that is of sufficient concern to be deemed a health effect has been decided upon and its seriousness described. *As EPA interprets the Clean Air Act, this determination, which is an important step in the process of setting National Ambient Air Quality Standards is a function that is to be served by a risk assessment* [emphasis added].

And indeed, EPA followed through on its word, later assessments of the NAAQS would rely more and more heavily on risk assessment models, rather than on measured harms observed in actual human populations. As we will see shortly, this was a turning point, from exposure studies to epidemiological studies, which are an entirely different kind of animal.

This pattern, of shifting from a reliance on observation, measurement, and physical characterization to one of theoretical risk modeling grounded in a vast array of assumptions, and projections of risk would hold for other risks that EPA and other governmental agencies would regulate in years to come, such as acid rain; cancer risks from chemicals of a zillion sorts; the ozone hole; climate change; and more.

Also in 2008, the EPA explicitly acknowledges that it has changed the rationale for the NAAQS for Ozone away from what we might call traditional science—the science of identification, measurement, characterization - all of the "what is this" questions that have led to the scientific advances of the last several centuries, to a "new science" based on modeling: long term studies in which one can only study a few small variables based on intermittent sampling over a lifetime, subjective endpoints that cannot be disentangled from confounding variables nor measured absolutely in any meaningful way (physically un-noticeable "decrements" of lung function in asthmatic individuals, and even more abstract and remote "endpoints" of exposure to ozone such as school absences, and premature mortality. As observed in the *Federal Register*:

The decision in the last review focused primarily on evidence from short-term (e.g., 1 to 3 hours) and prolonged (6 to 8 hours) controlled-exposure studies reporting lung function decrements, respiratory symptoms, and respiratory inflammation in humans, as well as epidemiology studies reporting excess hospital admissions and emergency department visits for respiratory causes. The Criteria Document prepared for this review emphasizes a large number of epidemiological studies published since the last review with these and additional health endpoints, including the effects of acute (short-term and prolonged) and chronic exposures to O3 on lung function decrements and enhanced respiratory symptoms in asthmatic individuals, school absences, and premature mortality.

Introducing its overview of Human Exposure and Health Risk Assessments in the 2008 NAAQS revision for Ozone, EPA:

…developed and applied models to estimate human exposures and health risks. This broader public health context included consideration of the size of particular population groups at risk for various effects, the likelihood that exposures of concern would occur for individuals in such groups under varying air quality scenarios, estimates of the number of people likely to experience O3-related effects, the variability in estimated exposures and risks, and the kind and degree of uncertainties inherent in assessing the exposures and risks involved.

Again, this marks a major shift away from the pragmatic air pollution research aimed at identification, qualification, determining concentrations, measuring exposures and metabolic responses, and the other scientific activities focused on the concrete, toward new scientific methodologies focused on the abstract, and assumed.

Interestingly, in discussing challenges to EPA's rationale for the revised standards in 2008, EPA made the decision to group questioners to its initial proposals into two categories: Basically, the "public health community," vs. "industry".

As EPA summarizes, "*Medical and public health commenters* [emphasis added] also expressed the view that EPA must not use uncertainty in the scientific evidence as justification for retaining the current O3 standard."

By contrast, "Another group of commenters *representing industry associations and businesses* [emphasis added] opposed revising the current primary O3 standard. These views were extensively presented in comments from the Utility Air Regulatory Group (UARG), representing a group of electric generating companies and organizations and several national trade associations, and in comments from other industry and business associations including, for example: Exxon Mobil Corporation; the Alliance of Automobile Manufacturers (AAM); the National Association of Manufacturers (NAM); [and] the American Petroleum Institute (API)."

Prior to 2008, there was no such dichotomy: challenges to EPA's proposed ozone standards were grouped by the technical nature of the challenge, with commenters listed alphabetically, whether their comments were in favor or opposed regarding a particular technical decision.

Somewhere, between 1997 and 2008, the battle lines over air pollution control regulations were firmly drawn: it was public health advocates arguing for models over measurement on the side of the Agency (and the angels, one presumes), and agents of industry arguing about the quality of the evidence (or lack thereof) that EPA was invoking to impose new costly regulatory burdens upon their historically legal, and valued activities in American society.

2015 Revision to the Ozone Regulations

The 2015 *Federal Register* publication of revisions to the ozone NAAQS essentially completed the shift in analytic focus of ozone health hazards from the tangible—studies based on actual exposures of living organisms to ozone—to theoretical models that estimate a theoretical risk to a theoretical person having theoretical characteristics that were compiled by the EPA itself (rather than published in peer-reviewed literature). This was the Health Risk and Exposure Assessment for Ozone, published by the EPA Office of Air and Radiation (OAR)→the Office of Air Quality Planning and Standards (OAQPS)→the Health and Environmental Impacts Division, Risk and Benefits Group (HREA). The HREA is available online for the masochistically inclined to peruse at leisure. Great, great leisure: the report itself, at over 500 pages long is essentially beyond any kind of cogent summarization. The executive summary is marginally better, at only 15 pages in length, and can also be read online.

In determining the 2015 revisions to the NAAQS for ozone, then, we are at three or more removes from actual studies published and confirmed in the peer-reviewed scientific literature that shows ozone poses a harm to animal and/or human life:

- Instead of actual quantitative measurements of harm, we have modeled estimates of harm based on a very limited pool of data.

- Instead of actually measuring ozone exposure to people directly, much less measuring exposure of biologically sensitive tissues, or having a defined mechanistic mode of potential harm, EPA modeled exposure based on broad data applied to broad swaths of the population over broad environmental conditions.

- Instead of the EPA administrator writing in the *Federal Register* how he or she interpreted the actual evidence used in crafting the standard, the Administrator evaluated a summary report, itself a summary report of other summary reports, and ultimately relied on her own judgement, and that of the EPA-appointed Clean Air Scientific Advisory Committee (CASAC), a group of selected scientists (many or most of whom had conducted research under EPA funding) to determine what the new ozone standard should be.

3.4   Particulate Matter

Particulate matter, refreshingly enough, comes without much of a chemistry lesson. It is pretty much exactly what it says it is, which is airborne particles of matter. The actual definition is based on particle size, rather than chemical composition. Particulate matter is generated by all sorts of chemical and physical phenomenon in the Earth's biogeochemical (yes, that's a word) system.

Our friends at NASA, who, of late, seems to spend more time looking down at the earth, rather than out into space, do have a nifty primer on particulate matter, with all kinds of pretty infographics. Figure 6 has a few helpful images from a NASA primer that explain particulate matter to the lay (very lay) audience.

There wasn't much mystery involving particulate matter at first, because, simply put, you could see it, and even feel it in the air. You could see it sluice off you after washing up a day working outside in a place with high particulate pollution, industrial or ambient. It was in your clothes, it settled on your car...you get the idea. At the same time, nobody actually knew much about what exactly made-up particulate matter: the chemical composition is too vast, with some elements organic, some inorganic, some chemically active, some inert, some toxic, some non-toxic, and so on. That's why, At first, scientists just measured total suspended particles (TSP) in a given volume of air.

Image 15. Particulate Matter

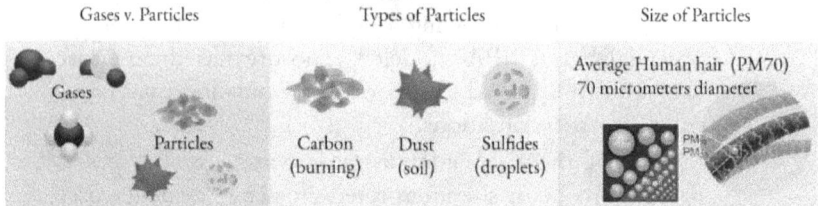

Source: NASA, Global Climate Change–Vital Signs of the Planet

The 1971 standards set the *Primary* standards for particulate matter at: 260 micrograms per cubic meter of air (abbreviated as ug/m3) averaged over 24 hours; and 75 ug/m3 as the annual average (measured as the geometric mean). The *Secondary* standards for total suspended particulates was set at 150 ug/m3 measured over 24 hours, and an annual geometric mean of 60 ug/m3.

Particulate matter standards were both redefined and revised in 1987. Beginning in 1987, only particulate matter that was 10 microns or less in average particle diameter were measured (called PM10), as these were deemed the most likely to be able to penetrate human lungs and cause harm. The 1987 Primary standard was set at a 24-hour threshold of 150 ug/m3 of PM10, this time when averaged over 3 years; and a 50 ug/m3 annual average value, calculated over 3 years. (I'm not going to get into the arcana regarding how the EPA chose 24-hour, annual, or 3-year averages, and that's just the tip of the iceberg. For the purposes of deciding if the standards are violated, EPA uses a variety of measurements settled on in the regulatory process as being the most accurate, or most useful metric for a given pollutant. Sometimes that's obvious, sometimes, it's quite obscure).

The standards were revised yet again in 1997, when still another category of particulates was introduced, PM2.5 which somewhat self-descriptively consists of particulate matter with an average particle diameter below 2.5 microns. The same rationale applied, research had shown that the smaller particulates were capable of penetrating still more deeply into the lungs, and remain there, potentially posing a greater threat than larger particulates that may be intercepted (and then expelled) by structures in the larger airways of the lungs. The 1997 standards were set at still lower concentration levels for both classes of particulates (PM10 and PM2.5), for both primary and secondary NAAQS and set somewhat lower still in 2012.

As with Ozone, let's look at the EPA's ultimate rationale, as published in the *Federal Register*, for Particulate Matter standards over the years.

Halcyon Days of 1971

Once again, in the halcyon days of 1971, the initiation of particulate matter controls was fairly pragmatic. In the introduction to the 1971 *Federal Register* entry, EPA Administrator William Ruckelshaus basically states that EPA staff proposed what they felt was a *reasonable standard* (see above), in the judgement of the Administrator, were "requisite to protect the public health" with an adequate margin of safety (fulfilling their mandate under the *Clean Air Act*), and were "requisite to protect the public welfare" from particulate matter. At this point in the development of particulate matter air quality standards, the focus was still almost exclusively on what could be seen and measured. There was not much question about whether or not particulates of a certain size could penetrate the lungs and airspaces of the respiratory system, and remain there for a good long time, you could (pardon the graphic example) just cut open the lungs of any number of: dead miners, dead smokers (my mother and father, for example), dead construction workers, dead firefighters, dead barbecue chefs, and dead chimney sweeps, for that matter, and you could see that particulate matter could indeed penetrate the respiratory system at a variety of depths, and stay there for various lengths of time. The chemical activities of this class of pollutants at the time, however, was largely unknown, they had barely been described as a physical class of objects, much less broken down by individual constituents, and paired up with demonstrated biological effects.

Still, however, it's hard to see anyone disputing that having a lung full of soot could be anything but bad for a person, that releasing such stuff into the atmosphere constituted an assault on people's bodies, and that it was reasonable as a society to prevent that from happening.

But even in these early days where empiricism was still the order of the day, we would see the troubling inclination of EPA administrators to open their envelope of potential fears far beyond what could be observed or measured. The national secondary standards for particulate matter would not only protect the "public welfare," (itself, a broadly undefined term), but would protect it from "any known *or anticipated* [emphasis added] effects associated with the presence of air pollutants in the ambient air."

We would also see the dynamic that would prevail upon any challenges to the scientific basis of the proposed (or enacted) regulations moving forward. Title 42 states "...current scientific knowledge of the health and welfare hazards of these air pollutants is imperfect...the validity of available research data has been questioned but not wholly refuted, the Administrator has in each case promulgated a national primary standard which includes a margin of safety adequate to protect the public health from adverse effects suggested by the available data."

Or, to put it succinctly, "Shut up, they explained," these are our standards, and we're sticking to them. If you cannot "wholly refute" the judgement of the agency and administrator, well, that's your problem. Some might observe that this would require challengers to prove the negative, which is, of course, an impossible hurdle to achieve. In retrospect, this would turn out to be a refreshingly honest statement of the rationale for the newly proposed NAAQS. It comes down to "our in-house experts suggested this, we like it, and we don't think people's criticisms of our proposals would get us in trouble it we ignored them."

1987: Re-Inspection of the Air Quality Standards

By 1987, the "process" had clearly come to take over the proceedings when it came time to re-inspect the air quality standards set in 1971. Gone were the simple days when the Administrator could write, in the *Federal Register*, that having reviewed the actual evidence regarding the potential harm of a pollutant and rendered his or her judgement. Instead, an utterly impenetrable process had been constructed in which agency staff, at several levels gathered, interpreted, sifted, accepted, or rejected evidence, and passed those judgements upward to still other groups of staff that would decide if they agreed with the lower-level staffers. From there, the process continued onward and upward until it passed over the transom of the Clean Air Scientific Advisory Committee (again, a body of experts that were largely dependent on increased attention to their work based on the pursuit of ever tighter air quality standards) to make a recommendation to the EPA Administrator, who then would use his or her judgement to call the ball.

Still, reading the 1987 *Federal Register* entry on the revised standards is illuminating. First, the EPA admits that frankly, the physical evidence they have linking particulate matter to human health risk is somewhat tenuous:

The criteria document and its addendum [EPA staff summary documents] identify a small number of community epidemiological studies that are useful in determining concentrations at which particulate matter is likely to affect public health. The staff used these quantitative studies to examine concentration-response relationships and to develop numerical "ranges of interest" for possible PM10 standards.

A number of uncertainties associated with use of these studies must be considered in selecting an appropriate margin of safety. As discussed in the staff paper and the criteria document, and the addenda to those documents, epidemiological studies are generally limited in sensitivity and subject to inherent difficulties involving confounding variables. Moreover, many of the quantitative studies were conducted in times and places where pollutant composition may have varied considerably from current U.S. atmospheres. Most also have used British Smoke [BS] or TSP [Total Suspended Particulate Matter] as particle indicators. None of the published studies used the proposed PM10 indicator. Thus, assumptions must be used to convert the various results to common (PM10) units.

But pursuing the "let's add more weak data to our existing weak data to make it look stronger," mentality, EPA staff cast the net more broadly, to include "an additional substantial body of scientific literature that, while not providing reliable concentration-response relationships for ambient exposures, does provide important qualitative insights into the health risks associated with human exposure to particles. This literature includes both quantitative and qualitative epidemiological studies, controlled human exposure experiments, and animal toxicological studies." Yes, we're back to the rat models. By 1987, the idea that the absence of evidence of harm would not be taken as meaning there was no harm. The zero-threat mentality is clearly stated:

The intent of the margin of safety requirement was to direct the Administrator to set air quality standards at pollution levels below those at which adverse health effects have been found or might be expected to occur in sensitive groups. Experience with the requirement has shown that the scientific data are often so inconclusive that it is difficult to identify with confidence the lowest pollution level at which an adverse effect will occur. Moreover, in cases such as the present one, the evidence suggests that there is a continuum of effects, with the risk, incidence, or severity of harm decreasing, *but not necessarily vanishing* [emphasis added], as the level of pollution is decreased.

In the absence of clearly identified thresholds for health effects, *the selection of a standard that provides an adequate margin of safety requires an exercise of informed judgment by the Administrator* [emphasis added]. The level selected will depend on the expected incidence and severity of the potential effects and on the size of the population at risk, as well as on the degree of scientific certainty.

In discussing challenges to its determination of the NAAQS for PM10, in the *Federal Register*, EPA chose to respond to "Salient Public Comments," submitted to the agency after preliminary proposed standards were published. Several of the challenges raised to the proposed standards, as well as EPA's answer, show an agency that is increasingly driven by speculative models of harm, rather than empirical demonstrations of harm. For example:

A number of commenters took issue with EPA's interpretation of the various analyses of London mortality data. These commenters suggest that[:] (a) the London data can be used to show only an association of excess mortality with high concentrations of pollution during unique episodes in which BS and SO levels exceeded 500 to 1000 $\mu g/m^3$, (b) a number of the analyses suffer from methodological flaws precluding valid conclusions, (c) the conclusion that effects may be possible at low pollution levels (e.g., <250 $\mu g/m^3$) or that there is a continuum of association with no identifiable threshold is not supportable, (d) the results of Mazumdar et al. (1982) and Ostro (1984) are more consistent with the hypothesis that particulate matter is acting as a surrogate for some other causal agent rather than as a causal agent itself, and (e) it is biologically implausible that mortality could be affected by particulate matter at levels below those shown by Lawther et al. (1970) to produce morbid effects in sensitive populations.

To put that in English, several critics of EPA's determination of the health threat of particulate matter were based on studies of incidents involving terrible air pollution in London, England that was poorly understood. EPA's response to this challenge was lengthy but contained this significant admission:

> In order to respond fully to these criticisms, EPA conducted more sophisticated re-analyses of the original London data to further determine the degree of reliance that can be placed on the published results. Each of these studies does suffer from limitations and uncertainties delineated in EPA's updated assessment; these limitations *preclude definitive conclusions with-respect to causality as well as identification of clear "no observed effects" levels* [emphasis added].

We won't get into EPA's rationales for the secondary particulate matter standards established to protect "public welfare," including, refreshingly enough, property rights, but if you're feeling somewhat masochistic, and like wading through relatively arcane discussions of whether or not soot on buildings and reduced visibility were determined to constitute harms worth regulating, reading the *Federal Register* entry might be worth your time.

A final interesting aspect of the 1987 standards is that the "cost is no object" focus of the EPA would survive an innovative requirement established by Executive Order 12291 (Reagan, 1981).

> In promulgating new regulations, reviewing existing regulations, and developing legislative proposals concerning regulation, all agencies, to the extent permitted by law, shall adhere to the following requirements: (a) Administrative decisions shall be based on adequate information concerning the need for and consequences of proposed government action; (b) Regulatory action shall not be undertaken unless the potential benefits to society for the regulation outweigh the potential costs to society; (c) Regulatory objectives shall be chosen to maximize the net benefits to society; (d) Among alternative approaches to any given regulatory objective, the alternative involving the least net cost to society shall be chosen; and (e) Agencies shall set regulatory priorities with the aim of maximizing the aggregate net benefits to society, taking into account the condition of the particular industries affected by regulations, the condition of the

national economy, and other regulatory actions contemplated for the future.

EPA acknowledged this new requirement in its *Federal Register* entry tightening the NAAQS on particulate matter, observing that a Regulatory Impact Analysis (RIA) was conducted for the proposed revisions, but in announcing the availability of the draft RIA, the Agency stated that

> ... neither the RIA nor the contractors' reports were considered in developing the proposed revisions...Consistent with its past practice, the Agency has not considered the final Regulatory Impact Analysis of National Ambient Air Quality Standards for Particulate Matter (EPA, 1986c) in reaching decisions on the final standards. [By the way this pesky requirement from the Reagan-era was *undone* by President Bill Clinton in Executive order 12866.]

1997: No-threshold of Safety Model

By 1997, it is safe to say that the choice of modeling, not measurement of air pollution health impacts, to set "health" standards was based on another model type, the "no-threshold of safety" model. This model aims to drive air quality regulations toward a non-possible world of zero-risk. The idea of "zero-risk" is, of course, a model of human omnipotence: that we can, through an act of will, render ourselves "safe" from any of the harmful aspects of physical reality, such as, for example, the reality that the universe itself does not tolerate purity, in air, in innocence, in evil, or in anything else.

It is also safe to say that by 1997, the process of assessing risk and selecting air quality standards had ballooned to the point that the process itself was impenetrable, and in a sense, immune to criticism, because at every layer, the "judgment" of succeeding layers of EPA staff, and ultimately the EPA administrator, became all that mattered. Remember the 1971 *Federal Register* entry that established the particulate matter standard? It took *one page* for EPA Administrator to set forth the reasoning behind the regulation. The next 14 pages were technical materials defining particulates, and how they would be measured.

The 1997 entry in the *Federal Register* was 110 pages long, and over half of that was about the process and rationale used in setting the revised Ambient Air Quality Standard for particulate matter, including some amazingly dismissive answers to challenges from outside the EPA. Once again, let's look at the Rationale for the Primary Standards. EPA invokes three classes of evidence in summarizing the basis for their rationale:

1. Health effects information, and alternative views on the appropriate interpretation and use of the information, as the basis for judgments about the risks to public health presented by population exposures to ambient PM.

2. Insights gained from a quantitative risk assessment conducted to provide a broader perspective for judgments about protecting public health from the risks associated with PM exposures.

3. Specific conclusions regarding the need for revisions to the current standards and the elements of PM standards (i.e., indicator, averaging time, form, and level) that, taken together, would be appropriate to protect public health with an adequate margin of safety.

One of these elements, the closest one to "we have measured some harm from particulate matter at the discussed concentrations," is conspicuously scant as the conversation continues. In fact, EPA states immediately after listing these three classes of evidence that, "In brief, since the last review of the PM criteria and standards, the most significant new evidence on the health effects of PM is the greatly expanded body of community epidemiological studies."

The thing to understand in this transition is that epidemiological studies are, by their nature, modeling studies, rather than empirical measurement studies. They neither specifically identify causes of harm, nor the specific mechanism of harm, they study associations between various groupings of the population and various negative health indicators. As EPA admits, they are at best, broadly indicative of the possibility of harm, rather than specifically indicative:

EPA emphasizes that it places greater weight on the overall conclusions derived from the studies—that PM air pollution is likely causing or contributing to significant adverse effects at levels below those permitted by the current standards—than on the specific concentration-response functions and quantitative risk estimates derived from them. These quantitative risk estimates include significant uncertainty and, therefore, should not be viewed as demonstrated health impacts. EPA believes, however, that they do represent reasonable estimates as to the possible extent of risk for these effects given the available information.

You may be wondering at this point, when the "belief" of a government agency, backed up by studies they themselves admit being non-quantitative and non-specific became a legitimate rationale for promulgating rules that would affect all of society, and impose the costs of meeting those rules on virtually all Americans? The NAAQS revisions of 1997 might not have been the beginning of that dynamic, but with regard to health, safety, and environmental protection, a good argument can be made that "faith in models" had replaced "faith in evidence," by 1997. Here are few more examples of choosing faith over fact:

While the lack of demonstrated mechanisms that explain the extensive body of epidemiological findings is an important caution, which presents difficulties in providing an integrated assessment of PM health effects research, a number of potential mechanisms have been hypothesized in the recent literature. Moreover, qualitative information from laboratory studies of the effects of particle components at high concentrations and dosimetry considerations suggest that the kinds of effects observed in community studies (e.g., respiratory and cardiovascular related responses) are at least plausibly related to inhalation of PM.

EPA's 1997 *Federal Register* entry on Particulate Matter Standards may also signify when "science by consensus" became a significant thing in the setting of important environmental health exposure standards:

For example, a group of 27 members of the scientific and medical community recognized as having substantial expertise in conducting research on the health effects of air pollution stated: Health studies conducted in the U.S. and around the world have demonstrated that levels of particulate and ozone air pollution below the current U.S. National Air Quality Standards exacerbate serious respiratory disease and contribute to early death.

And, pairing up science-by-consensus with the magic of round numbers, EPA observes that:

> Similar conclusions were reached in a letter signed by more than 1,000 scientists, clinicians, researchers, and other health care professionals. The cosigners to this letter argued that tens of thousands of hospital visits and premature deaths could be prevented with the proposed air quality standard revisions. In fact, these commenters argued that even stronger standards than those proposed by EPA are needed to protect the health of the most vulnerable residents of our communities.

Once again, in 1997, we also see the development of "us vs. them" evaluation of criticisms of the proposed new standards. On the one hand, organizations such as the above wanted the standards set even more stringently, and "Another body of commenters, including almost all commenters representing businesses and industry associations, many local governmental groups and private citizens, and some States opposed revising the standards." EPA's answer to those groups, whose concern was primarily that epidemiological models are not reliable indicators of risk, was basically, "well, we disagree." Or, in EPA speak:

> In summary, EPA notes that these commenters provided scientific advice and conclusions that are in substantial disagreement with the conclusions of the review reflected in the Criteria Document and Staff Paper. EPA stands behind the scientific conclusions reached in these documents regarding the appropriate use of the available community epidemiological studies.

The debate over whether or not it was appropriate for EPA to rely on epidemiological models of risk, rather than grounding their standards in empirical demonstrations of risk was protracted, both within the (stunningly huge) volume of reports and analysis generating during the NAAQS revision process, but also within the public policy community. The breakdown was indeed fairly clear: the "want to regulate tighter standards" side of the argument wanted to base them on epidemiological models alone, while the "about to be regulated" community wanted to see actual evidence that what they were doing was causing harm. But this was a hill that EPA was willing to die on:

> Having carefully considered the public comments on the above matters, EPA believes the fundamental scientific conclusions on the effects of PM reached in the Criteria Document and Staff Paper, and restated in the introduction to this unit, remain valid. That is, the epidemiological evidence for ambient PM, alone or in combination with other pollutants, shows associations with premature mortality, hospital admissions, respiratory symptoms, and lung function decrements. Despite extensive critical examination in the criteria and standards review, these findings cannot be otherwise explained by analytical, data, or other problems inherent in the conduct of such studies. *Although the evidence from toxicological studies available during the criteria review has not revealed demonstrated mechanisms that explain the range of effects reported in epidemiological studies, it does not and cannot refute the observation of such effects in exposed populations* [emphasis added]. Moreover, the effects observed in the recent epidemiological studies at lower PM concentrations are both coherent with each other and plausible based on the categories of effects observed at much higher concentrations in historic air pollution episodes, laboratory studies of PM effects at high doses, and particle dosimetry studies.

In other words, EPA basically said, "we like the findings of our models, and since you can't prove the negative—that is, you can't prove that what we're proposing is impossible, well, we're going with our models."

We could continue discussing the National Ambient Air Quality Standards at exquisite length, as the issue remains active today, and indeed, has branched out into ever finer distinctions between particle types and exposure estimates, but again, our point in this review is not to re-litigate disputes over individual studies, but to trace the timeline of divergence in the determination of what constitutes evidence of harm? Is it to be actual physical demonstrations that definitively link exposure to a substance to the development of a particular malady or is it to be estimates derived from assumption-laden statistical models that are, in fact, only tangentially influenced by such "hard evidence," of the sort you might want to insist on if someone accused you of causing harm in a court of law.

For those who are feeling somewhat masochistic, I would suggest reading the *Federal Register* entry for the 2013 revisions of the particulate matter standards, as well as the 2020 revisions at your leisure.

Models Make Me Breathless

It might surprise you to hear that for the first round of air pollution regulations under the *Clean Air Act*, on ozone, carbon monoxide, and larger particulate matter, I think the empirical evidence linking actions (air emissions) to demonstrable harms to persons and property would have risen to a standard of evidence that I'd be satisfied to have used against me in a court of law, were I accused of harming the neighbor's delicate children by the use of my 5 year-old lawnmower. That's not to say that I approve of the formulation and implementation structure that those regulations took– I rarely do–but one can at least make the case that in the beginning of the crusade to control air pollution, we were talking about measurable risks, having measurable impacts, on measurable humans, with measurable harms as a consequence.

Prior to the advent of risk modeling, when we were looking at gross biological harms that could be measured empirically, where a dose-response relationship between exposure and harms could be developed mechanistically, demonstrated empirically, and where there were, indeed, bodies filling hospital beds and mortuaries as a result of those air pollution exposures, I would assert that regulation was absolutely warranted. In fact, those regulations would fit into the category of "needful as fire" things.

But after 1979 in the case of ozone, and 1987 in the case of particulate matter, I would argue that the balance of evidence shifted unsupportable from the empirical, to the speculative. From the measurable, to the modeled. That's not to say that air pollution at those lower levels of harm regulated after those dates were not capable of doing some harm to some people (even a fair bit of harm to a fair number of people), but I'd say that the evidence of the risks posed to a smaller and smaller part of the population (which was itself often a generative source of those same risk) was not sufficient to warrant laying a massive edifice of regulation on society–at least not in those societies with a premise that one should not be unduly restrained by the force of government if one is not actively initiating harm to others. But again, like your emission levels from your vehicle…your mileage may vary.

Epidemiology Models and Their Limits

As we move forward in the Plague of Models to look at risks that are still more abstract than those of very-low-concentration air pollution, it is worth pausing to explore some of the limitations of epidemiology models, as the same limitations will plague virtually all environmental risk assessments that have been the basis for environmental law development for about 50 years now.

What I mean by their limits is not about whether or not epidemiological models are useful in some manner, they certainly are. What I am talking about is whether the outputs of epidemiological studies constitute "evidence," in a more legalistic/public policy standpoint: are the findings of epidemiological studies something you'd be willing to assume apply to your specific case, in your specific life, and would you approve of someone making that assumption for you in deciding what you legally are, or are not, allowed to do? Just as "models are not measures," epidemiology is not "evidence." It is, at best, an educated guesstimate, at worse, uninformed or biased speculation.

These two perceptions of modeling, that it is neither measurement, nor evidence, is important because, as we discussed at the beginning of our journey, that is the essence of public policy: it's the body of guidance, laws, rules, procedures, and even customs that impose restrictions on your behavior whether you consent to those restrictions or not. It is where the government brings its monopoly power to bear in ways that affect people concretely: the power to coerce.

Five Ways That Epidemiology Models Are Not Epidemiology Measures.

1. Epidemiology studies (or models) are broad population (or sub-group) studies involving averaged values of average people, average behavior, average health, average income, average...nearly everything. There are, undoubtedly, some people out there who fit that particular model specification, but there won't be very many. So, the assumption that you can look at say, an increased risk estimate generated from an epidemiology model will correspond to your actual risk is a mistaken assumption.

2. Trite as it may seem, this really is garbage-in-garbage-out modeling. In addition to relying on individual variables that

may or may not capture the major aspect of infectious disease transmission, epidemiological models include a vast array of assumptions, and data adjustments for commonly known "confounders." An example of accounting for cigarette smoking when doing epidemiology studies would be such an adjustment. Note that not to do this would be insane, as clearly, people who smoke are not going to be representative of the average population with regard to their response to say, air pollution exposure. But, making adjustments like this merely raise more questions, such as, "why do those people smoke?" "Is poverty also associated with smoking (yes, yes, it is)? And alcohol consumption, what about that? Yes. Are these people smoking because they have an underlying psychological condition (such as schizophrenia) which is actually medicated by smoking tobacco? How would this affect their risk profile compared to the "average risks" postulated for the entire population in epidemiology models?

3. Epidemiology models used in setting public policy are also usually forecast models. A traditional laboratory style measurement study may have identified a particular risk factor, but epidemiology models not only apply that risk broadly against populations it does so over time and space, with a vast array of assumptions about how myriad events will unfold in the future. Climate change modeling studies would be a good example of this. The relationship between greenhouse gases in the atmosphere and the retention of heat in the atmosphere has been measured (under specific circumstances in laboratories). That should be without question. However, the extrapolation of that dynamic to the entire world, which we can barely monitor significantly, which has a nearly infinite number of atmospheric subdomains, with confounding influences from non-greenhouse gas related "climate forcings," and the assumptions about the course of non-GHG related global atmospheric evolution as well as social development over time make these climate studies all about the model, and nothing about the measurement.

4. Most epidemiology model studies, as with most social science studies in general, are not repeatable, and have been shown to be wrong over time (Ioannidis). The track record of social science research is very coherent. Coherently wrong.

5. Nobody can predict the future, period. Modeling studies tend to get around this point by talking about "projections," and "scenarios," but the fact is, all models assume a world largely continuous with our own, and in a million ways that we know of ourselves - technologies unforeseen even 30 years ago, we know that is not reality.

Our next exploration of the plague of models will be about modeling that is done at yet one more removes from direct human harm, to look at proposed risks at the edge of Earth's atmosphere.

This is another 1000x zoom outward for the plague of models: In the beginning, we started with the most direct: apply a chemical to a biological tissue, and see what it does; to "feed a chemical to a biological organism and see what it does," to generalize a model of toxicity for a particular chemical to theoretically "similar" organisms; to population studies, then to ecological studies that can, in theory, feedback to harm humans.

4

Models That Blot Out the Sun

So, in Chapter One, we discussed the launch phase of the plague of models in the middle-1900s, which was the widespread acceptance of the idea, by the scientific, medical, and regulatory establishments of the United States (and other developed economies such as Canada and the European Community), that theoretical animal modeling of human health effects had reached a point of utility in the development of public policy equivalent to empirical demonstrations of causality.

That is, a belief became widespread that theoretical animal exposure models were, for all intent and purpose, just as "real" as empirically defined mechanistic or deterministic models of causality and were acceptable surrogates for "evidence" or "proof" of risk (or harm) to justify coercive public policies to mitigate a modeled harm.

The first step in that process (well, the first step in the modern era of public policy, at any rate), was the acceptance of the idea that animals were "good enough for government work," as models for how human beings actually worked. The idea here was, basically, since animals looked a lot like people in many ways, it was reasonable to *assume* that what would affect an animal would affect a human in similar ways.

And at gross scales of interaction, that certainly seems reasonable. Drop a building on a cow, you get a dead cow. Drop a building on a human, you get a dead human. Voila–model validation. But as we discussed in Section One, that assumption of comparability between animals and humans is a *model*, which breaks down quickly, and quickly becomes a layer-cake of stacked abstractions and assertions of questionable validity.

Now before you whip out the "you're an anti-vivisectionist, anti-science guy," trope, please read back and note that I explained earlier that I felt animal experimentation was both useful and moral and is certainly better than the available alternatives to help understand biology, and biochemical reactions to external stimuli, and that I engaged in such research myself as a biology student for several years. However, and this is important, even then, *I was aware that I was studying a surrogate for what I was really interested in and was relying on a model of similarity to gain any understanding about the biological systems I was studying.* I knew that we could not say, from research that I conducted on chicken embryo nuclear RNA, for example, that what I found was directly comparable to the same RNA in human beings, in either structure, or more importantly, function.

In chapter two, we discussed the first major zoom out of the idea wherein decision makers accepted model-based outputs as evidence, under the pretense that model-based suggestions of risk from exposures to potential harms from air contaminants could be assumed to scale up from extremely low exposures and harms to very small subsets of population, up to the entire population at all levels, over long periods of time, and vast periods of space. Again, I am in no way implying that this relationship is entirely false, and that air pollutants do not actually cause harm to some people. My receipts for asthma medications would conclusively show that I'm not an air pollution or asthma denier.

What I am arguing is that *defining evidence of harm went from the direct to the indirect, from the proximal to the distant, to the well-defined to the ill-defined (or undefined),* was to the detriment of public policy grounded in the rule of law: a system where people are "presumed innocent until proven guilty." Proven. Not modeled. A critically important element crept into public policy in this stage of the plague of models: the harms that are postulated are purely statistical harms: they cannot be proven or disproven either prospectively or retrospectively. This takes us out of the realm of *The Science,* at least it does if you've ever read Karl Popper, and believe that all science must be falsifiable.

In chapter three, we zoomed out yet again and looked at models which assumed that risks to various bio-geo-chemical systems only remotely related to human welfare can translate into risks to human beings, and in such a way as to legitimate the use of public policy to enjoin persons X from engaging in behavior Y, which might in turn somehow damage bio-geo-chemical system Z and harm your great grandchildren.

We'll look at the two highest of the high-profile examples of this expansion of the plague of models in chronological order of public attention: We'll start, once again, up in the ozone, this time with naturally forming ozone that floats at the very top of the atmosphere, shielding the Earth from ultraviolet radiation pouring from the Sun. Then, we'll come somewhat back down to earth, to talk about the 900-pound gorilla generally referred to as Climate Change, before examining the 9,000-pound Gorilla named COVID.

What makes ozone and climate change worthy of special attention is that both subjects are virtually 100 percent driven by computer modeling, as the nature of the proposed risks are far removed in space and time from any possibility of empirical measurement. That's an important distinction, so it's worth beating the deceased equine for a bit.

Prior to the concerns about the Ozone Hole and Climate Change, there were at least some empirically identifiable harms being done to people or their property that could be measured, tracked back to a specific potential cause, and therefore addressed in some manner consistent with the ideas of American (and previously Common Law) forms of jurisprudence and governance.

But with the Ozone Hole and Climate Change, the postulated risks to people and their property cannot be empirically determined: it can't be measured in any way that we would consider representative of reality. For one thing, in both cases, proposed harms are all far off in the future, and understanding the proposed causes of the harms requires an accurate understanding of the distant past, and complex systems that are far beyond current levels of human ability. With climate change, the risk is about changed weather patterns 50 to 100 years from now, affecting people entirely differently based on their wealth and technological capability at that time, and their ability to simply adapt to changes over time, none of which is predictable. In the case of the Ozone Hole, the risk to people is of possibly developing skin cancer and/or cataracts, again, problems that take decades to develop, and happen in a vast population of different sensitivities to UV radiation, different lifestyles, different technologies, different cultural habits…the list is nearly infinite.

So, at some crucial point (which we'll talk about more in depth as we go on) both the risks of climate change, and the risks of enhanced exposure to UV radiation caused by ozone depletion depend entirely on the use of model simulation: from gross conceptual models, to more complicated statistical and probabilistic models, these are risks that simply cannot, in the universe that we currently inhabit, actually be measured and understood by purely empirical means of measurement which, heretofore, your average person might have considered to be "evidence" for example, when someone was trying to show them why tractor X was better than tractor Y. I can assure you, that wasn't "Trust me, I have a model." Nor, for that matter, are any of these models subject to falsification in the conventional sense of the term.

And, as we've explored earlier, you can't simulate things without incorporating a vast array of assumptions about how you understand whatever empirical data that you do have, and even more assumptions of future events (which, rather by definition, must be considered to be 100% speculative, unless you are a psychic. Of course, if you're a psychic, you knew I was going to say that.)

So, let's get to our exploration of the Ozone Hole, particularly from a critical question which permeates this entire book, which is: *should our governments be able to use the outputs of simulation models as actual concrete evidence of harms being committed, person-to-person, that justifies the use of state force to intervene in either the economy, or personal choice of a person in a society that in theory at least, believes in the idea of inalienable, individual rights to life, liberty, property, and all that good stuff in the Western Operating System?*

4.1   The Other Ozone: At the Edge of Space!

Along about 1956, out at a research station in Antarctica, some intrepid (and thermally-hardy) researchers set about measuring the characteristics of the ozone that floats above the top of the stratosphere, that being the layer of the atmosphere that tops out at 50 km (31 miles) above sea level (the bottom of the stratosphere, though not quite as relevant to this story varies from 7 km to 20 km above sea level, depending on what part of the Earth you're talking about).

Yes, Ozone again. Didn't we deal with this already? And the answer is, yes and no. We are indeed talking about the same chemical as we discussed in chapter 3, but this ozone is found at a different level of the atmosphere, it is generated by different physical mechanisms, and it theoretically poses different risks to human health and the environment based on exposure to radiation, rather than exposure to chemical/physical pollutants such as particulate matter, or MSG.

Changes in the layer of ozone at the top of the stratosphere can affect how much solar radiation reaches the surface of the Earth, which in turn, affects the level of risk that surface-dwelling organisms (like people, plants, plankton, and polar bears) face from radiation-induced damage and mutation: sunburns and skin cancers, as well as cataracts. And no, before you ask, this won't be our last discussion of ozone, as it also plays a role in climate change.

High-altitude ozone, called "the good ozone," by those who champion the ozone layer, is formed when high-energy ultraviolet radiation strikes bimolecular oxygen way up high in the atmosphere, ripping the two oxygen atoms apart, and letting some of it reform as ozone, or trimolecular oxygen. The chemistry is daunting, so we won't get into it except to show the two-step production process in Image 16. Suffice to say, global satellite observations of the stratospheric ozone over the Antarctic started in 1978.

Why, you might ask, were scientists studying the ozone layer way up there, over the Antarctic (where the atmosphere is thinnest?). It certainly wasn't for the pleasure of experiencing the climatic characteristics of the region. That's a great question, and I didn't find a direct answer, other than the implication that stratospheric ozone research was triggered by a study in 1974 showing that *chlorofluorocarbons* (a steadily growing air contaminant since its discovery and use in the 1930s), abbreviated CFC's, could catalytically break down ozone in the presence of high-frequency UV light: exactly the conditions at the top of the stratosphere. That "catalytically" part is important because it suggests that one molecule of a CFC not only breaks down one molecule of ozone, but is regenerated over the course of the reaction, and can do it over and over and over again. There are, by the way, a large number of different CFC's capable of breaking down ozone. The EPA has a very lovely and extensive list (if you are interested).

Image 16. Two-step Stratosphere Ozone Production

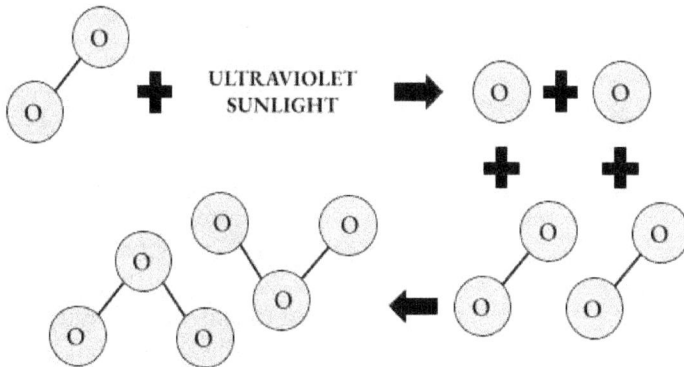

Source: NOAA Chemical Sciences Laboratory

Now that you know entirely more about ozone at both upper and lower levels of the atmosphere than you probably ever wanted to, what are CFCs, and why did (do) we love them and fear them so much? We love CFCs because they help us keep things cold, and make things fluffy, not to mention, being biologically inert propellants for all sorts of gases used industrially, commercially, and by consumers around the world. We love CFCs because keeping things cold has been of overwhelming importance in the advance of human civilizations, by way of preserving everything from foods to medicines, cooling homes, businesses, cars, and industries via their use in refrigeration and air conditioning systems. They are valuable for more than simply refrigeration and cooling: CFCs are used extensively in the development of aircraft and aerospace coatings, as well as for the production of foam used in packaging and transporting of delicate goods. And your childhood pool toys, most likely.

Chlorofluorocarbons as you might guess from the name, are organic chemicals (they are carbon-based) but have atoms of Chlorine and Fluorine in their molecular structure. Chlorine and Fluorine are highly reactive elements in the Periodic Table scheme of things. I'm not going to go into depth on CFC chemistry because, mostly, it's far too complex to get into here and even the "gee whiz" elements that I might find interesting, you probably won't. Instead, we'll focus on what CFCs' do, rather than what are CFCs, and give a few examples.

Most people's first-hand experience with CFCs would have come in with their exposure to modern (electric powered) refrigerators and modern (electric powered) air conditioning (We're not talking about evaporative coolers, or swamp coolers as we used to call them, nor iceboxes which were insulated boxes with actual wet or dry ice in them, but rather, modern "compressed cooling gas" type fridges and air conditioners. People born before the 1970s may have had their first experience with CFCs when using aerosol canisters to spray things around, such as deodorants, shaving creams, oven cleaners, whipped cream, and a few thousand other products best used aerated. But we'll start with air conditioning and refrigeration because I live in Las Vegas, a city which would almost certainly not exist without both of these technologies. And were it also not for spray deodorant, I would aver that Las Vegas would not be Las Vegas of today either. Phew!

According to the American Society of Heating, Refrigerating and Air-Conditioning Engineers, or ASHRAE, (and really, who would you look to for information on this?) Alexander Catlin Twining (And G-d Bless him) began experimenting with "vapor-compression refrigeration and ice-making in 1848. But it would be almost a hundred years later (1928) before a research team at General Motors synthesized CFCs for the Frigidaire company, whose shortened name (The Fridge) would forever be associated with the modern ice-box [see Image 17].

And how do we know this was really the beginning of modern refrigeration, you will ask? Because the very next year, in 1929, according to ASHRAE, an electrically refrigerated vending machine was developed by the Vendometer Corporation of New York. That same year, Frigidaire would debut an indoor electrically powered air conditioner (see Image 18). (Ironically, the size hasn't changed that much from one that would cool your home today.)

And in 1930, an absolutely pivotal year in the history of American civilization, the Kelvinator company installed an air conditioner in a Cadillac. If that is not the definition of a turning point in human history, I don't know what would be.

But as I mentioned above, over succeeding decades, environmental scientists became concerned that CFCs might pose a threat to the thin layer of ozone that protects us all from a bunch of UV radiation and began to regulate them. Sweden went first, banning aerosol canisters that used CFCs in 1978, which may have given birth to the American perception of smelly Europeans. Even though, Swedes are not technically Europeans. Nor are they technically smelly (well, some are) But there you go.

Image 17. History of F-12 (1928 Article)

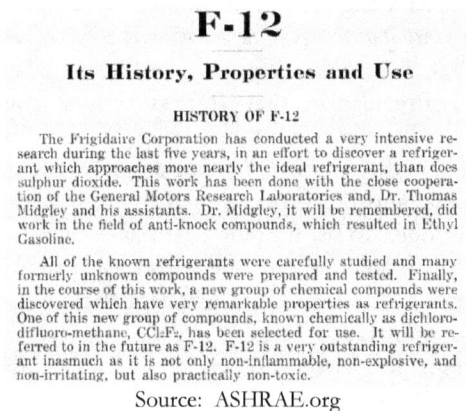

F-12

Its History, Properties and Use

HISTORY OF F-12

The Frigidaire Corporation has conducted a very intensive research during the last five years, in an effort to discover a refrigerant which approaches more nearly the ideal refrigerant, than does sulphur dioxide. This work has been done with the close cooperation of the General Motors Research Laboratories and, Dr. Thomas Midgley and his assistants. Dr. Midgley, it will be remembered, did work in the field of anti-knock compounds, which resulted in Ethyl Gasoline.

All of the known refrigerants were carefully studied and many formerly unknown compounds were prepared and tested. Finally, in the course of this work, a new group of chemical compounds were discovered which have very remarkable properties as refrigerants. One of this new group of compounds, known chemically as dichloro-difluoro-methane, CCl_2F_2, has been selected for use. It will be referred to in the future as F-12. F-12 is a very outstanding refrigerant inasmuch as it is not only non-inflammable, non-explosive, and non-irritating, but also practically non-toxic.

Source: ASHRAE.org

The United States Environmental Protection Agency followed Sweden's in the same year, and the US would go on to enact the CFC phase out program outlined in the Montreal Protocol on Substances that Deplete the Ozone Layer. Perhaps you didn't know it (I certainly didn't), but apparently:

September 16th is World Ozone Day, marking the anniversary of the signing of the Montreal Protocol on Substances that Deplete the Ozone Layer, the landmark international agreement focused on helping heal the ozone layer and protecting our planet from harmful ultraviolet (UV) radiation. [You'll want to mark your calendars appropriately.]

Image 18. Frigidaire Room Cooler (1929)

Source: ASHRAE.org

But what's most interesting about the Ozone Hole from our perspective, *is how the models of stratospheric ozone depletion were used as evidence to justify the elimination of CFCs,* a process that still continues today, proliferating a veritable volcano of regulations that affect everything from the refrigerator you buy, the air conditioner you buy, the propellants in the medical devices (like asthma inhalers) that you use, the packing materials that cushion your consumer products, and the process used to apply paint to your planes, trains, and automobiles, to say nothing of missiles, supersonic jets, rockets, and all that cool stuff. So strap on your rocket pack, and get ready to travel into the realm of the EPA's "Atmospheric and Health Effects Framework," also known as AHEF.

AHEF traces its roots back to 2006 but has been updated several times since then. The 2020 update report from the US EPA will be my primary source for the discussion of AHEF, though we'll look at some of the documents referenced in that report as critical to the estimation of the human health risks of stratospheric ozone depletion. For future reference, CFCs and related chemicals capable of destroying Ozone in the stratosphere are referred to as Ozone Depleting Substances, or ODS. As EPA explains:

> The United States Environmental Protection Agency (EPA) uses its Atmospheric and Health Effects Framework (AHEF) model to assess the adverse human health effects associated with a depleted stratospheric ozone layer. The AHEF estimates the

probable difference in skin cancer mortality, skin cancer incidence, and cataract incidence in the United States between different ODS emission scenarios.

And AHEF 2020 does paint a scary picture of the risk of stratospheric ozone depletion, as well as the expectations of salvation to come from the enforcement of the Montreal Protocol on Ozone Depleting Substances, mentioned earlier:

> With the current set of updates to the AHEF, the Montreal Protocol as amended and adjusted—compared with a scenario of no controls on ODS to reduce or avoid emissions—is now expected to prevent approximately 443 million cases of skin cancer, 2.3 million skin cancer deaths, and 63 million cataract cases for people in the United States born in the years 1890–2100.

> The strengthening of the original Montreal Protocol with its subsequent amendments and adjustments accounts for a significant portion of these benefits, resulting in an estimated 230 million fewer skin cancers, 1.3 million fewer deaths, and 33 million fewer cataract cases than the original 1987 Montreal Protocol over the same period.

And now…it's time for another disclaimer!

Author Context Box 6.

Lest anyone think that I don't treat the risks of skin cancer, cataracts seriously, I'll just observe that my mother had cataracts, as did her mother, and several of my family and friends had minor skin cancers removed over the years. I grew up, as much as I can be said to have grown up, in Los Angeles, the San Fernando Valley, specifically, and I spent every summer of my boyhood in the intense sun of the Valley (frequently, with temperatures over 100F), almost never with sunscreen.

Modern sunscreens didn't exist in the 1970s, apart from some zinc oxide that made people look like clowns, and was only worn by lifeguards, skiers, and well, clowns. I spent my formative teen years

---

driving around the Valley, left arm hanging out the window of my non-air-conditioned cars, and I only have to look down at that arm to see the effects of sun damage over those years. The base color of that arm is several shades darker than my right arm, and the skin is considerably more distressed by the passage of time. I am quite intensely aware that skin cancer is a constant risk for me, as are cataracts, and I check myself for potential skin cancers on a regular basis and am quite diligent about getting my eyes checked for cataracts every year.

As I mentioned about earlier risks, we explored (food additives, conventional air pollution), I am not a skeptic of the actual potential harms of things, especially those that can be documented with resort to simple, mechanistic, physics-based science, of the sort that led to the development of all the wonderful devices, medications, agriculture, and computers that underpin modern life.

So, in the case of stratospheric ozone depletion, I have zero problems with the science that starts at the top of the atmosphere, where the stratospheric ozone later exists, and traces the passage of sunlight down through the atmosphere to the surface of the Earth. And when you think about it, that's no small bit of science, given that it requires being able to measure things that originate in the sun (photons), randomly walk their way out of the sun to beam down to the Earth, hit the Earth at varying angles over the course of the day and year due to orbital mechanics, and complex climatic factors (including some that are not all that well understood, such as cloud cover), and then impinge on human, animal, and plant tissues living on the surface of the Earth. I have no problem with any of that science at all, really, though AHEF itself assigns an uncertainty factor to even those best understood aspects of ozone of about five percent.

So AHEF, as the EPA explains, was developed in the 1990s, and "The EPA uses AHEF to estimate the probable changes in skin cancer mortality, skin cancer incidence, and cataract incidence in the United States that result from different ODS emission scenarios when compared to a baseline scenario."

Unpacking that a bit, "Changes in health effects are calculated either for (a) incremental changes associated with one policy scenario relative to another or (b) relative to a 1979–1980 baseline. The 1979–1980 baseline refers to conditions pertaining to un-depleted ozone, or in other words, the health effects that would have occurred if the ozone concentration that existed in 1979–1980 had been maintained through the time period modeled."

And in that one statement, really, we move from what I'd consider the "science" part of the ozone hole/health hazard scenario into a realm of discussion much more worthy of some skeptical attention, which is the Model World.

The AHEF has five main computational steps contained in sub-models that together calculate estimates for incidence and mortality for various UV radiation-related health effects for a given ODS emission scenario. The sub-model computations are as follows:

1. Emissions Sub-model: *Simulates* [emphasis added] the past and future global emissions of 16 different ODS that are being phased out under the Montreal Protocol.

2. Ozone Depletion Sub-model: *Models* [emphasis added] impacts of ODS emissions on stratospheric ozone via changes in stratospheric chlorine and bromine.

3. UV Radiation Sub-model: *Models* [emphasis added] the induced instantaneous changes in ground-level UV radiation.

4. Exposure Sub-model: *Models* [emphasis added] the cumulative personal exposure to UV radiation by year, age, and location.

5. Effects Sub-model: *Derives* [emphasis added] dose-response relationships for incidence and mortality of health effects from baseline incidence data and projects changes in population-based future incidence and mortality.

In a nutshell, moving conceptually inward from the outer edge of the atmosphere, AHEF takes estimates of past and future CFC emissions, uses a model to estimate how that will thin the ozone layer, models the change in UV-radiation at ground-level from that ozone layer thinning, then models exposure to human beings at the Earth's surface, and finally, estimates how much that additional exposure to UV radiation might cause skin cancer in humans.

I've italicized a few words in the description above to emphasize that AHEF is not about *measurement* of the effects of ozone depletion and consequent increased UV radiation upon sensitive biological tissues (that's not practically possible), it is about *estimating* them in the past, present, and future via mathematical models that are, as we'll discuss, laden with assumptions. To start you off, lest you think that I'm just making stuff up, here's just one of those assumptions:

> The standard operating assumption in the AHEF is that individuals' sun exposure behavior remains the same in the scenario and baseline scenario. Human behavior to sun exposure is a source of uncertainty that is not easily quantified, so the AHEF assumes that human exposure behavior remains constant through time and does not explicitly take into account innovations in sun protection technology (e.g., improved sunglasses and sunscreens), increased public awareness of the effects of overexposure to UV radiation, or increased sensitization to the need for early treatment of suspicious lesions.

In other words, AHEF assumes that people will not react as people have acted through all of history, since the first primitive hominid draped "themselves" with animal skins and took to the shade to avoid having their skin burned. I'd have to argue that is a fairly large assumption.

Now, we could dig into AHEF for many dozens of pages, as in fact, EPA does in publicly available reports in 2010, 2015, and 2020. And, if you're intensely interested, I suggest reading those reports, though I should issue a mental health warning about this, as the reports are highly technical, and are about as bland and dry as the Gobi Desert, where, you would certainly get a sunburn, and place yourself at risk of cataracts.

But instead of going through all the voluminous details of how EPA estimates the past, present, and future of humanity's (and nature's) cutaneous health history, I'm going to focus in on what I consider to be the critical nexus of the issue: What evidence is used to assess how much risk UV radiation poses to human tissues? I'll give you a hint: it's not something that's going to scream out at you when you read EPAs reports about AHEF, and in fact, you'll have to do some digging (as I did) to find it, but, believe it or not, it brings us back all the way to our origins in this book: research conducted exposing animal tissue to some potential harm (in this case, UV radiation), and then using a pile of assumptions to extrapolate the impact that similar UV exposures would have on human tissues in both present day, and the future.

How many studies, you ask? About half a dozen, from the 1970s. On hairless mice, eye lenses taken out of young pigs, and, oh, a population of people from Salisbury, Maryland. And no, I'm not making that up either. How can I prove that? EPA's own words from AHEF 2020, p. 22:

> "This section describes the method for calculating future ground-level UV irradiance and relating these values to changes in human health effects. First, the predicted future ozone concentrations under various policy scenarios (as discussed in the previous section) are used to model the change in UV radiation reaching the ground for the latitudes across the United States. Those predicted changes in ground-level UV radiation intensity are then *biologically weighted using action spectra to reflect the extent to which different UV wavelengths cause a particular health effect* [emphasis added] (see Box 3)."

What is *Action Spectrum*, You Say?

An action spectrum describes the relative effectiveness of energy at different UV wavelengths in producing a particular biological response, such as development of melanoma, basal cell carcinoma, squamous cell carcinoma, or cataract. The AHEF and the Tropospheric Ultraviolet-Visible (TUV) model rely on action spectra for each health effect because action spectra provide information regarding which wavelengths of the total UV spectrum are most effective at causing the particular health effect. For example, UV-B wavelengths (280–320 nm) are known to cause erythema, as well as the development of skin cancer, cataract, and suppression of components of the immune system. UV-A radiation (320–400 nm) is not as readily absorbed by ozone (EEAP, 2019) and is not as potent as UV-B in the etiology of UV radiation damage-related health effects.

The AHEF uses the SCUP-h action spectrum (Spectrum Combined Utrecht/Philadelphia data, corrected for Human transmission) for modeling all types of skin cancer. *The SCUP spectrum was derived on the basis of the induction of squamous cell carcinoma in hairless mice (denoted as*

> *SCUP-m*). Because mouse skin and human skin have different absorption spectra for UV light, the action spectrum was corrected for human skin transmission by making adjustments to account for differences in epidermal thickness and the number of hair follicles per unit area. This adjusted action spectrum is denoted as SCUP-h (de Gruijl et al., 1993).
>
> *For cataract, the AHEF uses the Oriowo action spectrum* due to both its coverage of optimum wavelengths and the similarity of the pig lens to the human lens in composition and UV response (Oriowo et al., 2001). The Oriowo action spectrum is based on the *in vitro* induction of cataract in whole, cultured pig lenses spanning across wavelengths from 270 to 370 nm, thus extending into the UV-A spectrum.
>
> The UV Radiation Sub-model models the relationship between ozone and the amount of UV radiation reaching the Earth's surface using "look-up tables" generated with the Tropospheric Ultraviolet-Visible (TUV) atmospheric radiative transfer model"

The AHEF report explains further that:

> The UV Radiation Sub-model models the relationship between ozone and the amount of UV radiation reaching the Earth's surface using "look-up tables" generated with the Tropospheric Ultraviolet-Visible (TUV) atmospheric radiative transfer model. The TUV model was developed and is maintained at the National Center for Atmospheric Research and is available at: https://www2.acom.ucar.edu/modeling/tuv-download.
>
> The TUV model *first computes the amount of UV radiation reaching the Earth's surface as a function of solar zenith angle (SZA) and atmospheric composition including stratospheric ozone; this is done at each of 120 UV wavelengths from 280 to 400 nm. Next, the ground-level irradiance of each wavelength is multiplied by the biological effectiveness (action spectrum) of that wavelength and summed (integrated) over all contributing wavelengths, to yield the biologically effective irradiance* [emphasis added]. This is repeated over a grid of different solar angles and ozone columns, to generate a two-dimensional look-up table—one for each biological endpoint. The TUV model's look-up tables are

interpolated in the AHEF to estimate exposure at different locations and times.

And the next step is to ask how that additional UV radiation affects human health (p24):

> Once the appropriate action spectrum is selected for each health effect and the UV radiation dose of biologically active radiation and morbidity or mortality across latitudes are identified, statistical regression analyses are used to estimate the dose-response relationship, known as the BAF, for each health effect. The BAF measures the degree to which changes in exposure to UV radiation weighted by the appropriate action spectrum (as measured in Watts/m^2) cause incremental changes in health effects (incidence or mortality), estimated after accounting for the influence of birth year and age, as necessary.
>
> BAFs are defined as the percent change in a health effect resulting from a one-percent change in the intensity of UV radiation (weighted by the chosen action spectrum). For each health effect, the AHEF applies the BAF to predict future incidence and mortality. Estimated ground- level effective UV irradiance from the TUV model is combined with a selected BAF to translate changes in exposure to UV radiation to a percentage change in expected health effects.

Sorry to expose you to all that, but I anticipate some pushback on my claim that the entire edifice of risk-estimates of human harm from increased UV radiation as a result of Ozone Depletion rests on this small body of animal research. And yet, there it is, in EPA's own words, as of 2020.

So, let's dive into this whole "action spectrum," "biologically effective irradiance" thing (the latter is sometimes referred to, confusingly, as the BAF, or Biological Amplification Factor, elsewhere in the literature).

Way back in 1991, an article published by Hugh M. Pitcher and Janice D. Longstreth, *Melanoma Mortality and Exposure to Ultraviolet Radiation: an Empirical Relationship* studied the "relationship of melanoma deaths to ambient ultraviolet radiation levels for the United States. This was a fairly straightforward study that correlated estimated ambient levels of UV radiation, with data from EPA on melanoma death rates over a 30-year period. This was essentially a correlation study (from abstract): "Estimates of effective dose were derived by applying different weighting functions to the ambient UV energy levels predicted by the NASA model for 215 Standard Metropolitan Areas (SMA), thereby developing estimates of *active UV energy which would penetrate the epidermis of individuals at various locations* [emphasis added]." The "empirical" findings of the Pitcher and Longstreth article are not, in retrospect, surprising:

> A highly statistically significant association between all measures of dose and death rates is found, with dose estimates based on application of a weighting function derived from the action spectrum for DNA-damage (DNA-weighted dose) providing (very marginally) the strongest relationship. Controls for ethnicity, income, education, and occupation reduce the size of the effect, but the effect remains significant. The death rates in males show a greater response than those in females to changes in estimated dose. [Yes, indeed, too much sunshine causes skin cancer.]

However, Pitcher and Longstreth do not stop there, despite the title of the paper emphasizing that it is "empirical":

> Variations in the duration of the exposure measure (e.g., peak, or cumulative dose), the authors report, have a large impact on the *estimates* [emphasis added] of the effects that ozone depletion will have on cutaneous malignant melanoma (CMM) mortality. For a *dose estimate* [emphasis added] based on the amount of DNA-weighted UV energy received on a clear day in June ("peak dose"). Results imply a 1% reduction in ozone will result in a 1.6% increase in male death rates and a 1.1% increase in female death rates. *A dose estimate based on an annual amount of DNA-weighted UV energy ("annual dose")* [emphasis added] implies mortality changes of 0.82% for men and 0.57% for women for a 1% change in ozone.

Pitcher and Longstreth were, appropriately (and refreshingly) cautious in caveating their work. They conclude:

> Finally, the potential impacts on mortality caused by decreases in ozone in the 10-20% range are quite large if no other changes occur. In contrast to many other risk assessments, the change in

radiation levels associated with 10-20% depletions is well within the range of exposure for our data set. Barring other changes, a depletion of 10% would increase the death rate by 16%...for males and 11% for females.

However, other changes are bound to occur. Simple preventative measures, like wearing a sunscreen can sharply reduce exposure, especially the peak exposures which the weight of the current evidence suggests providing the best explanation of the role of UV in affecting melanoma death rates.

4.2   We're Feeling the Burn! Send in the Mice!

In a 1993 article published in the Journal of Cancer Research, a research team led by Frank R. de Gruijl, then listed as being with the Department of Dermatology, and the University of Utrecht, in the Netherlands, set out to assess the relationship between exposure to UV radiation, and the development of skin cancer, a topic of no small importance in the pale-skinned, Northern latitude country of outdoor exercise fanatics.

As de Gruijl et al. observe, although the relationship between CFCs and stratospheric ozone had been elucidated in the 1970s; and the later measurements of the ozone hole confirmed that the chemical reactivity of CFS seemed to actually be depleting the ozone layer (leading to a regional thinning of the layer referred to as the "ozone hole"); and a mechanism was proposed for potential causation of skin cancer by researcher R.B. Setlow in 1974 (DNA mutation via transdermal penetration of UV radiation); it wasn't until the early 1990s that efforts were made to empirically determine that relationship, with the work of de Gruijl and his team.

The challenge was, as de Gruijl observed in the 1993 article, "Direct information on the dependence of UV carcinogenesis *can only be obtained from animal experiments. It is not possible to extract such information for humans from epidemiological data* [emphasis added] …Protracted monochromatic irradiation of animals to induce skin cancers is not feasible, and the experiments are therefore carried out with broadband UV sources of various spectral compositions." In other words, because of the lengthy time it takes for skin cancers to develop, along with the ethical matter of zapping people until their skin burns was considered unethical for some strange reason (after all, people pay good money for that in tanning salons...go figure), previous research looked primarily at animals exposed to standard sun lamps and used sunburn as a surrogate indication for cancer risk.

But de Gruijl wanted to narrow things down a bit, and so, in came the mice. Specifically, hairless mutant mice, to be zapped with UV radiation from a filtered Xenon arc lamp. Most people are, blissfully, unfamiliar with hairless mice, which are a generally unattractive little breed of the rodent sort. So first, about those mice and their spa-like conditions. As the 1993 paper explains:

> The experiments were carried out between 1978 and 1991 under standardized conditions in order to maximize reproducibility. Both male and female hairless albino SKH:HR1 mice were used, and they entered the experiments at ages varying between 6 and 10 weeks. All mice originated from the breading stock of the former Skin and Cancer Hospital in Philadelphia. The animals were housed individually and had continuous free access to laboratory chow and tap water. The animal rooms were kept at 25°C and illuminated with yellow lamps (no UV output) in a 12-h day/night cycle.

Again, it has to be observed that people would have paid perfectly good money for this kind of treatment. At any rate, the one study mentioned in the 2020 AHEF report as being central to the "modeling of all types of skin cancer" is this one:

Frank. R. de Gruijl et al. (1993). *Wavelength dependence of skin cancer induction by Ultraviolet Irradiation of Albino Hairless Mice. Journal of Cancer Research*, Volume 53, p pp. 53-60, January 1993.

Abstract:
> Information on the variation in carcinogenicity with wavelength is crucial for risk assessments for skin cancers induced by UV radiation. Until recently, the wavelength (lambda) dependency of other detrimental UV effects, such as sunburn, have been used as substitutes. Direct information on the (lambda) dependency can only be obtained from animal experiments. To this end we accumulated a large data set on skin tumors induced by chronic UV exposure of albino SKH:HKI mice (14 different broadband UV sources and about 1100 mice): the data come from the Photobiology unit of the former Skin and Cancer Hospital in Philadelphia and from the Department of Dermatology of the University of

Utrecht. The (lambda) dependency was extracted from this data set (a statistically satisfactory description with $X^2 = 13.4$, df = 7) and represented by the Skin Cancer Utrecht-Philadelphia action spectrum, i.e., a set of factors to weight the exposures at different wavelengths according to their respective effectivenesses (inversely proportional to the daily exposure required for a median tumor induction time of 300 days). The fits obtained with other already available action spectra proved to be poor ($x^2 > 60$, df = 11). The maximum effectiveness was found at 293 nm, and above 340 nm the effectiveness showed a shoulder at about 10^{-4} of the maximum. A sensitivity analysis of the final solution for the (lambda) dependency showed a large margin of uncertainty above 340 nm and an information gap below 280 nm. The large variation in tumor responses in the present data set can be transformed to a coherent, common dose-response relationship by proper spectral weighting with this single action spectrum.

The authors generously also penned a Review article (that is in somewhat more readable, or at least, as readable as these things get, which is here:

Frank R. de Gruijl and Donald Forbes (1995). *UV-induced skin cancer in a hairless mouse model.* Review Article, *BioEssays*, Vol. 17, no. 7.

Summary:

Ultraviolet (UV) radiation is a very common carcinogen in our environment, but epidemiological data on the relationship between skin cancers and ambient solar UV radiation are very restricted. In hairless mice the process of UV carcinogenesis can be studied in depth. Experiments with this animal model have yielded quantitative data on how tumor development depends on dose, time and wavelength of the UV radiation. In combination with epidemiological data, these experimental results can be transposed to humans. Comparative studies on molecular, cellular and physiological changes in mouse and man can further our fundamental understanding of UV carcinogenesis in man. This is likely to improve risk assessments such as those related to a stratospheric ozone depletion, and to yield well-targeted intervention schemes, e.g., prescribing a specific drug or diet, for high-risk individuals.

As the 1993 de Gruijl study explains, "the experiments" [exposing hairless mice to UV radiation] ran from 1978 to 1991 and included both male and female hairless rats of the strain SKH:HR1 (more on them below) and the mice entered the experimental protocol between the ages of six to ten weeks.

Without going into the gruesome details, suffice it to say that the mice were exposed to a variety of UV radiation wavelengths for a range of times and intensities, during which their skin was visually examined for the development of tumors over 1 mm in size. It is worth noting here that these particular hairless mice were known to NOT spontaneously develop skin cancers, and only rarely develop other benign skin tumors or papillomas.

Surprisingly, to me at least, is that the final paragraph of the Summary of the 1993 de Gruijl paper is quite tentative, and it seems strange that it would be included into EPAs AHEF model as a definitive work. Here's the critical paragraph. It is technical, but I think, important (I'm going to trim out some of the detailed numerical data for better understanding):

> For the present data set various UV sources have been used to induce skin tumors in SKH:HR1 hairless mice: ranging from low UV exposures from sources with UVB radiation to excessive UV exposures from sources with mainly long wave UVA radiation.
>
> The time lapses until 50% of the animals bore tumors in different experiments varied from 2 months to 2 years. A proper spectral weighting with the SCUP action spectrum focuses these scattered data points (Fig. 1) on a common dose-time relationship. *Evidently, such an action spectrum is operationally useful for a definition of the carcinogenic UV dose* [emphasis added].

So far, so good. But what does not seem to have carried through to the inclusion of the de Gruijl actions spectrum into the AHEF risk model are the strong caveats given by the authors at the end of their summary:

> It should be stressed, however, that it *is an operationally defined action spectrum that does not yield direct and unambiguous information on the photochemical reactions leading to tumor formation* [emphasis added].

The overall shape of the SCUP action spectrum below 340 nm roughly resembles what one would expect with UV-induced mutations, but the shoulder above 340 nm appears somewhat high. *The definition of the action spectrum above 340 nm is not very accurate* [emphasis added], and an extension into the visible may be necessary, but we lack sufficient data to quantify the carcinogenicity of wavelengths larger than 390 nm. As UV carcinogenesis is probably an intricate, dynamical multistep process, the *interpretation of the present action spectrum is by no means straightforward* [emphasis added]. The poor results we obtained thus far with action spectra constructed from data on mutagenesis and epidermal transmission appear to underline the complexity of the spectral response.

In other words, the landmark study included in the biological risk module of the EPA's integrated risk model found some limited connection between certain exposures to certain wavelengths of UV radiation and to the formation of skin tumors in hairless mice which might be useful "operationally," but is quite limited in its accuracy and utility.

I should note here that I have absolutely no problem with the nature of the de Gruijl study: to my eye, having studied biology and environmental science for about 16 years in the classroom and lab, and another 20 years reading such studies as part of my policy research, the study looks like a fairly typical cellular and molecular biology study. The researchers were very explicit about the findings of the study, and their utility for understanding the relationship between UV radiation exposure and skin cancer in hairless mice, used as a surrogate for studying the potential for skin cancer formation in humans based on comparable UV exposures.

I say this because, once again, I want to make it extremely clear: I do not have a problem with the studies that were done to elucidate the risk of skin cancer (and cataracts) from exposure to UV radiation. I am not bashing the science, or the scientists in anything relating to this subject at all. In fact, I laud the researchers for doing the work: it was highly relevant, and important knowledge to gather at the time of serious concern about a dreaded human sickness.

What I consider to be a part of the plague of models is how such research is then incorporated into complex abstract models that give such research findings an aura of greater utility than is warranted, and usually proclaimed by the original researchers themselves.

The de Gruijl summary paper is by far the more readable of the two and answers some questions people might have about the previous study, and the general idea behind them. So, for example, on the question of "okay, so why study mice, rather than people, or pigs (often used to test things related to human skin reactivity) or donated human tissue samples for that matter. It's not clear from the previous de Gruijl paper, nor for that matter, from the entire literature why exactly human tissue samples were off the table for studies like this. The de Gruijl summary seems to capture the essence of the reason, however, which was "convenience: (p652)":

> Mice are convenient representatives of mammals in experiments on toxic effects: they are easy to breed and maintain and, most of all, they are small, which facilitates attaining sufficient statistical power by large enough numbers of tested individuals. Mice are by far the most used animals in experimental carcinogenesis, including experimental skin carcinogenesis. For the latter the fur is a handicap, especially with UV irradiation, because the hairs form an impenetrable shield. Shaving off the fur to expose the underlying skin could introduce a confounding stimulatory effect on tumor formation by the carcinogenic agent under investigation. Hairless skin is exceptionally well-suited for experiments on carcinogenesis in general: the animals need not be killed to assess the tumor load as is necessary with internal tumors. The tumors are readily observable at very small sizes (a trained observer has no problem in spotting tumors smaller than 1 mm across), and multiple tumors per mouse can be followed in their progression without any serious discomfort for the animals. Moreover, the carcinogenesis by low-level chronic UV exposure of hairless skin has a direct analogy in everyday human life.

That is, of course, if you assume that humans wear no clothes; don't use any skincare products that might alter the skin's reaction to UV radiation; or might alter their behavior due to discomfort, or, I don't know, concerns about developing tumors on their skin (much less wrinkles - I don't think mice much care about wrinkles). But otherwise, mice are just like humans. Besides, nobody really cares too much if you kill a few of them. Or a few thousand, for that matter.

One might also observe that these mice were somewhat unlike human beings in that they were genetically pure-bred, whereas humans are not, and of course, those mice were actually unlike most other mice, in that they were hairless. And, of course, there were indications that the researchers knew that hairless mice were not perfect (or even near-perfect) analogues for human skin (p653):

> Among the SKH-2 hairless phenotype, there are two pigment variants: brown and black. The brown variant is less susceptible to UV carcinogenesis, while strangely enough, the blacks appear to be as susceptible as the closely related SKH-1 albino hairless mice. In contrast to humans, where the melanocytes (pigment cells) are located in the epidermis, most of the melanocytes and their melanin are located in the dermis in non-irradiated pigmented (hairless) mice. Upon UV exposure the SKH-2 mice do, however, develop epidermal melanocytes, and pigment is deposited in the epidermis.

Read that carefully. In the hairless mice, more heavily pigmented skin is as susceptible to UV exposure as in the albino mice. Meanwhile, brown variants are less susceptible to UV radiation than either black or albino mice. And there's the small qualification that in fact, humans and mice do not even have their melanocytes (melanin-generating cells) in the same layers of their skin. And of course, there are still other differences. For example, human skin thickens at higher UV radiation levels, and becomes more pigmented (we tan). These hairless mice don't do that (p655).

De Gruijl's summary article also has a quite cautiously worded conclusion, and also points out something interesting: de Gruijl's research was not particularly intended to reveal how reducing ozone-depletion might reduce skin cancer risks to humans. Team de Gruijl was on the hunt for better sunscreens and medications to prevent skin cancers (p658):

> In many respects UV carcinogenesis appears to be similar in mouse and man, e.g., at the level of DNA damage and resulting mutations in the p53 tumor suppressor gene, effects of fat diet and implications of UV-induced modification of the immune system (most notably a lasting antigen-specific tolerance). Thus, testing the carcinogenic potency of certain lamps (e.g., halogen lamps) or certain photo-sensitizing agents in the hairless mouse model is very relevant for a proper assessment of the carcinogenic risk in humans. In making the extrapolation to humans, the fundamental differences in sensitivity between the two species have, of course, to be taken into account.

Epidemiological data enable us to make crude estimations of differences in sensitivity and in responses. A fundamental understanding of these differences in sensitivities and responses is now emerging, and are likely to refine the risk assessments, and open up new possibilities for well-targeted interventions to lower carcinogenic risk from UV exposure in our indoor and outdoor environments.

Now at this point in the discussion, you're observing that, well, this was all so 30-years ago, so 1990s, and you'd be correct. But notice that this research is still what is cited (and presumably used) to estimate risk to human beings from predicted heightened UV-B radiation exposure as a result of stratospheric ozone depletion. One might think there would have been some progress in pinning all this down in 25 years (certainly, de Gruijl thought there would be), for such an important subject. However, to remind you, this is EPA, AHEF 2020 (p22):

The AHEF uses the SCUP-h action spectrum (Spectrum Combined Utrecht-Philadelphia data, corrected for Human transmission) for modeling all types of skin cancer. The SCUP spectrum was derived on the basis of the induction of squamous cell carcinoma in hairless mice (denoted as SCUP-m). Because mouse skin and human skin have different absorption spectra for UV light, the action spectrum was corrected for human skin transmission by making adjustments to account for differences in epidermal thickness and the number of hair follicles per unit area. This adjusted action spectrum is denoted as SCUP-h (de Gruijl et al., 1993).

4.3 Cataract Risks: From Sunbathers in Maryland to in a Pig's Eye

In 1998, as concerns about the ozone hole, UV exposure, skin cancer, and cataracts was in full foment, an epidemiological study was conducted in Salisbury, Maryland, by a team of researchers led by Sheila K. West (West, et al. hereafter).

Sunlight Exposure and Risk of Lens Opacities in a Population-Based Study and The Salisbury Eye Evaluation Project, Sheila K. West, PhD; Donald D. Duncan, PhD; Beatriz Munoz, MSc; Gary S. Rubin, PhD; Linda P. Fried, MD, MPH; Karen Bandeen-Roche, PhD; Oliver D. Schein, MD, MPH (1998).

The Salisbury study followed 2520 people, aged 65-84 years old, in Salisbury Maryland for 2 years, from 1993 to 1995. (26.4% were African Americans). The data for the study was partly empirical, but mostly survey based. The empirical part consisted of measuring the "cortical opacity," (an indicator of cataract development) of the study participants, which was then matched with survey-based data to develop a relationship between "Maryland sun-years of exposure" and the development of cortical opacity. These were the results:

> The odds of cortical opacity increased with increasing ocular exposure to UV-B (odds ratio [OR], 1.10; 95% confidence interval [CI], 1.02-1.20). The relationship was similar for women (OR, 1.14; 95% CI, 1.00-1.30) and for African Americans (OR, 1.18; 95% CI, 1.04-1.33). Analyses of the ocular dose by each age group after the age of 30 years showed no vulnerable age group, suggesting damage is based on cumulative exposure.

Unpacking that a bit requires additional explanation. First, about the survey: to estimate how much UV-B the survey participants were exposed to, they were asked to complete a survey. A "random sample of residents of Salisbury, Md, aged 65 to 84 years was recruited for a home interview and an examination at the SEE clinic, which included lens photography and administration of a questionnaire about sun exposure during leisure and work times over the lifetime of the participant since the age of 30 years." Yes, you read that right, a bunch of elderly folks were asked to look back and estimate how much time they'd spent in the sun over the previous 30 years. The screeners asked: "For the job you held longest in your life, did you spend more than 2 hours outside during daylight in the summer months?" Another question "asked respondents to self-rate their vision status on a scale of 1 to 10, with 10 being excellent." I certainly could not meaningfully answer such a survey question myself, and I'm only 60. Of course, in those 30 years, I lived in California, Texas, Virginia, Nevada, British Columbia, and Alberta, where climatic conditions were rather radically different with regard to being willing to spend much time out in the sun. (Not to mention the actual intensity of the sun in those locations).

And now, some explanation of statistical terms. The "odds-ratio" expresses the relationship between in this case, exposure to UV-B at a certain level, and the development of cortical opacity. So, an odds-ratio of

1.10 would indicate that, basically, a person exposed to the amount of UV radiation estimated over the span of exposure time covered in the survey people completed were about 10 percent more likely to show cortical opacity on examination. The "confidence interval" of 95% (which is considered the gold-standard for most scientific research) means that the researchers are confident that their results would only have happened because of random factors 5% of the time. As an aside, while this sounds really cool, if you think about it, a 5 percent chance that randomness would account for your results means that if you ran that same experiment 20 times, one of those times you'd find a result that was interesting, but meaningless. Now, a cynic might observe that for many studies, you could run 20 cycles of the calculations, and if there were any probabilistic components to the mathematical calculations involved, you could get the one "worth publishing" by accident, and nobody would need to know about the other 19 runs…but of course, we know that scientific researchers are beyond the temptations of bias or wishful thinking.

And a bit more on that odds ratio thing. Is an odds-ratio of 10% (it was almost 20% for the African Americans in the sample) found in an epidemiology study of this sort meaningful in a real-world sense? Well, not particularly. As the CDC (an agency now sadly fallen into a crisis of credibility partly because of the plague of models) explains:

An odds ratio of
- (or close to 1.0) indicates that the odds of exposure among case-patients are the same as, or similar to, the odds of exposure among controls. The exposure is not associated with the disease.
- greater than 1.0 indicates that the odds of exposure among case-patients are greater than the odds of exposure among controls. The exposure might be a risk factor for the disease.
- less than 1.0 indicates that the odds of exposure among case-patients are lower than the odds of exposure among controls. The exposure might be a protective factor against the disease.
- the magnitude of the odds ratio is called the "strength of the association." The further away an odds ratio is from 1.0, the more likely it is that the relationship between the exposure and the disease is causal. For example, an odds ratio of 1.2 is above 1.0, but is not a strong association. *An odds-ratio of 10 suggests a stronger association* [emphasis added].

Ten? Does an odds ratio of 10 suggests a stronger association? Then what does an odds-ratio of 1.10 mean in the bigger scheme of things?

Rather than get too deep into the statistical weeds on all this (despite having had several classes in statistics, I'm not a statistician, nor would I ever play one on television), I'm going to leave this discussion in the hands of my absolutely favorite science writer of all time, Gary Taubes, famous for skewering the sacred cows in the War on Salt, and the War on Fat, and the idea of "A Calorie is a Calorie is a Calorie."

Writing in Science, in 1995, Taubes explores the growing problem of statistical misunderstanding of study results regarding environmental exposures to possible health hazards. In *Epidemiology Faces its Limits,* Taubes observes that a flurry of studies being covered breathlessly in the media were causing an "epidemic of anxiety." Risks were seemingly everywhere, Taubes observes, from "hair dyes (lymphomas, myelomas and leukemia) to coffee (pancreatic cancer and heart disease, to oral contraceptives and other hormone treatments…."

Worse as Taubes quotes the editors of the New England Journal of medicine, "Americans increasingly find themselves beset by contradictory advice. No sooner do they learn the results of one research study than they hear of one with the opposite message."

I'll leave the readers to track down Taubes article and read the whole thing, as they will marvel at how little has seemingly changed in the way that the media, and the regulatory community treat studies indicating relatively small risks from environmental causes. This paragraph is the one that I remembered, 25 years later, as I was writing this book:

> As a "general rule of thumb," says Angell of the New England Journal, "we are looking for a relative risk of three or more [before accept publication], particularly if it is biologically implausible or if it's a brand-new finding." Robert Temple, director of drug evaluation at the Food and Drug Administration, puts it bluntly: "My basic rule is if the relative risk isn't at least three or four, forget it." But as John Bailar, an epidemiologist at McGill University and consultant for the NEJM, former statistical points out, there is no reliable way of identifying the dividing line. "If you see a 10-fold relative risk and it's replicated and it's a good study with biological backup, like we have with cigarettes and lung cancer, you can draw a strong inference," he

says. "If it's a 1.5 relative risk, and it's only one study, and even a very good one, you scratch your chin and say maybe.

If you'd like a bit more statistics with your statistics, another illuminating (though much less easy-to-understand) article about this was written by Henian Chen, Patricia Cohen, and Sophie Chen, in the journal "Communications in Statistics - Simulation and Computation, in 2010. The basic conclusion of their study, "How Big is a Big Odds Ratio? Interpreting the Magnitudes of Odds Ratios in Epidemiological Studies," is that a study should be considered of only low significance if the odds ratio is below 1.68, of medium significance if the odds ratio is between 1.68 and 3.47, and of strong significance if the odds ratio is over 6.71.

In context then, one would have to say that while vaguely interesting, the Salisbury study was nothing to hang one's sun hat on, much less justify a world-spanning treaty to phase out a stupendously useful and popular class of chemicals used to manufacture a vast range of useful materials and devices that saved humanity much suffering and deprivation. Now, back to the studies.

Model of Risk of Cortical Cataract in the US Population with Exposure to Increased Ultraviolet Radiation due to Stratospheric Ozone Depletion, Sheila K. West, Janice D. Longstreth, Beatriz E. Munoz, Hugh M. Pitcher, and Donald D. Duncan. (2005).

Abstract:

The authors modeled the possible consequences for US cataract incidence of increases in ultraviolet B radiation due to ozone depletion. Data on the dose-response relation between ocular exposure to ultraviolet B radiation and cortical cataract were derived from a population-based study (the Salisbury Eye Evaluation Project, Salisbury, Maryland) in which extensive data on cataract and ultraviolet radiation were collected in persons aged 65–84 years. Exposure estimates for the US population were derived using estimated ultraviolet radiation fluxes as a function of wavelength. US Census data were used to obtain the age, ethnicity, and sex distribution of the population. Predicted probabilities of cataract were derived from the age-, sex-, and ethnicity-specific ocular ultraviolet exposure data and were modeled under conditions of 5–20% ozone depletion. The analysis indicated that by

2050, the prevalence of cortical cataract will increase above expected levels by 1.3–6.9%. The authors estimate that with 5–20% ozone depletion, there will be 167,000–830,000 additional cases of cortical cataract by 2050. Because of the high prevalence of cataract in older persons, at a 2003 cost of $3,370 per cataract operation, this increase could represent an excess cost of $563 million to $2.8 billion.

But while West et. Al. uses one of their own prior papers ("Sunlight Exposure and Risk of Lens Opacities in a Population Based Study: The Salisbury Eye Evaluation Project, JAMA, 1998) to define the action spectrum (The 2016 West paper makes some major assumptions about extrapolation capability from that sample. For example:

> In order to predict changes in cataract prevalence for the United States under varying levels of ozone depletion, *we had to assume that populations across the United States had ocular exposure behaviors (hat wearing, use of glasses, percentage of time spent outside, etc.) similar to those of our sample in Maryland. Moreover, for our predictions relative to the year 2050, we also assumed that these behaviors would not change over time* [emphasis added].

I'd say that these are two very large assumptions, the first being that small samples can be hand-waved as representing larger populations, and the second being what I call the "static fallacy," that critical variables one absolutely *will* change over time are held as constants. As an aside, you see this all the time in public policy analysis, such as with electric vehicles for example. EV boosters love to predict how the technology for electric vehicles will evolve, but they usually assume that for some reason, internal combustion engine technology would be static. In other variations, governments make assumptions all the time that people will not react to things they do even though they know, with absolute certainty, that they will. See also, black markets.

Another assumption: "Since the basis for the dose-response function is cumulative exposure over the year and there is little empirical basis on which to estimate the spatial pattern of ozone depletion at middle or low latitudes, where estimates of current ozone depletion are low, we chose to assume that ozone depletion would occur at the same percentage rate from baseline levels for all locations for which estimates were made. This assumption is consistent with a well-mixed increase in stratospheric halogens and has the advantage of clearly illustrating the nonlinear relation between ozone levels and annual ultraviolet exposure levels." How do we know that stratospheric halogens are "well-mixed," they don't say.

And finally…These estimates were based on the assumption of stable changes in ozone depletion—that is, *that people will live for 40 or more years under the same amount of ultraviolet radiation*—while in actuality ultraviolet radiation is likely to fluctuate (although the degree is uncertain). As I mentioned earlier, I'm not the "average person," having lived in 5 US States (NJ, CA, TX, VA, and NV) and 2 Canadian Provinces (BC and AB), it still seems to be a rather large assumption, particularly when paired with the assumption that the people will also not change their behaviors over time. I suppose we could call this a double-static assumption, otherwise known as the "frog in a warming pot" theory of human behavior. (That like frogs, the humans will just stay where they are as they progressively fry without moving or changing behavior, until they die).

Enough with the rats, now let's move onto something a bit juicer. Bacon! No, not really, but it does involve pigs. Specifically, what research on pigs (or parts of pigs) can tell us about the risk of cataract development in the context of a diminishing ozone layer.

4.4   In a Pig's Eye!

Trigger warning: if you are particularly squeamish, and you couldn't handle that whole "dissection of a frog and fetal pig" thing in high school biology (Yes, I know, I'm dating myself), then you might want to skip over this part and go to the concluding paragraphs of the section. We'll start with this study, that I'll abbreviate as "Oriowo" for the last name of the primary author.

Action Spectrum and Recovery for In Vitro UV-Induced Cataract Using Whole Lenses, Olanrewaju M. Oriowo, Anthony P. Cullen, B. Ralph Chou, and Jacob G. Sivak

The purpose of Oriowo was "To establish the in vitro action spectrum for acute UV cataractogenesis using whole cultured lenses. The recovery pattern of the induced cataract was also investigated." That's pretty straightforward. Cataractogenesis is a term for "Cataract induction" (the formation of a cataract), which is what I'll use as we go forward.

The way this was done was by exposing the lenses of the eyes, taken from young pigs (6 to 8 months old) that had been slaughtered at a local abattoir, presumably, for food, though the study doesn't go into details. The lenses of the eyes were "aseptically dissected" (meaning, the dissection conditions were sterile to avoid contamination) and the lenses were placed into a "culture medium," a mixture of "porcine serum," preservatives, and antibiotics, the details of which we don't need to get into, and which probably would not be overly illuminating to discuss anyway. The critical assumption of Oriowo, is *"Because the pig's embryological growth and development are typical of mammals and its shape and size are similar to the human lens, some inferences may be made to the human lens."* Given the rather large number of variations between species, I'd have to say that this is a somewhat slim reed to hang a giant, global-harm reduction treaty, on, but that's just me.

This is the part where things get a bit icky. The isolated lenses of the piglets were then zapped with UV energy at a range of wavelength bands in the UV spectrum, ranging from 270 to 370 nanometers, using reflected radiation from a Xenon Arc lamp for periods ranging from 49 seconds to approximately 22 hours. The irradiated spots on the lenses were then monitored (eyeball to eyeball, via dissecting microscope) every 6 to 12 hours, up to 48 hours post-irradiation, to detect the presence of any UV-induced opacity, which was considered an indicator of cataract induction. *Oriowo* found that certain wavelengths of UV light (specifically 270, 300, and 365 nanometer wavelengths) caused opacities at a "threshold" radiation value of 0.057, 0.069, and 137.19 Joules per exposed square centimeter. Permanent damage, however, was found to occur only at twice the threshold for damage, interestingly enough, radiation in the UV-A spectrum actually repairs damage caused by UV-B.

Approximately 648 lenses were used in the study, though no mention is made whether they were in matched sets, or mix-and matched, nor otherwise graded for size, thickness, density, or other variables that might be of relevance. Hence, we have to assume that the researchers were assuming that "a lens is a lens is a lens," regardless of exactly which particular animal it came from, after the animal had lived for between 6 and 8 weeks, and were slaughtered, one assumes, under less-than-ideal conditions for ensuring their stability.

There are a variety of assumptions used in the *Oriowo* study, however, that may or may not have made it all the way down the line to inclusion in AHEF, such as, pigs have a lot in common with humans, but other than some notable examples related to Hunter Biden, they don't have all that much in common behaviorally. Another assumption is that a lens dissected out of the eyeball of a pig, kept in a solution unlike the native solution in which it would exist, and without the protections of external and adjacent tissues (like, eyelids and corneas) were comparable to lenses in intact pig's eyes, and by extrapolation, to intact human eyes.

That brings us back to AHEF, and to EPA's model which is the nexus connecting everything from ozone thinning the top of the stratosphere to the risks of human mortality.

According to EPA, "Of the major sources of uncertainty associated with the AHEF, the total quantified uncertainty is roughly 60 percent," as summarized in table 5.

As can be seen from the table, the uncertainties in the study are sharply different when we move from considering the empirical elements of AHEF (the passage of UV radiation through a thinned stratospheric ozone layer down to human eye exposure at ground level), which was only estimated at 5% uncertain, to the translation of those exposures to human health effects, which is estimated at 60%. A full 80% of that risk is concentrated in the "biological amplification factors" used to extrapolate estimates of mortality and morbidity due to UV-B exposures (presumably based on the *Salisbury* study) and another 10% from uncertainty about the choice of the UV action spectra discussed above.

Table 5. Major Sources of Quantified Uncertainty

Source of Uncertainty	Quantified Uncertainty
Translating column ozone to ground-level UV: TUV Model	$\approx 5\%$
Translating UV exposure to human health effects: Uncertainty in the BAFs • CCM mortality (6%) • NMSC mortality (5%) • NMSC incidence (30%)	$\leq 30\%$
Uncertainty with choice of action spectrum	$\approx 50\%$
Early life exposure v. whole life exposure	$\approx 10\%$
Total $\sqrt{(5^2 + 30^2 + 50^2 + 10^2)}$	$\approx 60\%$

Source: Global Programs Division, Office of Air and Radiation, U.S. EPA.

EPA 2006 also explains that "The last two sources of quantified uncertainty-the age-weighted exposure scenario assumption and the estimated BAFs (the extrapolations from UV exposure estimates to mortality and morbidity incidence) also introduce relatively modest variation in the estimated health effects, of about 11 percent and up to 30 percent, respectively.

Table 6. Factors with Unknown Contributions to Uncertainty

Factor	Parameter
Change in Ozone Estimates	• Composition of future atmosphere • Ability to model atmospheric processes accurately • Response of ozone layer to changing ODS concentrations • Effect of climate change on ozone depletion • Global Compliance with modeled policy scenarios • Changes in composition and quantity of ODS emissions
Change in UV Radiation	• Long-term systematic changes in atmospheric opacity (e.g. clouds, aerosols, other pollutants)
Change in Health Effect Estimates	• Changes in Human UV exposure behaviour • Laboratory techniques and instrumentation for deriving an action spectrum • Improvements in medical care and/or increased longevity • Changes in socioeconomic factors (e.g. demographics and human behavioural changes) • Baseline information (e.g. misreporting of skin cancer incidence and mortality data) • Changes in population composition and size

Source: Global Programs Division, Office of Air and Radiation, U.S. EPA.

Other unquantified sources of uncertainty EPA attributes to AHEF can be seen in table 6. Some of them, such as the assumptions of unchanging human behavior, the potential development of new medical technologies, the assumption of non-mobility, and others are rather large stretches, as we discussed above.

4.5   Model Malpractice and the Ozone Hole

When you ask the question of "how do we know that eliminating CFCs in order to stop ozone layer thinning to prevent human risks of skin cancer and cataracts," after more than 40 years, (and even I find this amazing) it still comes down, according to the EPA, to studies on a small group of people in Maryland, studies of the effect of UV radiation on the back-skin of mutant hairless mice, and the effect of zapping naked lenses of the eyes of piglets with enough UV radiation to cause them to cloud up.

As with the lower level regulations of conventional air pollutants, I would not say that the causal chain of effect from "Peter in Pennsylvania put Freon in his car," to "70-year old Mary in Maryland developed cataracts" was clear enough to constitute evidence that would warrant telling Peter he had to shell out major bucks to upgrade his air conditioner to run on something else (or forego his air conditioner, as modern-day environmentalists would insist) because doing so posed some significant risk to Mary, who may or may not have worn sunglasses, worn hats, slathered on sunscreen, and spent various amounts of time outdoors over the course of her life, and who may have had any number of other potential causes of her cataracts, and who, in fact, may have moved all over the place within and beyond Maryland based on her recollection of life over the last 30 years. By the same rationale, I wouldn't judge that the empirical case was solidly made to support any of the coercive regulations on industry or individuals that were instituted to sever the chain of events that the government believed justified on the basis that people were harming other people by using ozone-depleting chemicals or were particularly likely to do so in the future.

But once again, I suggest you form your own judgment, and choose your sunscreen, hat, sunglasses, lava-lava, umbrella, or tan-enhancer wisely, as you choose.

And now, for the penultimate example of the plague of models (this would have been top dog until 2019 and COVID-19) …man-made, or person-made, or anthropogenic Catastrophic Climate Change.

5

Models Take over the World

T he threat of catastrophic anthropogenic Climate Change, and the Godzilla of Regulatory Schemes that accompanies it, represents, for the moment, the most expansive outward expansion of the plague of models.

We started at the smallest level of the plague of models, exploring the risk and regulation nexus inside the intestines of the human body, then zoomed out of the body to exposures to toxins in the ambient air, then outward again to ambient UV radiation, we now turn to a model that's truly global in scope: from the depths of the oceans, to the very fringes of space, we are told that anthropogenic climate change poses historically unprecedented levels of risk to everything: people, animals, insects, plants, fungi, corals, and everything else that exists within the fringes of Earth's atmosphere. It is the Mother-of-All-Risks (MOAR). Even bigger than COVID-19 (which is coming, I promise). But first, we need, yes, another Author Context Box.

Author Context Box 7.

Though it pains me to do this, as I have had to do this so many, many times in discussing climate change science and or policy, I have to re-state my basic "position" on climate science. Am I an "accepter," or "denier" of climate change science? That is, do I accept that what's postulated as the "science" of climate change reflects societies best empirically based, scientifically derived understanding of how climate change operates in the physical world? The answer to that is pretty much a big "YES," but let me be even more explicit.

Do I think that the *physics* of climate change as we currently understand it solidly describes how the climate actually functions in the tangible universe?

Yes, I do. Have I studied that? Yes, for several years in college, and I maintained at least a survey-level awareness of developments in the field ever after.

Do I think that the *chemistry* of climate change as we currently understand it solidly describes how climate chemistry actually functions in the tangible universe? *Yes, I do.* Have I studied that? Yes, I studied chemistry for about 4 years in college, and again, maintained at least a survey-level awareness of developments in the field ever after.

Do I think that the *biology/ecology* of climate change as we currently understand it solidly describes how climate biological and ecological impacts actually play out in the real world? *That would be a qualified "mostly."* Have I studied that? Yes indeed, in fact, biology, specifically applied molecular biology and environmental science and engineering was my entire academic focus leading to the doctorate. I studied biology and environmental science and engineering for about 16 years in college, and again, maintained at least a survey-level awareness of developments in the field ever after. The reason I rate this one a "mostly," is because biology and ecology are applied physics and chemistry of living things, and living things feature massive non-linearity and challengingly emergent functions that cannot be precisely captured or well understood, even relatively simple biological systems, such as a moderate-sized ecosystem like a single river valley, much less the global ecosystem.

Do I think that *climate modeling* as we currently use it is an empirical or scientific endeavor that describes physical reality as we know it? *Not in the least.* In fact, I think that representing abstract mathematical as science is itself a denial of what science actually is both epistemology and practically.

Do I think that *climate policy* and disputes over climate policy have anything to do with *science acceptance* and *science denial*? No. And I'd go so far as to say that anyone who tries to bring science denial into policy discussions is an ignoramus.

Climate change is, of course, a rather large topic to address in any shelf full of books, much less one section of one book. So, to make the discussion manageable, and to stick with our primary focus, which is the nexus of risk models and coercive regulation, we're going to focus on one element of the climate change debate, which is, broadly, *can models predict the future, and should they be accepted as the basis for implementing policies, rules, and regulations intended to stave off various predicted possible future realities.*

But before we can get to that, we must unpack things a bit, because projected (and proclaimed) climate risks that humans face from our enrichment of greenhouse gases in the atmosphere actually rests on a nested cluster of models. So, let's take a break to talk about oysters. Yes, Oysters. I love oysters and could talk about them and extol their gustatory qualities at some length, having lived in, and having to learned how to shuck oysters in Oyster Paradise, also known as British Columbia, Canada.

Pearls form in oysters when some irritant has penetrated the flesh of an oyster. Most often, not surprisingly, this is a tiny grain of sand, though it can be all kinds of fascinating things, like parasites, tiny insects, and what have you. Anyway, in a response to the irritation, the oyster coats the grain of sand in layer after layer of nacreous material called "nacre," until, after a time, you have the lovely spherical beauties that have inspired so many paeans, wars, marital joys, marital woes, and cost so many people so much money over the ages.

For the *modeled pearl beyond price,* which is climate change, the grain of sand at the center is a simple physical relationship between carbon dioxide, or CO_2, and radiation.

As it happens, if you hit a molecule of CO_2 with a photon of radiation in the infrared (or near-infrared) parts of the radiation spectrum, energy is absorbed by the CO_2 molecule for a short time, which agitates the molecule, "heating" the environment around it. After a short period of time, the excited molecule re-radiates the energy onward as even longer-wavelength (lower energy) radiation. This same relationship holds true for the other gases known as "greenhouse gases:" they capture incoming long-wave radiation, get excited, that excitement is measured as "heat," and they eventually re-release some of that energy to the environment around them. The different greenhouse gases have different lifetimes of survival in the atmosphere and have different affinities for capturing and re-emitting radiation than does CO_2, which makes it quite complicated to figure out the net "warming" impact that the various gases have over various lengths of time. If you ever read the term "CO_2 equivalents," that's a common measure for discussing greenhouse gases that lumps them all together and normalizes their heat-trapping capability to that of carbon dioxide. If that's not confusing enough, most people just refer to GHGs, or CO2, or worse still, "carbon emissions."

So that's really it, right there, the beating heart of the entire issue of climate change. That's the hardest of the hard-science part of the subject, so don't worry, it gets less abstract as we go on. Well, no it doesn't, really, but I don't want you to give up yet and skip ahead to COVID.

At the global level, that *CO2/radiation* relationship is a mixed blessing, but in the main, it's mostly a blessing. When you consider the Earth as a ball floating in space that only stays warm enough to sustain life because incoming radiation (and some outgoing radiation from the Earth itself) lingers in the layer of gases we call the atmosphere, carbon dioxide and the other greenhouse gases are a good thing.

But as the saying goes, "too much of a good thing can be bad for you," and so it is with the greenhouse gases. If we enrich them in the atmosphere, all things being equal (which, admittedly, they never actually are), we will trap extra heat in the atmosphere, causing what is colloquially known as "global warming." And that extra warming, again, all things being equal, would be expected to add energy to all kinds of atmospheric processes and natural energy fluxes that the earth experiences, increasing the frequency and severity of things like storms, and worsening things like heat waves, droughts, and so on. It would also, in theory, lessen those things in some places because energy is not transferred around the Earth uniformly through the atmosphere (and hydrosphere). So yes, despite all the chortling this inspires in those skeptical of the entirety of climate change science, enriching the atmosphere with greenhouse gases really can causing cooling in some areas and warming in others.

Beyond this part of the subject, however, the rest of the subject of climate change is much less "hard science" than is the grain of sand inside at the center of our climate pearl. Radiating outward from the central relationship between "trapping heat" and atmospheric greenhouse gas enrichment, things get less and less directly mechanistic. They steadily evolve away from the mechanistic explanations of things that most people would think of as "science," (or would have until relatively recently) and into more and more *abstracted simulations of physical reality.*

Each stage outward, from the *CO2/radiation* interaction at the heart of climate change science requires abstractions and assumptions, from the atmospheric lifecycles of greenhouse gases, to the natural activity cycles of the sun, to the orbital variations of the earth, to the myriad of other biogeochemical processes going on in the atmosphere at the same time, to the transfer impacts of the trapped radiation on other parts of the environment, to the impacts those changes will have on the human-experienced biosphere to what will happen in 100 years. At one level or another, all these things are about abstract models.

A quick aside: as I mentioned earlier, even the idea of a global average temperature (or any measure of central tendency, such as median, mean, or mode), is itself is a model. An average is an abstracted value that estimates the distribution of variables in a set of things. There may, in fact, be no members of the set of measured things that exactly match the value of the average. Or, as I like to put it, "Reality gives us only temporal point data. Humans give it curves in space and time.

Fortunately, we don't have to explore all of the intricacies of climate science, in order to see the impact of the plague of models, because first, we would not have enough time or space to do it even if we had a few thousand pages (any more than the United Nations Intergovernmental Panel on Climate Change manages to do), and because we're concerned with the *nexus* of where abstracted model outputs and abstracted model predictions interact with the proliferation of regulation. That lets us narrow things down a bit to two key questions. The first question is "*If humans enrich the concentration of greenhouse gases in the environment by X, how much heat will be trapped in the atmosphere.*" And the second-order question is "*How, where, and when will that heat retention manifest itself in changes to the climate to the detriment of human health and well-being?*"

Both of these questions are (mostly) dependent on modeling exercises, since there's really no way to actually measure the causes and effects of greenhouse gas enrichment of the atmosphere in real time or over the passage of time, nor is there a way to measure all of the factors that feed into climate sensitivity, itself, and, of course, the future is the future: we don't know anything about that until we get there, beyond the most gross expectations that processes in motion will remain in motion according to the laws of physics.

5.1   Now, to Climate Sensitivity

So, first to the sensitive subject of climate sensitivity, the smaller model that infuses the bigger models of climate Armageddon. To remind the reader, climate sensitivity is a measure of how sensitive the climate is to be increasing the concentration of greenhouse gases in the atmosphere.

The reason that we can't simply measure the climate sensitivity to greenhouse gases is because the heat retained by the atmosphere around

Earth is the product of heat-retention by multiple gases with different modes and efficiencies of heat-trapping in the atmosphere, that feature different duration times in the atmosphere and have different distributions through the atmosphere, and each of which is somewhat different in its response to other climate factors changing simultaneously, such as the temperature itself, and feedbacks related to the temperature, such as the formation of water vapor in the atmosphere, and its impact on precipitation...and on and on. A few of these factors are somewhat measurable, while most of them must be estimated, modeled, or simply stipulated.

The question of climate sensitivity has a fairly lengthy history, which I'll summarize courtesy of our friends at the University Center for Atmospheric Research (UCAR). For more detail, I recommend visiting their website on the topic.

- 1640 - Flemish alchemist Johann Baptista van Helmolt discovers that air is a mixture of gases, and studies carbon dioxide, which he called "the spirit of wood," because it comes off burning wood.
- 1754 - Joseph Black, a medical student in Edinburgh, figured out how to measure CO_2
- 1824 - Jean-Baptiste Fourier a mathematician working for Napoleon (Vive la France!) described how the greenhouse gases in the atmosphere trapped heat near the surface of the Earth, rendering it warmer than it would be as an uninsulated ball hanging in space. Fourier forever confused the heck out of people by comparing this phenomenon to a greenhouse, which, in fact, it is almost nothing like.
- 1856 - Eunice Foote, an American Scientist, discovered that regular sunlight could be trapped by a mixture of water vapor and carbon dioxide, and warm the air around them.
- 1859 - John Tyndall, a British physicist, put the finger on carbon dioxide, ozone, and water vapor as the heat-trapping culprits that kept us warm
- 1896 - Svante Arrhenius, a Swedish chemist who gets disproportionate recognition in this process (in my humble opinion), observed that burning coal released CO_2 into the air, and speculated that it would warm up the planet.

- Post-1900: British coal engineer George Callendar established that atmospheric CO2 levels were increasing in the industrial revolution; American chemist Roger Revelle, with Austrian born Hans Suess, pointed the finger of blame at industrial processes, and in 1988, American climate scientist James Hansen made the case to the United States Congress that humans were causing climate change, and that it posed a danger to humanity.

Now, on to the people who estimated just how sensitive the atmosphere was to greenhouse gas enrichment. The year 1896 takes us back to the Swede, Arrhenius, who in the journal *Science* (p269) wrote:

One may now ask, How much must the carbonic acid vary according to our figures, in order that the temperature should attain the same values as in the Tertiary and Ice ages respectively? A simple calculation shows that the temperature in the arctic regions would rise about 8° to 9°C., if the carbonic acid increased to 2.5 or 3 times its present value. In order to get the temperature of the ice age between the 40th and 50th parallels, the carbonic acid in the air should sink to 0.62–0.55 of its present value (lowering of temperature 4°–5°C.).

If you are looking for someone to blame for the fact that we are constantly talking about the impacts of "doubling the concentration of CO2 from pre-industrial levels," you can blame Arrhenius.

But that's basically where we got the current way of discussing the sensitivity of the climate to greenhouse gas emissions. If CO2 levels were to double from its level in 1896, Arrhenius calculated, the climate would warm by somewhere between 4-5 °C, which, for you Imperial sorts, would be around 7.2 - 9 degrees Fahrenheit. (One-degree Celsius equals 1.8 degrees Fahrenheit).

Since the United Nations Governmental Panel was kind enough to publish their 6th Assessment report on the Scientific Basis of Climate Change (aka AR6) as I was writing this chapter, I'll start by give you their take on climate sensitivity. But first, a few words about the United Nations Intergovernmental Panel on Climate Change.

The United Nations Intergovernmental Panel on Climate Change, is considered the ultimate authority on all things relating to climate change past, present, and future. And who better to explain their origins than the IPCC itself:

> The establishment of the IPCC was endorsed by UN General Assembly in 1988. Its initial task, as outlined in UN General Assembly Resolution 43/53 of 6 December 1988, was to prepare a comprehensive review and recommendations with respect to the state of knowledge of the science of climate change; the social and economic impact of climate change, and potential response strategies and elements for inclusion in a possible future international convention on climate. Since 1988, the IPCC has had five assessment cycles and delivered five Assessment Reports, the most comprehensive scientific reports about climate change produced worldwide. It has also produced a range of Methodology Reports, Special Reports and Technical Papers, in response to requests for information on specific scientific and technical matters from the United Nations Framework Convention on Climate Change (UNFCCC), governments and international organizations.

For the record, I've followed the IPCC reports since 1995, reading the Second Assessment Report in its entirely, was an expert reviewer on the "Science of Climate Change" volume for the Third Assessment report, and also reviewed a special report of the IPCC on "Aviation and the Global Climate." I have read the summaries of all the subsequent reports as well, but while I do love my science, my masochism only goes so far. If you are desperately in need of a sleeping aid, I highly recommend any of these volumes.

There has been, for as long as the IPCC has published its reports, considerable controversy about whether or not the widely read and widely cited "Summaries for Policymakers" are an unbiased representation of what it in the underlying technical reports. In my experience, the answer to that is a resounding no, and I've written about that a fair bit over the years. Generally speaking, in my opinion, the Summaries for Policymakers tend to emphasize high-end risks, and exaggerate the confidence of the estimations of long-term climate risk to a serious extent. Serious enough that I do not consider the Summaries for Policy Makers attached to the IPCC technical reports to be authoritative representations of "Climate Change Science," as defined by the full body of experts who write the underlying technical reports. Those are generally far more nuanced, more heavily caveated, and much more "conservative," in giving credence to more extreme predictions and assumptions. More about this to follow.

Anyway, here is the summary paragraph from the technical summary of AR6 on climate sensitivity (pTS-57), defined as the Earth's "Equilibrium Climate Sensitivity," which we'll define in a bit. For context, the two-common metrics of climate sensitivity are:

1. *The Transient Climate Response* (TCR), which estimates how much the climate will warm at the time that atmospheric greenhouse gas concentrations reach twice the pre-industrial concentration; and

2. *The Equilibrium Climate Sensitivity* (ECS), which estimates how much the climate will warm after enough time for the atmosphere to equilibrate to having a concentration of greenhouse gases at twice the pre-industrial level.

The ECS is usually about 2-3 times higher than the TCR. Confusing? Yes. Not my fault though. In general, most people simply discuss climate sensitivity in terms of "how much warming will result from doubling the CO2 level of pre-industrial times or, as I think of it, $\Delta t2xC$, or "temperature change for doubling pre-industrial GHG levels." That's a fairly gross metric, but it's a convenient one for most people to latch on to.

And note that AR5 was the 5th Assessment Report which preceded AR6. (And yes, there was an AR5, and an AR4, but for some reason, the first assessment report was called the FAR, the second was called the SAR, and the third was called the TAR. It's almost as if they want to be confusing. Anyway, here's the *nut graf*:

Since AR5, substantial quantitative progress has been made in combining new evidence of Earth's climate sensitivity, with improvements in the understanding and quantification of Earth's energy imbalance, the instrumental record of global surface temperature change, paleoclimate change from proxy records, climate feedbacks and their dependence on time scale and climate state. A key advance is the broad agreement across these multiple lines of evidence, supporting a best estimate of equilibrium climate sensitivity (ECS) of 3°C, with a *very likely* range of 2°C to 5°C. The *likely* range of 2.5°C to 4°C is narrower than the AR5 *likely* range of 1.5°C to 4.5°C.

And there's are charts below (see Figures 5-7) that underlies the above summary. A bit of explanation will probably help the reader to understand these three charts. Figure 5 shows the estimated range of climate sensitivity as it evolved in the reports of the Intergovernmental Panel on Climate Change over time, from a predecessor report by the US National Academies of Science called the Charney report, through the First Assessment report in 1990, through to the Sixth Assessment report of 2021. The vertical solid bars show the possible ranges of climate sensitivity—that's how much the climate would warm if you doubled CO2 levels from pre-industrial levels, in Celsius (reminder, one degree Celsius is equivalent to 1.8 degrees Fahrenheit.) the cross bars on the top panel represent IPCC's best estimate of where climate sensitivity lies within the range. The dashed lines, that came in with the Fifth Assessment report represent the extreme possibilities of climate sensitivity as assessed plausible by the IPCC. Important note here: the dashed lines, while they are described as "Very Likely" mean that the IPCC thinks that it's "Very likely" these are physically plausible realities, not that they are very likely to actually be reality. And that particular debate will have to wait for another time, though it is both scientifically and politically important. Anyway, for now, you need to focus on the solid vertical bars with the cross piece.

The reason I'm subjecting you to this figure is because first, I don't want to be accused of misrepresenting what the IPCC, which is (both rightly and wrongly) considered the ultimate touchstone on climate science, is saying.

Here's the takeaway: from panel one: over the decades, the IPCC's estimates of climate sensitivity haven't diverged all that much from Arrhenius original estimate. The extreme values, as determined by models (See the bulleted list in panel one of the figure to see what that includes) have fluctuated over time, mostly because different groups of modelers have focused on assessing the possibility of "long-tails" in the distribution of climate sensitivity, which could lead to somewhat lower, or sharply higher estimates depending on how much credence they are given.

A key element of the figure below is the acronym "CMIP6 ESMs" What that stands for is "Coupled Model Intercomparison Project, phase 6," which employs a large ensemble of "Earth Simulation Models" of climate sensitivity to greenhouse gases (free migraine at the reference). These are not empirical measurements asking, "how much have we emitted, and how much has it warmed?" Rather, these are a what-if question which goes something like this: "If we understand all of the various components of the climate, and the physics of the Earth's atmosphere, and *if* we understand the influence of adding (or subtracting) additional units of certain gases to the atmosphere, *then* this is the potential range of climate sensitivities that we'd get from an ensemble of distributions) are given, which have twice the probability of being outside the maximum/minimum value at a given end, compared to ranges (i.e., two tailed distributions) which are given for the other lines of evidence. For example, the *extremely likely* limit of greater than 95% probability corresponds to one side of the *very likely* (5% to 95%) range. Best estimates are given as either a single number or by a range represented by grey box. CMIP6 ESM values are not directly used as a line of evidence but are presented on the Figure for comparison.

So that is the modeled version of climate sensitivity that will feed forward into models that estimate how that sensitivity will play out as the atmosphere is enriched by manmade greenhouse gases over time. Of course, I should mention, at this point, that there is a quite lively dispute about whether the IPCC's assessment of the sensitivity of the climate to changes due to anthropogenic greenhouse gas emissions reflects reality. This is another peg that some "climate skeptics" focus on when expressing doubts about the entire paradigm of climate change.

Figure 5. Evolution of Equilibrium Climate Sensitivity Assessments

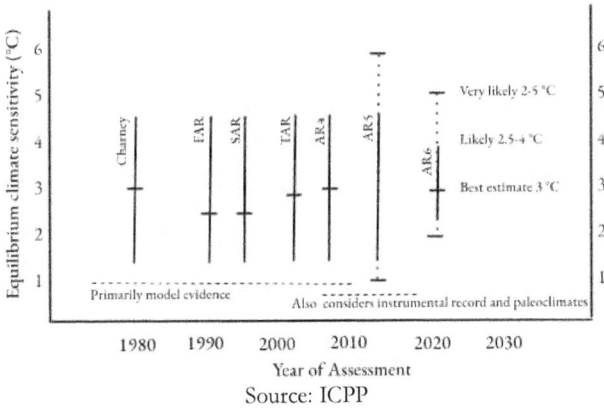

Source: ICPP

Figure 6. Equilibrium Climate Sensitivity (°C)

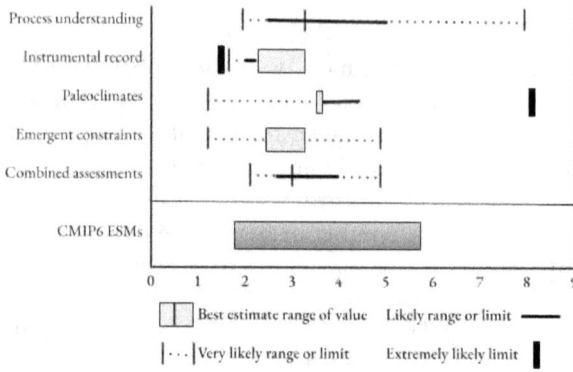

Source: ICPP

Figure 7.
Transient Climate Response (°C) Assessed in AR6
and Simulated by CMIP6 ESMs

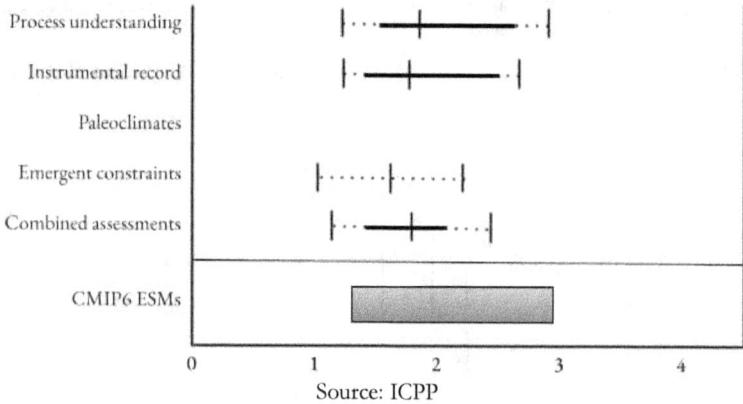

Source: ICPP

To be specific, the debate over-estimates of climate sensitivity come down to "can't we measure it more directly, or do we have to model it, and what gets us the most accurate picture of what's happening?"

I'm not going to go into a great deal of depth on that debate since first, it would take us still further afield from our core focus on the nexus of risk and regulation, second, I am not a physicist, and third, I'd like my readers to stay semi-conscious as we move onto the last sections of this little volume, and I can pretty much guarantee that whether it influenced one's views on the understanding of climate change or not, a protracted discussion of the nuances of measuring or modeling climate sensitivity would not increase the probability of that desire. But one study worth noting, one of a continuing series of peer-reviewed studies authored by climate researchers Nic Lewis and Judith Curry, tries to estimate the climate sensitivity in a more empirical way, by correlating actual observed changes in greenhouse gases in the atmosphere, with observed temperature changes over time.

The Lewis and Curry approach to estimating the Earth's climate sensitivity has generally concluded that the climate is less sensitive to greenhouse gas enrichment than is estimated by the models of the IPCC. This is the executive summary from Lewis and Curry 2018, (mostly in English!) in the peer-reviewed journal *Climate Dynamics* (Note that the K in the temperature readings stands for degrees on the Kelvin scale, which are the same as degrees on the Centigrade scale. I know, it's confusing. Again, not my fault.):

> Energy budget estimates of equilibrium climate sensitivity (ECS) and transient climate response (TCR) are derived using the comprehensive 1750–2011 time series and the uncertainty ranges for forcing components provided in the Intergovernmental Panel on Climate Change Fifth Assessment Working Group I Report, along with its estimates of heat accumulation in the climate system. The resulting estimates are less dependent on global climate models and allow more realistically for forcing uncertainties than similar estimates based on forcings diagnosed from simulations by such models. Base and final periods are selected that have well matched volcanic activity and influence from internal variability. Using 1859–1882 for the base period and 1995–2011 for the final period, thus avoiding major volcanic activity, median estimates are derived for *ECS of 1.64 K and for TCR of 1.33 K. ECS 17–83 and 5–95 % uncertainty ranges are 1.25–2.45 and 1.05–4.05 K; the corresponding TCR ranges are 1.05–1.80 and 0.90–2.50 K* [emphasis added]. Results using alternative well-matched base and final periods provide similar best estimates but give wider uncertainty ranges, principally reflecting smaller changes in average forcing. Uncertainty in aerosol forcing is the dominant contribution to the ECS and TCR uncertainty ranges.

The key take-away here is, according to the findings of Lewis and Curry using an empirical approach to measuring climate sensitivity, the computer models used by the United Nations Intergovernmental Panel on Climate Change run hot. They suggest an atmosphere more sensitive to greenhouse gas enrichment than can be seen from studies that actually analyse the physical response of the climate.

The ranges of potential climate sensitivity published by Lewis and Curry are important not simply because they are half or less than those of the IPCC, but because, if the Curry and Lewis calculation of climate sensitivity is correct, the risk of likely future warming is far lower than that estimated by the IPCC, and usually assumed to be correct by world governments. In fact, at the lower ranges of warming that we would expect if Lewis and Curry are correct, anthropogenic climate change for a doubling of pre-industrial levels of greenhouse gases would be largely benign except in a few climatically precarious places on Earth.

Table 7. Best Estimates (Medians) and Uncertainty Ranges for ECS and TCR

Base Period	Final Period	ECS best estimate (K)	ECS 17%-83% range (K)	ECS 5%-95% range (K)	TCR best estimate (K)	TCR 17%-83% range (K)	TCR 5%-95% range (K)
1869-82	2007-16	1.50	1.2-1.95	1.05-2.45	1.20	1.0-1.45	0.9-1.7
		1.66	1.35-2.15	1.15-2.7	1.33	1.1-1.6	1.0-1.9
1869-82	1995-2016	1.56	1.2-2.1	1.05-2.75	1.22	1.0-1.5	0.85-1.85
		1.69	1.35-2.25	1.15-3.0	1.32	1.1-1.65	0.95-2.0
1850-1900	1980-2016	1.54	1.2-2.15	1.0-2.95	1.23	1.0-1.6	0.85-1.95
		1.67	1.3-2.3	1.1-3.2	1.33	1.05-1.7	0.9-2.15
1930-50	2007-16	1.56	1.2-2.15	1.0-3.0	1.20	0.95-1.5	0.85-1.85
		1.65	1.25-2.3	1.05-3.15	1.27	1.05-1.6	0.9-1.95
LC15 results for comparison							
1859-82	1995-2011	1.64	1.25-2.45	1.05-4.05	1.33	1.05-1.8	0.9-2.5
1850-1900	1987-2011	1.67	1.25-2.6	1.0-4.75	1.31	1.0-1.8	0.85-2.55

Source: Lewis and Curry (2018)

Figure 8.
Estimated Probability Density Functions for ECS
Using Each Period Combinations

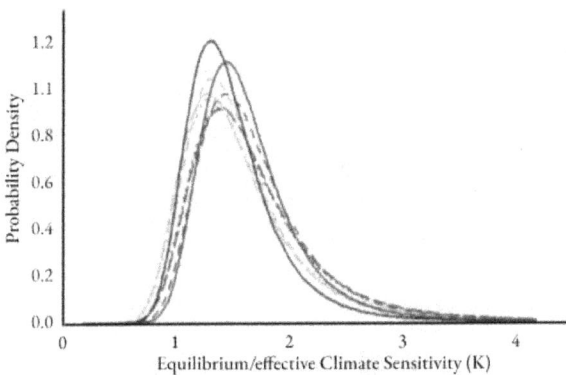

Source: Lewis and Curry (2018)

Figure 9. Estimated Probability Density Functions for TCR
Using Each Period Combinations

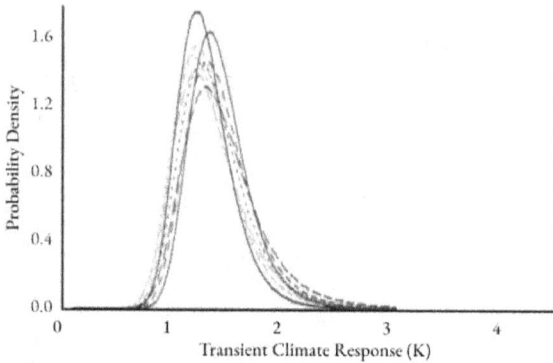

Source: Lewis and Curry (2018)

Figure 10.
Period Combinations Used to Estimate Probability Density
Functions for ECS and TCR

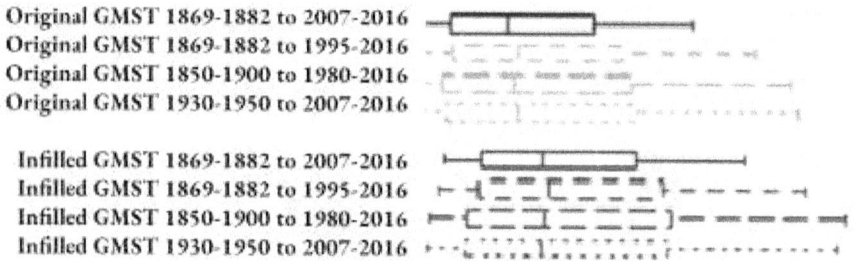

Original GMST 1869-1882 to 2007-2016
Original GMST 1869-1882 to 1995-2016
Original GMST 1850-1900 to 1980-2016
Original GMST 1930-1950 to 2007-2016

Infilled GMST 1869-1882 to 2007-2016
Infilled GMST 1869-1882 to 1995-2016
Infilled GMST 1850-1900 to 1980-2016
Infilled GMST 1930-1950 to 2007-2016

Source: Lewis and Curry (2018)

5.2 Break Out the Delorean, We're Back to the Future!

Having clarified (I hope) the nature of how sensitive the climate is to enrichment by manmade greenhouse gas emissions, we can now turn to the major nexus in the *risk and regulation relationship*, which is the estimations of future harms that would come from greenhouse gas enrichment of the atmosphere. And if you thought that simply figuring out climate sensitivity involved making a lot of assumptions, estimates, guesstimates, and the like, you haven't seen anything yet.

So, let's start at the beginning of this sub-question: How does the "climate science" community estimate what enriching the atmosphere with greenhouse gases today will impact the temperature, and temperature-related climate phenomenon in the future?

The answer to that little question was mentioned earlier, because the same models used to estimate how sensitive the atmosphere is to enrichment with greenhouse gases are, coincidentally, the same climate models that are used to predict what effect that greenhouse-gas-induced warming will have on the global average temperature, and derivative climate and weather dynamics as we project forward in time.

Since none of us are physicists nor climate modelers, we're not going to get into the nitty gritty details of how those climate models work. Instead, we're going to cut to the chase, and focus on the assumptions that are fed into the predictive climate models, and assess whether or not those assumptions are largely based on empirical data (which, for the future, is no), mechanistically-predictable future events (again, mostly not), or are simply speculative extrapolations from our general theory of the climate, working from speculative futuristic science-fiction scenarios laid out by a giant interdisciplinary panel of experts (in the hard sciences, social sciences, and non-sciences) commissioned by the United Nations Intergovernmental Panel on Climate Change.

I'll give you a hint: the predictions of what will happen to the climate because of greenhouse gas emissions of past, present, and future are not based on empirical understanding: they are, in fact, in the latter category of speculative futuristic science-fiction scenarios primarily concocted by a giant panel of experts. So, let's talk about the evolution of future climate scenarios.

5.3   Climate Prognostication in Climate Policy

As we discussed earlier, the idea of predicting what would happen in the future if we were to double the concentration of greenhouse gases in the atmosphere (compared to their pre-industrial level) started with that Swedish fellow, Arrhenius, who told us that doubling CO2 levels in the atmosphere (from those pre-industrial levels at the time) would likely cause a warming of the global atmosphere somewhere between 4 and 5 degrees Celsius. In the several hundred years since Arrhenius, and despite untold billions of dollars, and trillions of person-power hours and computer processing time, the understanding of the "official" climate science community, the IPCC, is actually much less certain: Now, the expected range of warming is between 2.5 and 4 degrees Celsius. But you might well ask, when will that doubling of greenhouse gas concentrations happen?

And what will happen to the climate along the way, before we hit that doubling point, or even afterward? That is the 64-trillion-dollar question.

That question takes us back into the canonical literature of the United Nations Intergovernmental Panel on Climate Change. For this discussion, however, we will rely on a particular sub-stream of that literature which lives at the nexus of risk and regulation, which the IPCC designates as "Synthesis Reports." This requires a bit of back story, looking into how the IPCC process works, so bear with me.

Each volume of the IPCC's encyclopedic assessment reports on climate change are used to create several summary documents. One of them (for each of the three main volumes of the assessment report) is a Technical Summary (moderately lengthy and well, technical). Another one is a Summary for Policymakers (relatively short and more accessible). And finally, the three-volume set for each Assessment Report and all their summaries, is followed by a synthesis report.

The synthesis report is the critical report that the IPCC makes to the world's governments in fulfillment of its obligations under the United Nations Framework Convention on Climate Change. The latest synthesis report as of this writing, was for the Fifth Assessment Report, abbreviated, as with the previous reports, AR5. The AR6 synthesis report, according to the IPCC, will not be available until 2022, when the three underlying volumes have been completed, summarized, and published (some would say, after a post-hoc massage to ensure conformity with the final recommendations of the Synthesis report, but those people would be cynical in the extreme). The Summary for Policymakers for the Sixth Assessment Report was, however, published just in time for the writing of this section, and while not as integrally tied in with the nexus of risk and policy, will serve to bring us up to date on the key question of "how are the risks of climate change modeled, and are they of suitable relationship to reality to be used as data, or evidence of harm so as to justify world-girdling massive regulation of the entire global energy system?"

Author Context Box 8.

I should mention here that there is a great deal of controversy about the, let us say, fidelity of the IPCC reports to the underlying scientific literature that it ostensibly sums up in its encyclopedic manner, as well as how those encyclopedic volumes are dithered down into summary reports, synthesis reports, and special reports of the IPCC that tend to actually dominate the debate over climate change in the world's popular and political discourse.

I'll just give my opinion here of how that works. In the technical volumes of the IPCC assessment reports, I think that there is a genuine effort made by the scientists who participate in the production of the reports to do a rigorous job in summarizing the underlying climate change literature (peer reviewed and non-peer-reviewed) that is considered to be the most robust and rigorous information we have about climate change in all its myriad dimensions. It's a herculean task and having read several of the full technical volumes cover to cover (and served as an official reviewer on two of them), it's actually amazing to me that they were accomplished at all. These technical reports are not perfect of course, as they are written by humans with their own biases and imperfections, and by committee, to boot, but I can't imagine a better way to summarize such a vast body of scientific knowledge in order to find the "weight of the evidence," so, I accept the underlying technical reports as being sound summaries of the state of knowledge of climate change, and always have. That's not to say that I think they are absolute truth: a lot of the underlying science of some areas involving understanding climate change is in its infancy, or very early childhood, and all of those involving forecasting are heavily dependent on the social sciences and/or are based on more speculative modeling than I'm comfortable with.

The summaries of the three underlying technical reports, however, are a very different story. The summaries (Summaries for Policymakers, and Synthesis Reports) that are all that most people will ever get a glimpse into in the popular discourse on climate change are a very different creature. In my experience in studying them, the summary reports tend to be much more selective in focusing on things interesting to politicians and supportive of government action and tend to both over-simplify important issues while overstating the confidence that the IPCC has in the rigor of its confidence.

In other words, the Summaries of the IPCC Assessment Reports, which inform the nexus of risk and regulation in the global war on climate change, focus on all the scary parts of the climate bible and relay them as verities, compared with the usually cautious and caveated treatments of the subject that you'll find in the technical volumes of the IPCC. And that's quite enough about that.

5.4   The UN Speaks

So, as we did with ambient air pollution, let's trace the way that the *estimation* of and *projection* of climate risks (don't call it prediction, or the modelers will become upset) has evolved over the past few decades of the IPCC's synthesis reports. And to simplify things a bit, we'll abbreviate the synthesis reports as SR1 through SR6.

SR1: The First Synthesis Report (1992)

The first synthesis report of the IPCC (SR1), published in June 1992 is actually very interesting reading for anyone interested in the subject of climate change science as well as policy, because it shows just how quickly a relatively modest report on the science of climate change and its attendant risks evolved into the massive, gloomy-and-doomy, yet supremely self-confident reports we see published by the IPCC today. SR1 was drafted as a post-hoc supplement to the 1990 First Assessment Report at the request of various member governments of the United Nations Framework Convention on Climate Change (P.ix). The authors of SR1 were given six tasks to fulfill by the IPCC (p5):

> Task 1: Assessment of national net greenhouse gas emissions;
> Task 2: Predictions of the regional distributions of climate
>   change and associated impact studies including model
>   validation studies;
> Task 3: Energy and industry related issues;
> Task 4: Agriculture and forestry related issues;
> Task 5: Vulnerability to sea-level rise; and
> Task 6: Emission scenarios.

For our discussion, we'll focus mainly on tasks 2 and 6, and these are most directly at our favorite nexus of risk assessment, and its utility for forming public policy. We'll follow a similar pattern of focus for the other synthesis reports, so I won't list all their individual focal areas repeatedly, but the later synthesis reports focus on all of the same tasks, and more as they evolved over time.

A cynic might observe that the genesis of the Synthesis reports was based on the fact that the first set of technical reports, while interesting, didn't call for much of anything in the way of actions beyond "more research." Policymakers, not having much use for such things, demanded that the IPCC address the questions above in the framework of "what should be do," rather than simply focusing on "what do we know," so that they'd have a more clear pathway on taking more aggressive actions, spending more money, and having more international meetings in exotic locales featuring flights on private jets, gourmet dining, hobnobbing with celebrities, and all that fun stuff. And hence, the genesis of Synthesis Reports. But as I said, pointing that out could be considered cynical. SR1 starts off on familiar ground in its major conclusions (p6):

> ...emissions resulting from human activities are substantially increasing the atmospheric concentrations of the greenhouse gases: carbon dioxide, methane, chlorofluorocarbons, and nitrous oxide, and the evidence from the modeling studies, from observations and the sensitivity analyses indicate that the sensitivity of global mean surface temperature to doubling CO2, is unlikely to lie outside the range 1.5° to 4.5°C.

Prominently, in the major conclusions of the first synthesis, is that admission that "there are many uncertainties in our predictions particularly with regard to the timing, magnitude and regional patterns of climate change due to our incomplete understanding," and "the size of this warming is broadly consistent with predictions of climate models, but it is also of the same magnitude as natural climate variability. Thus, the observed increase would be largely due to this natural variability; alternatively, this variability and other human factors could have offset a still larger human-induced greenhouse warming." The final major conclusion in SR1 was "the unequivocal detection of the enhanced greenhouse effect *from observations* [emphasis added] is not likely for a decade or more."

But that bit of humility is not the most important element of SR1, because it is also in SR1 that we set the stage for how the IPCC will treat the future, and the risks that climate change poses to people and the planet. Rather than simply extrapolating from existing trends in greenhouse gas concentrations and climate patterns into the future, the IPCC establishes a process of modeling what those greenhouse gas concentrations might be like under a variety of "scenarios" that are based on potential political actions and then models what impacts that GHG-induced global warming would have on the climate.

This conscious decision, to create a framework of futuristic predictions, and then work backward from those predictions with modeling is where, in my opinion, the IPCC's "scientists" left the "science" part behind and embraced something more akin to science fiction. Still, at this point in Climate Change's plague of models, there was at least a fair bit of humility about the decision (p11):

> Scenario outputs are not predictions of the future and should not be used as such: they illustrate the effect of a wide range of economic, demographic and policy assumptions. They are inherently controversial because they reflect different views of the future. The results of short-term scenarios can vary considerably from actual outcomes even over short time horizons. Confidence in scenario outputs decreases as the time horizon increases, because the basis for the underlying assumptions becomes increasingly speculative. Considerable uncertainties surround the evolution of the types and levels of human activities (including economic growth and structure), technological advances, and human responses to possible environmental, economic, and institutional constraints. Consequently, emission scenarios must be constructed carefully and used with great caution.

This humility, while refreshing, would not, of course, prevent the world's policymakers nor the world's media, and climate activist community from acting as though the IPCC's scenarios were indeed ironclad predictions of the future, especially those predictions at the extremes of what would be considered harmful.

The original six IPCC scenarios for future greenhouse gas emission trajectories can be seen in the Table 8. As you can see from the table, the scenarios estimate future population levels, levels of economic growth, future energy supplies, and the expected impacts of various political agreements controlling emissions of other pollutants that contribute to climate change. *It is from these assumed futures that the expected atmospheric concentrations of greenhouse gases are derived, not from extrapolation forward of any observed or empirical trends.*

But with warts and all, the summary conclusions of SR1 were both modest and relatively humble. After an acknowledgement of the many uncertainties involved in their summation of the state of knowledge about climate change, most of the recommendations related to assessing the extent of, and potential impacts of climate change were calls for (not surprisingly) more research and more funding (p20/21):

Reduction of these uncertainties requires:

- improvements in the systematic observation and understanding of climate-forcing variables on a global basis, including solar irradiance and aerosols.
- development of comprehensive observations of the relevant variables describing all components of the climate system involving as required new technologies and the establishment of data sets.
- better understanding of climate-related processes, particularly those associated with clouds, oceans, and the carbon-cycle.
- an improved understanding of social, technological, and economic processes, especially in developing countries, that are necessary to develop more realistic scenarios of future emissions.
- the development of national inventories of current emissions.
- more detailed knowledge of climate changes which have taken place in the past.
- sustained and increased support for climate research activities which cross national and disciplinary boundaries; particular action is still needed to facilitate the full involvement of developing countries.
- improved international exchange of climate data.

But from such humble beginnings, the ability to predict the future of greenhouse gas emissions and their environmental impacts, and the confidence in the accuracy of the IPCC's reflections of global reality as established by "The Science" of climate change will grow more and more through subsequent synthesis reports, while this early symptom of climate reporting: a tendency to be honest about the limitations and utility of the information in IPCC reports will steadily be reduced, and replaced with louder and louder emphasis on the idea that the reports are steadily more accurate, reliable, and useful representations of hard reality, rather than speculative what-if models, backward-derived from science fiction scenarios could ever warrant.

Table 8.
Summary of Assumptions in the Six IPCC Alternative Scenarios

Scenario	Population	Economic Growth	Energy Supplies
IS92a,b	World Bank 1991 11.3 billion by 2100	1990-2025: 2.9% 1990-2100: 2.3%	12,000 EJ conventional oil 13000 EJ natural gas Solar costs fall to $0.075/kWh 191 EJ of biofuels available at $70/barrel*
IS92c	UN Medium-Low Case 6.4 billion by 2100	1990-2025: 2.0% 1990-2100: 1.2%	8,000 EJ conventional oil 7,300 EJ natural gas Nuclear costs decline by 0.4%
IS92d	UN Medium-Low Case 6.1 billion by 2100	1990-2025: 2.7% 1990-2100: 2.0%	Oil & gas the same as IS92c Solar costs fall to $0.065/kWh 272 EJ of biofuels available at $50/barrel*
IS92e	World Bank 1991 11.3 billion by 2100	1990-2025: 3.5% 1990-2100: 3.0%	18,400 EJ conventional oil Gas same as IS92a,b Phase out nuclear by 2075
IS92f	UN Medium-Low Case 17.6 billion by 2100	1990-2025: 2.9% 1990-2100: 2.3%	Oil & gas the same as IS92e Solar costs fall to $0.083/kWh Nuclear costs increase to $0.09/kWh

Source: IPCC (1992)

SR2: The Synthesis of the IPCC Second Assessment Reports (1995)

The second synthesis report of the IPCC (SR2) was published in 1995, after the publication of the IPCC's landmark 3-volume Second Assessment Report on climate change but relies on the same futuristic scenarios listed above as the basis for modeling expected impacts of manmade greenhouse gas enhancement of atmospheric greenhouse gas concentrations, so there's not much of to go over again regarding the issues of prognosticative modeling. But what is interesting about the SR2 is what it provides by way of context as to the genesis, process of production, and purpose, of the entire IPCC climate change reporting process.

At the outset of the report, SR2 seeks to clarify the nature and genesis of the IPCC's Synthesis Reports. The explication of the Synthesis Report process is revealing (though often overlooked), as it documents just how integrally tied the IPCC's climate change assessment process is tied in with, well, politics.

First, here is what is synthesized in the synthesis:

- the Report of Working Group I of the IPCC, the Science of Climate Change, with a Summary for Policymakers (SPM).
- the Report of Working Group II of the IPCC, Scientific-Technical Analyses of Impacts, Adaptations and Mitigation of Climate Change, with SPM.
- the Report of Working Group III of the IPCC, the Economic and Social Dimensions of Climate Change, with SPM.

That's a lot of synthesizing. The three reports of the three Working Groups are extremely lengthy, and complex documents, running to several thousand pages long as a set. There is ample room there for all the subtlety in the world (and for what it is worth from my reading, all that subtlety is present), but the synthesis reports attempt to digest all of that in a way that has utility (and comprehensibility) to policy makers.

That process is illuminating because it shows how the ultimate representations of the IPCC's climate research makes its way into the public policy (and global regulatory) process. Here are a few tidbits to help the reader understand the integration of the scientific and political components that lead to the IPCC synthesis reports, and the three Summaries for Policymakers that ultimately feed into the synthesis reports:

- The *leadership of the IPCC "at the outset decides the content* [emphasis added], broken down into chapters, of the report of each of its Working Groups. A writing team of three to six experts (on some rare occasions, more) is constituted for the initial drafting and subsequent revisions of a chapter. *"Governments and intergovernmental and non-governmental organizations are requested to nominate individuals with appropriate expertise for consideration for inclusion in the writing teams"* [emphasis added] (p. viii);
- *The selected writing teams draft the chapters* [emphasis added] and the material for inclusion in the SPMs (Summaries for Policymakers);

- The drafts are reviewed by "tens of experts" worldwide for expert review, chosen *"from nominations made by governments and organizations* [emphasis added]*;"*
- The draft is then revised, and sent to governments for review, after which it is revised again;
- And then the underlying working groups (or at least, the lead authors of the underlying working groups) receive the draft, "approves the SPM line by line."

You might think that would be the end of the process, but you would think wrongly. After this session, world governments get a draft to study for a month (and comment upon) before the final acceptance of the report at a meeting of the IPCC.

To put this process in simpler terms, rather than being an objective product of the world's leading climate scientists, and experts in climate economics, climate anthropology, climate hydrology, or what have you, the *IPCC reports are a political document that may involve such experts, but does not, per se, reflect only what they believe to be correct or important. Instead, a group of political actors get together and solicits the opinions of a few hundreds of global scientists (and then working through a smaller group of government-selected coordinating authors) about the science, risks, potential impacts, and potential policies that might address manmade climate change.* Those summaries of underlying technical literature (both peer-reviewed and non-peer-reviewed are turned out as three very lengthy, more than 200 pages each, volumes of what will become the international Bible of Climate Change. Then another small group of government-selected writers create Summaries for Policymakers for those technical volumes that are only required to be "consistent," with them rather than strictly representative of them. After that, a third team of government selected, authors draw all three of the Summaries for Policymakers together into a Synthesis report, which, packaged together, constitute the official report of the IPCC to world governments.

An astute reader will note that at the end of the day, the IPCC process, which represents itself as the very voice of science on the issue of climate change, is governed, at every step, from conception of the initial questions through review of the underlying reports and summaries, by national governments of the United Nations. Indeed, this is made explicit (p. vii):

> The reader may note that the IPCC is a fully intergovernmental, scientific-technical body. All States that are Members of the United Nations and of the World Meteorological Organization

are Members of the IPCC and its Working Groups. As such, governments approve the SPMs and accept the underlying chapters, which are, as stated earlier, written, and revised by experts.

An additional important context is provided in SR2 as to the overall purpose of the synthesis reports, which is, to inform policymakers that are working toward a pre-determined end, that being the mission of Article 2 of the United Nations Framework Convention on Climate Change, which has a primary mission of (p.3):

> ...stabilization of greenhouse gas concentrations in the atmosphere at a level that would prevent dangerous anthropogenic interference with the climate system. Such a level should be achieved within a time-frame sufficient to allow ecosystems to adapt naturally to climate change, to ensure that food production is not threatened and to enable economic development to proceed in a sustainable manner.

Again, the reader will note that many of these terms are highly subjective and take the discussion far afield from what most scholars of "science" would include within the domain of scientific inquiry.

Finally, lest the political influence over the IPCC Synthesis reports is still unclear, the IPCC explains that "The report then addresses issues related to *equity* and to ensuring that economic development proceeds in a *sustainable* manner. This involves addressing, for instance, estimates of the likely damage of climate change impacts, and the impacts, including costs and benefits, of adaptation and mitigation;" and that its recommendations are based on a preconceived, dare I say, global collectivist approach to problem solving, which is known as the "precautionary principle," that calls on all the Parties of the IPCC to

> ...take precautionary measures to anticipate, prevent or minimize the causes of climate change and mitigate its adverse effects. Where there are threats of serious or irreversible damage, lack of full scientific certainty should not be used as a reason for postponing such measures, taking into account that policies and measures to deal with climate change should be cost effective so as to ensure global benefits at the lowest possible cost. To achieve this, such policies and measures should take into account

different socio-economic contexts, be comprehensive, cover all relevant sources, sinks and reservoirs of greenhouse gases and adaptation and comprise all economic sectors. Efforts to address climate change may be carried out cooperatively by interested Parties.

As I mentioned, SR2 uses the same approach to future scenarios as SR1, and even though the second assessment report represents a massive expansion of efforts to summarize the state of knowledge about climate change, and the risks of manmade climate change, it might surprise the reader to see just how modest and, to use a term of art, "market-based," greenhouse gas mitigation was originally conceptualized by the IPCC.

A number of policies, many of which might be used by individual nations unilaterally, and some of which may be used by groups of countries and would require regional or international agreement, can facilitate the penetration of less greenhouse gas-intensive technologies and modified consumption patterns. These include, *inter alia* (not ordered according to priority):

- Putting in place appropriate institutional and structural frameworks; Energy pricing strategies—for example, carbon or energy taxes and reduced energy subsidies.
- Phasing out those existing distortionary policies which increase greenhouse gas emissions, such as some subsidies and regulations, non-internalization of environmental costs, and distortions in agriculture and transport pricing.
- Tradable emissions permits.
- Voluntary programmes and negotiated agreements with industry.
- Utility demand-side management programmes.
- Regulatory programmes including minimum energy-efficiency standards, such as for appliances and fuel economy.
- Stimulating research, development, and demonstration to make new technologies available.
- Market-pull and demonstration programmes that stimulate the development and application of advanced technologies.
- Renewable energy incentives during market build-up.

- Incentives such as provisions for accelerated depreciation and reduced costs for consumers.
- Education and training; information and advisory measures.
- Options that also support other economic and environmental goals.

SR3: The Synthesis of the Third Assessment Reports of the IPCC (2001)

The third Synthesis report of the IPCC (SR3) follows in the footsteps, and along the progressive pathway of increasing estimations of risk and using modeled scenarios of the future as a basis for quantifying those risks, as well as quantifying how those risks might be modified by certain sets of policy choices embodied in the forecast scenarios. But SR3 introduces a few new twists, one of which has received insufficient attention: how the IPCC expresses the strength of their conclusions about climate change. In SR3, this process was made explicit (from box SPM1, p 5):

> Where appropriate, the authors of the Third Assessment Report assigned confidence levels that represent their collective judgment in the validity of a conclusion based on observational evidence, modeling results, and theory that they have examined. The following words have been used throughout the text of the Synthesis Report to the TAR relating to WGI findings: virtually certain (greater than 99% chance that a result is true); very likely (90–99% chance); likely (66–90% chance); medium likelihood (33–66% chance); unlikely (10–33% chance); very unlikely (1–10% chance); and exceptionally unlikely (less than 1% chance). An explicit uncertainty range ($\pm$) is a likely range. Estimates of confidence relating to WGII findings are: very high (95% or greater), high (67–95%), medium (33–67%), low (5–33%), and very low (5% or less). No confidence levels were assigned in WGIII.

What is important in this description is to understand that in context of how the overall IPCC report process works, these assignments of confidence levels must be understood as being completely objective. They are the opinions, primarily of the authors, in how confident that they are in their own work that was included in the overall reports of the IPCC. These confidence ranges are not based on statistical tests of whether or not various claims are actually correct, as in, they have been demonstrated empirically to reflect reality in some non-transitory manner. Remember this as we move along, because later, the IPCC will kick this up a notch, and introduce a new confidence term of "incontrovertibly."

The next important development in climate risk assessment within the context of the IPCC is also reflected in SR3, where the process for modeling future risk scenarios is substantially revised. Rather than going forward with the six futuristic scenarios previously described, the IPCC adopted a new set of forward-looking scenarios that were developed for them in a Special Report on Emission Scenarios, abbreviated, SRES. This time around, there were four primary "Storylines" used to characterize different futures, which were then each detailed in a "family" of scenarios spun off from each storyline. There were 40 different scenarios put forward at the end of the process.

The approach used in authoring SRES is described in the Summary for Policymakers that accompanied the (again), several hundred-page technical report. SRES was written by a team that "included more than 50 members from 18 countries who represent a broad range of scientific backgrounds, and non-governmental organizations." Again, lest you think I'm exaggerating the science-fiction nature of this entire endeavor, this is how the SRES were prepared, in the IPCC's words, in the preface, the SRES preparation included six major steps:

- analysis of existing scenarios in the literature;
- analysis of major scenario characteristics, driving forces, and their relationships;
- formulation of four narrative scenario "storylines" to describe alternative futures;
- quantification of each storyline using a variety of modeling approaches;
- an "open" review process of the resultant emissions scenarios and their assumptions; and
- three revisions of the scenarios and the Report subsequent to the open review process, i.e., the formal IPCC Expert Review and the final combined IPCC Expert and Government Review.

The next time that someone abuses you for "not following the science," if you express disbelief in one of the futures painted by the IPCC under the rubric of "the science," you might want to show them this statement. It probably won't change their minds, but it might make you feel better. Better still, show them this statement, from the first page (numerically page 3) of the Summary for Policymakers which reads:

> A set of scenarios was developed to represent the range of driving forces and emissions in the scenario literature so as to reflect current understanding and knowledge about underlying uncertainties. They exclude only outlying "surprise" or "disaster" scenarios in the literature. Any scenario necessarily includes subjective elements and is open to various interpretations. Preferences for the scenarios presented here vary among users. No judgment is offered in this Report as to the preference for any of the scenarios and they are not assigned probabilities of occurrence, neither must they be interpreted as policy recommendations.

The highly impressive chart (see Figure 17) shows how the new scenarios model future greenhouse gas emissions (direct and indirect via land-use changes), as well as how those estimates compare with the scenarios used in the First and Second IPCC assessment reports.

Figure 11. Annual Anthropogenic Carbon Dioxide Emissions under the IS92 Emission Scenarios

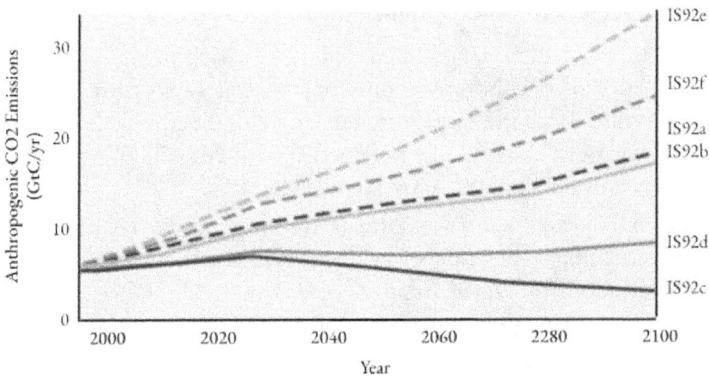

Source: IPCC Second Assessment Report

Once again though, I want to draw an important distinction that may be lost in my criticism of how the IPCC handles the nexus of risk and regulation. I am in no way blaming the authors of the reports (scientists and non-scientists alike) for how their information was ultimately used in the policy process or represented to the public via global media. The authors of SRES, as with most of the other IPCC technical reports, were quite explicit (p11):

> There is no single most likely, "central", or "best-guess" scenario, either with respect to SRES scenarios or to the underlying scenario literature. Probabilities or likelihood are not assigned to individual SRES scenarios. None of the SRES scenarios represents an estimate of a central tendency for all driving forces or emissions, such as the mean or median, and none should be interpreted as such. The distribution of the scenarios provides a useful context for understanding the relative position of a scenario but does not represent the likelihood of its occurrence. [And yet. How many times have we heard that "the science tells us that we have only 10 years to save the earth from *Climageddon*?"]

5.5 About Those 10-Years to Save the World Headlines

Much of the popular debate around manmade climate change and the timing and stringency of public policies intended to manage the risk of manmade climate change is based on the perception that the irreversible descent into catastrophic climate degradation seems to always be about ten years away. Here are a few examples from media coverage over the years:

- "A senior U.N. environmental official says entire nations could be wiped off the face of the Earth if the global warming trend is not reversed by the year 2000" (by Peter James Spielmann, Associated Press, 1989).
- "UN scientists warn time is running out to tackle global warming - Scientists say eight years left to avoid worst effects" (by David Adam, *The Guardian*, 2007).
- "IPCC climate report gives us 10 years to save the world" (Greenpeace, 2018).
- "Ocasio-Cortez: 'world will end in 12 years' if climate change not addressed" (by John Bowden, *The Hill*, 2019).
- "We have 10 years left to save the world, says climate expert" (Laura Paddison, *Huffpost*, 2020).

It all sounds terribly worrying, despite the fact that the 10-year bracket seems to keep propagating forward in time, rather than actually running out, as time generally does.

But where do these tipping point ideas come from? Are these claims based on looking at actual data about greenhouse gas emissions, and the rise in atmospheric temperatures and cautiously extrapolating forward from existing empirical trends in temperature and atmospheric GHG concentrations?

The short answer to that question is *no, they do not.* The "We have 10 years to save the Earth" mantra comes from a set of speculative computer models generated in the vast laboratories of climate change science, as filtered through the IPCC.

There are three discrete sets of forward-looking, or predictive models (created and run by largely discrete but somewhat overlapping modeling communities) that underpin the 10-year tipping point paradigm of climate change. Those model sets are:

- Ecological impact models that estimate what impact a warmer climate will have on a variety of ecosystems (human and non-human) *in the future*;
- Models of greenhouse gas (GHG) emissions that are expected *in the future*; and
- Models of warming caused by those GHG emissions expected to manifest *in the future*.

I emphasized the "in the future" part to highlight that these models, because they are about the future, cannot in any way be considered normative, empirical science. They are not in any way about measuring or characterizing "what is," they are all about speculating about "what may happen."

The outputs of these three types of modeling have varied over time as they have evolved since they first took the stage in the Second Assessment Report of the IPCC (SR2), but it was not until the Third Assessment Report of the IPCC in 2001 (SR3) that the triad of models would assemble to create the new "tipping point" paradigm.

In SR3, three key figures show the evolution of the separate model components. These figures, (figures 12, 13, 14) shows the 2001 estimated range of outputs for the three sets of models.

Figure 12. Radiative Forcing (Wm⁻²)

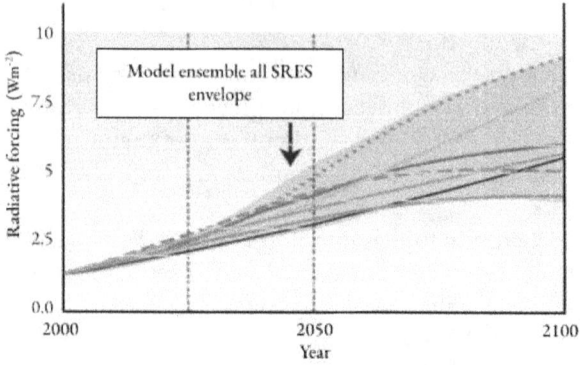

Source: IPCC AR3 Synthesis Report, p11.

Figure 13. Temperature Change (°C)

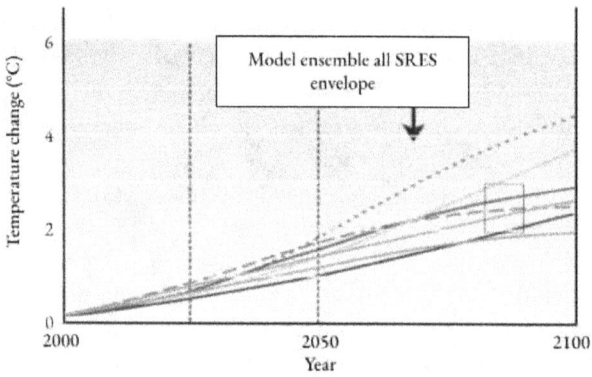

Source: IPCC AR3 Synthesis Report, p11.

Figure 14. Reasons for Concern (M) Impacts

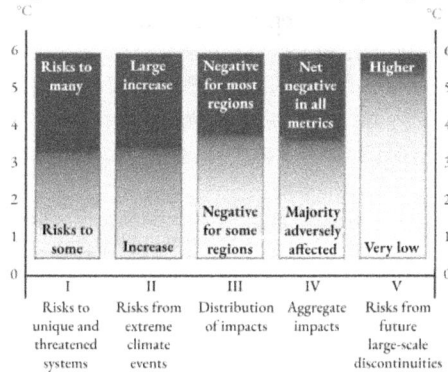

Source: IPCC AR3 Synthesis Report, p11.

Figure 12 shows how increased concentrations of greenhouse gases over time are predicted by computer models to capture more heat in the atmosphere (expressed as increased "radiative forcing") under a variety of different speculative scenarios of global development (see Figure 20) (We'll dig into those scenarios a bit more below). The black line in these charts represented a model that was basically "business as usual," in that it was mostly just an extrapolation forward from existing empirically documented trends). How that radiative forcing is modeled to produce temperature change in the global average temperature under those same futuristic scenarios is depicted in the middle (see Figure 13); and Figure 14 shows a summary of how ecological models used by the IPCC estimate the risks posed by various degrees of warming.

The panel on the right is essentially the origins of the *maximum warming targets* that would come to define the goals for global policies to control greenhouse gas emissions. The fourth bar from the left is the most important in this debate, showing the point at which impacts from climate warming become "Net negative in all metrics," which, as you can see back in 2001, wasn't predicted to be reached until the increase in global average temperature reached about 3.5° C. That temperature point was not predicted to be breached, as you can see in panel k, until around the year 2100, and even then, only under extreme scenarios of future greenhouse gas emission levels. However, in panel k, we also see that the IPCC has given us a dropline at the magic number of 2°C, scheduled to arrive in 2050, under several of the modeled projections of greenhouse gas accumulation used by the IPCC.

The equivalent climate-damage model ensembles as displayed in the IPCC Fourth Assessment Report, Synthesis Report, 2007 (SR4) is somewhat less visually alarming.

But the text accompanying this graphic emphasizes the risks of lower levels of warming still more strongly than did the SR3. For example, the description of the ecosystem impacts of climate change state:

> For increases in global average temperature exceeding 1.5 to 2.5°C and in concomitant atmospheric CO2 concentrations, there are projected to be major changes in ecosystem structure and function, species' ecological interactions and shifts in species' geographical ranges, with *predominantly negative consequences* [emphasis added] for biodiversity and ecosystem goods and services, e.g., water and food supply.

The 2°C threshold, in the Fourth Assessment Report is predicted to be breached in 2020—only some 13 years away.

To sum up how the "we have only X years to avoid the dreaded climate tipping point of Y" evolved in subsequent IPCC reports.

- In the IPCC Fifth Assessment Report of 2014, The net-harm threshold drops to about 1.6C, to be breached in 2030 (Figures SPM10 and SPM11)

- In the IPCC Special Report Global Warming of 1.5C of 2018, the critical net-harm threshold drops to 1.5C, estimated to be reached by 2030. This remains the case in the most recent report of the IPCC, the Sixth Assessment Report (technical summary, draft) of 2021. (Infographic, p. TS-53).

Table 9. Impacts Associated with Global Temperature Changes

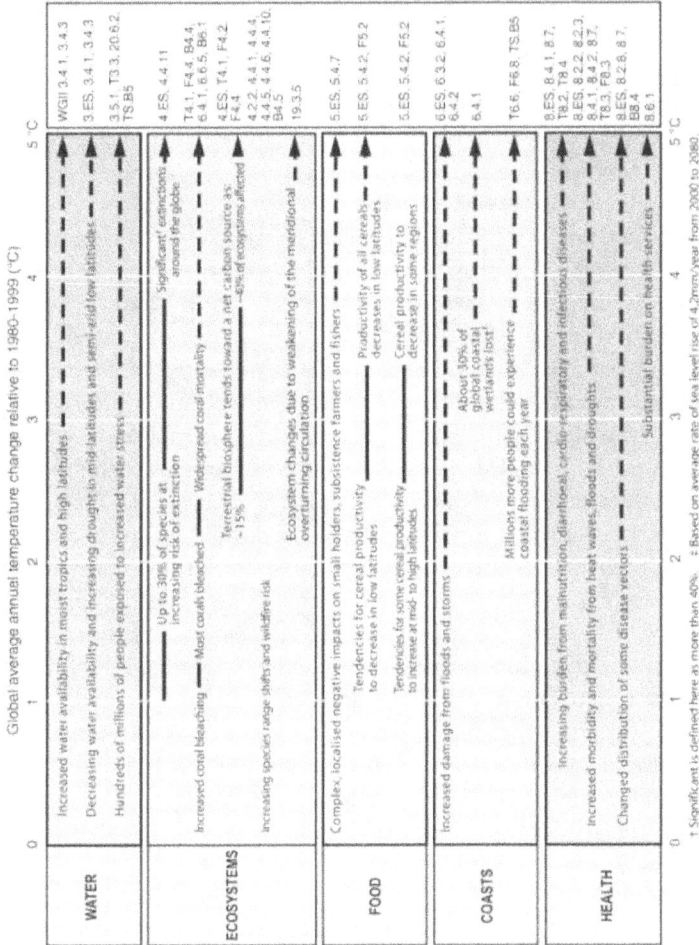

Global average annual temperature change relative to 1980-1999 (°C)

0   1   2   3   4   5 °C

WATER
- Increased water availability in moist tropics and high latitudes
- Decreasing water availability and increasing drought in mid-latitudes and semi-arid low latitudes
- Hundreds of millions of people exposed to increased water stress

References: WGII 3.4.1, 3.4.3 ; 3.ES, 3.4.1, 3.4.3 ; 3.5.1, T3.3, 20.6.2, TS.B5

ECOSYSTEMS
- Up to 30% of species at increasing risk of extinction
- Significant† extinctions around the globe
- Increased coral bleaching — Most corals bleached — Widespread coral mortality
- Terrestrial biosphere tends toward a net carbon source as: ~15% ... ~40% of ecosystems affected
- Increasing species range shifts and wildfire risk
- Ecosystem changes due to weakening of the meridional overturning circulation

References: 4.ES, 4.4.11 ; T4.1, F4.4, B4.4, 6.4.1, 6.6.5, B6.1 ; 4.ES, T4.1, F4.2, F4.4 ; 4.2.2, 4.4.1, 4.4.4, 4.4.5, 4.4.6, 4.4.10, B4.5 ; 19.3.5

FOOD
- Complex, localised negative impacts on small holders, subsistence farmers and fishers
- Tendencies for cereal productivity to decrease in low latitudes
- Productivity of all cereals decreases in low latitudes
- Tendencies for some cereal productivity to increase at mid- to high latitudes
- Cereal productivity to decrease in some regions

References: 5.ES, 5.4.7 ; 5.ES, 5.4.2, F5.2 ; 5.ES, 5.4.2, F5.2

COASTS
- Increased damage from floods and storms
- About 30% of global coastal wetlands lost‡
- Millions more people could experience coastal flooding each year

References: 6.ES, 6.3.2, 6.4.1, 6.4.2 ; 6.4.1 ; T6.6, F6.8, TS.B5

HEALTH
- Increasing burden from malnutrition, diarrhoeal, cardio-respiratory and infectious diseases
- Increased morbidity and mortality from heat waves, floods and droughts
- Changed distribution of some disease vectors
- Substantial burden on health services

References: 8.ES, 8.4.1, 8.7, T8.2, T8.4 ; 8.ES, 8.2.2, 8.2.3, 8.4.1, 8.4.2, 8.7 ; T8.3, F8.3 ; 8.ES, 8.2.8, 8.7, B8.4 ; 8.6.1

† Significant is defined here as more than 40%.   ‡ Based on average rate of sea level rise of 4.2mm/year from 2000 to 2080

Source: IPCC

So, according to the evolved model ensembles of the IPCC, we have 10 (maybe 12) years to save the Earth from a tipping point into uniformly destructive climate changes caused by greenhouse gas emissions.

As I mentioned briefly above, all three of the predictive exercises used in the IPCC reports are not simply extrapolations forward from observed physical trends in the climate, or greenhouse gas concentrations. They are predictive models built from sets of possible scenarios of the future, as dreamed up by special groups within the IPCC research community. To put it very simply, a bunch of people sit together and speculate about what the world will look like 100 years from now, in terms of, well, everything imaginable. What will the global population be? How much energy will humanity consume? How much food? How much water? How much transportation will there be? How will agricultural productivity progress, or fail to progress? How will technology to control greenhouse gas emissions develop? How will lower-greenhouse-gas producing forms of energy come into being? It is a very, very long list.

We will not go into the detailed contents or evolution of these scenarios, which only grow more detailed, more fractionated, and more fanciful. In the UN's own words, in later reports, rather than simply speaking about future scenarios, the UN creates sets of "Storylines" of the future and derives detailed Scenarios from those Storylines of how the future will unfold. The largest explication of this whole exercise in predicting the future can be found in the IPCC Special Report on Emission Scenarios (SRES), published in 2000. Only a serious masochist who wish a detailed understanding of the amazing process that the IPCC goes through to create speculative scenarios and storylines of the future Earth should read this report. At a mere 608 pages, it is one of the slimmer technical volumes among the IPCC climate reports. As an aside, while the IPCC is concerned with many things, such as greenhouse gas emissions, they seem to be completely unconcerned about the exploding proliferation of humongous, and almost impenetrable compendium reports of climate change research that are published every five years or so. Someone should really point out to them that even downloading those things, much less reading them, is no doubt a considerable contributor to global greenhouse gas emissions (not to mention narcolepsy and strabismus) that ought to be contained.

This figure below, from SRES, encapsulates the entire predictive scheme used in IPCC forecasting since 1990. The more astute reader will focus on the legend of the figure below, which contains an important (and some might say amusing) caveat: *"Altogether 40 SRES scenarios have been developed by six modeling teams. All are equally valid with no assigned probabilities of occurrence* [emphasis added]. *"*This is equivalent to saying that all are equally meaningless but pointing that out might get one labeled a climate denier, so we won't do that.

Image 19.
The Main Characteristics of the Four SRES Storylines and Scenario Families

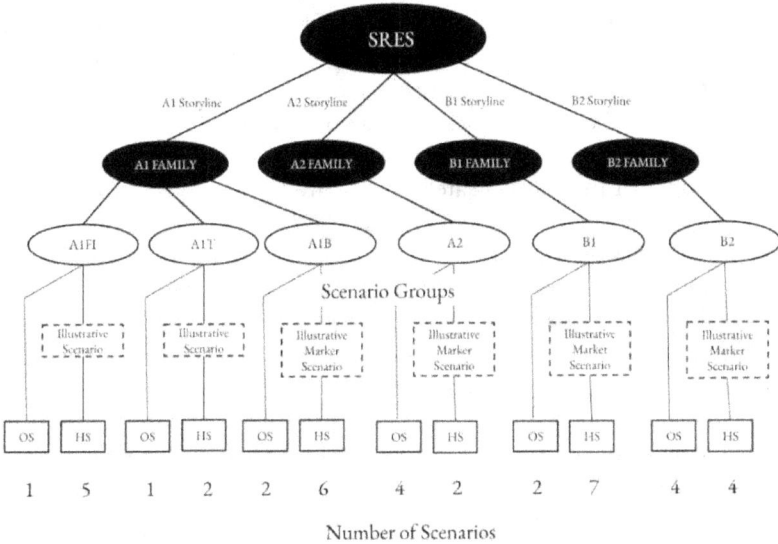

Number of Scenarios

Image Note: Schematic illustration of SRE S scenarios. Four qualitative storylines yield four sets of scenarios called "families": Al, A2, Bl, and B2. Altogether 40 SRE S scenarios have been developed by six modeling teams. Al l are equally valid with no assigned probabilities of occurrence. The set of scenarios consists of six scenario groups drawn from the four families: one group each in A2, Bl, B2, and three groups within the Al family, characterizing alternative developments of energy technologies: AlFI (fossil fuel intensive), AlB (balanced), and AIT (predominantly non-fossil fuel). Within each family and group of scenarios, some share "harmonized" assumptions on global population, gross world product, and final energy. These are marked as "HS" for harmonized scenarios. "OS" denotes scenarios that explore uncertainties in driving forces beyond those of the harmonized scenarios. The number of scenarios developed within each category is shown. For each of the six scenario groups an illustrative scenario (which is always harmonized) is provided. Four illustrative marker scenarios, one for each scenario family, were used in draft form in the 1998 SRE S open process and are included in revised form in this report. Two additional illustrative scenarios for the groups AlFI and AIT are also provided and complete a set of six that illustrate all scenario groups. Al l are equally sound.

Source: IPCC

There is only one major problem with all these prognostications of the future. Several researchers, including those of University of Guelph Professor Ross McKitrick, show that when compared with empirical measurements of the climate, most of the IPCC model simulations based on these scenarios' over-estimate the impact of greenhouse gas concentrations on the Earth's climate.

To give but one example, a research letter published in the journal *Earth and Space Science*, climate researchers Ross McKitrick and John Christy (co-developer of the Earth's satellite-measured global average temperature set at the University of Alabama, Huntsville) show that virtually all of the models used to project climate warming as a result of increasing greenhouse gas concentrations exceed observations of the actual climate response of the last 35 years. The figures below represent different modeled estimates of warming that were expected to occur from 1980 to 2015, with the dashed line (— —) representing the average of the estimated model warming. The chain-thick line (— - —), however, shows the actual empirically measured temperature trend over those same years, derived from global satellite measurements of the average temperature in the most sensitive parts of Earth's atmosphere—the global troposphere. The discrepancy between predicted and observed temperatures post 2000 are quite plain to see. Note that if one were to extrapolate forward from the "observed" temperature record, the thresholds of climate change defined as dangerous: 1.5-2°C look considerably further in the future than the next 10 years.

Figure 15. Global Lower Troposphere Temperature

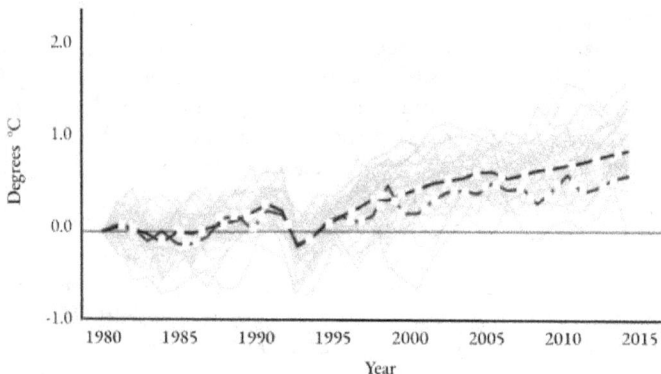

Figure Note: Time series model and observation temperature anomalies. Individual model runs (grey lines), model mean (— —), observational mean (— - —). All series shifted to begin at 0 in 1979.
Source: agupubs.online.wiley.com

Figure 16. Global Mid Troposphere Temperature

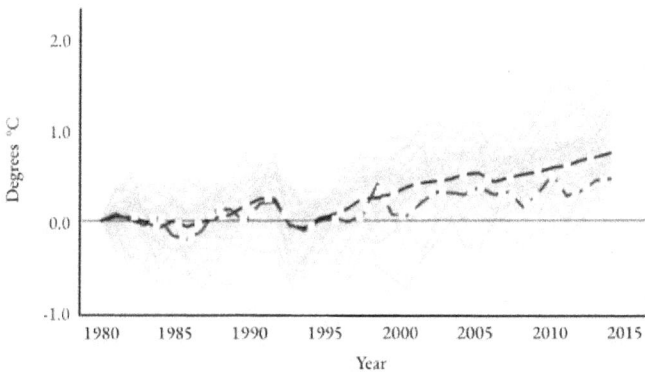

Source: agupubs.online.wiley.com

5.6   Models that Mangled Climate Policy

The prevailing wisdom that underpins the sense of climate urgency in today's policy debates—10 years to save the world—stems from three sets of speculative models developed over the last 30 years by scientists working under the umbrella of the United Nations Intergovernmental Panel on Climate Change.

If those models are to be believed, we have until 2030 to prevent the current trajectory of greenhouse gas emissions from tipping the world over the critical threshold of 1.5C, which necessitates immediate, and sharp reductions in global greenhouse gas emissions. Yes, after some 40 years of alarm, despite little or no progress in reducing global greenhouse gas emissions, we are still about 10 years from Armageddon. This alone should tell one that the claim is based on changeable assumptions in modeling, rather than real-time changes in observable data that could indicate risk. If in fact, the climate was oscillating that fast, we would be seeing vastly larger climatological problems than we have been.

But empirical evidence from the real world suggests that the IPCC's estimates of future warming are overstated, and what scientists have seen from looking at actual measurements of increased greenhouse gases in the environment, and the recent rise in global average temperatures makes it clear that these "10-years to save the planet" invocations are based more in ever changing speculative scenarios of what the future will look like—models, and not on observed reality.

6

COVID-19: Models to the Max!

S o, I know what you're thinking. "If you were going to write a book on how mistaken acceptance of computer models as accurate representations of past, present, or future empirical realities has buggered up various EHS policies and regulations, shouldn't you have started this book with a discussion of COVID-19?

Anyway, I'm glad you asked. To be brutally honest, when I first conceived of, and began plotting out this book in late 2019/early 2020, I rather hoped that I wouldn't have to write about COVID-19 at any length because it would simply be another virus that hit, did its viral thing, ran its typical viral course, and moved along into the category of "icky, but run-of-the-mill viruses endemic to human populations."

Unfortunately, that did not come to pass. Well, it did, after a while: as of this writing, COVID-19 looks to be entering into a state of tolerable mutual existence with the human species as all previous viruses that afflicted humanity eventually have–the proof of that is in our continued existence as a species. However, also as of this writing, COVID-19 and its variants have not been normalized that way. In fact, it is still driving a lot of people barking mad.

I was also hoping to put off writing about this until passions had cooled, and I thought it was safe to share thoughts that might not be 100% in tune (well, okay, might be jarringly out of tune) with the narrative of the moment, and consequently avoid being cast out by friends, family, acquaintances, and institutions as some kind of heretic, a risk that has only grown in recent decades of social division and strife. That is probably also a forlorn hope, but having reached the last chapters of this book, I have to take on the subject, despite the risk of peeving off still more friends, colleagues, and acquaintances.

Finally, I was also hoping that while I wrote the first parts of this book, we would have put Covid policy behind us (if nothing else) as an scientifically/technologically evolving issue (that is, we'd have solved it, or reached some kind of stable equilibrium), and I'd be able to write about all of the modeling that was done, and the policies that were enacted, and the consequences of said policy in a retrospective way, preferably drawing on authoritative post-hoc documents and research that had guided all of that policy, as I did with food additives, ambient air pollution, ozone-depleting chemicals, and climate change. Alas, no such luck.

Instead, nigh on three years into the insanity of the Covid19 pandemic, we are nowhere near being able to look at it through the rear-view mirror, and if anything, our rear-view mirror has become cracked, blurry, and to overwork a metaphor, is dangling from one loose screw in front of the windshield.

It should also be stated that our governments, and Public Health agencies dealing with COVID-19 have played so fast and loose with the various metrics one might use, as to conceivably make true understanding of events impossible, even in retrospect. Starting from the beginning of the pandemic with blurred distinctions between exposure, infection, illness, serious illness, hospitalization because of COVID-19, hospitalization with or while infected with COVID-19, tested for COVID-19 (virus), tested for COVID-19 antibodies, tested for differential strains of COVID-19 (extremely rare), died with COVID-19, died from COVID-19, reinfected with COVID-19, reinfected by a variant of COVID-19, was protected by one vaccine shot, or two, had adverse effects from one vaccine shot, or two, or three, or by vaccine brand, or type…it horrifies me to say it, but it seems as if the data of events from the very beginning of COVID-19, this critical event in modern human history may never be trustworthy for use in rigorous post-hoc analysis, or detailed determinations of what terms were appropriate, how they were defined, and so on.

And of course, the very first lockdown or guidance about social distancing, handwashing, and mask-wearing took us out of any possible reality predicted by most of the early mortality models of COVID-19, most of which were predicated on the assumption that no significant actions would be taken to slow the progress of the virus as it made its way through humanity. We have lived in the world of the counterfactual ever since, and for good or ill, we always will.

6.1   Intervention Effectiveness

We must start somewhere, and so we shall, with the risk-estimations that kicked the whole insanity off, which came from models of COVID-19 potential fatality. The modeled estimate that triggered the global panic over the not-yet named COVID-19 was found in a report, blandly titled, Report

4 on the Severity of the 2019 novel coronavirus. Here is the summary from Report 4:

> We present case fatality ratio (CFR) estimates for three strata of COVID-19 (previously termed 2019-nCoV) infections. For cases detected in Hubei [China], we estimate the CFR to be 18% (95% credible interval: 11%-81%). For cases detected in travelers outside mainland China, we obtain central estimates of the CFR in the range 1.2-5.6% depending on the statistical methods, with substantial uncertainty around these central values. Using estimates of underlying infection prevalence in Wuhan at the end of January derived from testing of passengers on repatriation flights to Japan and Germany, we adjusted the estimates of CFR from either the early epidemic in Hubei Province, or from cases reported outside mainland China, to obtain estimates of the overall CFR in all infections (asymptomatic or symptomatic) of approximately 1% (95% confidence interval 0.5%-4%). It is important to note that the differences in these estimates does not reflect underlying differences in disease severity between countries. CFRs seen in individual countries will vary depending on the sensitivity of different surveillance systems to detect cases of differing levels of severity and the clinical care offered to severely ill cases. All CFR estimates should be viewed cautiously at the current time as the sensitivity of surveillance of both deaths and cases in mainland China is unclear. Furthermore, all estimates rely on limited data on the typical time intervals from symptom onset to death or recovery which influences the CFR estimates.

To put that in plainer English, if you were one of the people who caught COVID-19 in Hubei China, during the earliest days of the pandemic, the Ferguson team calculated that you were at rather high risk of death: the case fatality rate for those people was estimated at 18 percent (though, the possible range of values for the case fatality rate even in this early measurement ranged from a worrisome 11 percent, to a potential "we're all gonna die" scenario of 81%). If you were one of the folks that managed to get out of mainland China, your estimated case-fatality rate was much lower, ranging between 1.2 to 5.6 percent, still with "substantial uncertainty around these central values." But by the end of January, using data collected from air travelers being repatriated to Japan and Germany, the case-fatality estimate had declined to about 1 percent (still highly substantial), with a potential range of from 0.5 percent to 4 percent. To Ferguson et.al. credit, they did emphasize that these CFR estimates should be used cautiously, and, surprisingly, they were not all that far off.

As of January 2023, some 2.5 years out, according to the World Health Organization's COVID-19 dashboard, "Globally, as of 8:18pm CET, 19 January 2023, there have been 663,248,631 confirmed cases of COVID-19, including 6,709,387 deaths, reported to WHO." Again, the math is simple: 6.6M/6.7M= about 1 per cent. And yes, I'm taking the WHO count at face value in this situation, which assumes that it's counting cases of COVID, rather than something else, like seasonal influenza. On the other hand, given that I'm sure Ferguson et al would assume that WHO would get this count right, it is somewhat of an apples-to-apples comparison to pair Ferguson's estimate with WHO's current count.

Ferguson's team also deserves some credit for getting something right that, in retrospect, was probably the worst-handled, and worst-internalized characteristic of COVID-19 risk – that it would be stratified by age. This was published in Lancet in June of 2020, but released earlier in February via the Imperial College London website (italics mine):

> Using data on 24 deaths that occurred in mainland China and 165 recoveries outside of China, we estimated the mean duration from onset of symptoms to death to be 17·8 days (95% credible interval [CrI] 16·9–19·2) and to hospital discharge to be 24·7 days (22·9–28·1). In all laboratory confirmed and clinically diagnosed cases from mainland China (n=70 117), we estimated a crude case fatality ratio (adjusted for censoring) of 3·67% (95% CrI 3·56–3·80). However, after further adjusting for demography and under-ascertainment, we obtained a best estimate of the case fatality ratio in China of 1·38% (1·23–1·53), with substantially higher ratios in older age groups (0·32% [0·27–0·38] in those aged <60 years vs 6·4% [5·7–7·2] in those aged ≥60 years), up to 13·4% (11·2–15·9) in those aged 80 years or older. Estimates of case fatality ratio from international cases stratified by age were consistent with those from China (parametric estimate 1·4% [0·4–3·5] in those aged <60 years [n=360] and 4·5% [1·8–11·1] in those aged ≥60 years [n=151]). Our estimated overall infection fatality ratio for China was 0·66% (0·39–1·33), with an increasing profile with age. Similarly, estimates of the proportion of infected individuals likely to be hospitalised increased with age

up to a maximum of 18·4% (11·0–37·6) in those aged 80 years or older.

And indeed, Covid mortality turned out to be even more sharply stratified by age. Table 10 illuminates how the risk of infection, hospitalization, and death from COVID-19 vary by age group (CDC, 2022).

Table 10.
Risk for COVID-19 Infection, Hospitalisation, and Death by Age Group

Rate compared to 18-29 years old	Years old								
	0-4	5-17	18-29	30-39	40-49	50-64	65-74	75-84	85+
Cases	0.5x	0.7x	Reference Group	1x	0.9x	0.8x	0.6x	0.6x	0.6x
Hospitalization	0.6x	0.2x	Reference Group	1.5x	1.9x	3.1x	4.9x	8.9x	15x
Death	0.3x	0.1x	Reference Group	3.5x	10x	25x	60x	140x	350x

Source: US Centers for Disease Control

Notice that the risk of being infected is the same in all age groups over 5 years of age. Some might find this surprising (if they did not read the earlier discussion thoroughly!), though, the only bit of surprise from a biological perspective is that the children under five don't even seem to let the virus get enough of a toehold in their bodies to register as an actual infection. The virtues of a truly robust immune system, one supposes. The fact that all of the other age groups show the same risk of infection is simply a reflection of the fact that everyone has, essentially, the same cellular and immune structures that allow COVID-19 to enter and infect one's cells, and COVID-19, being a small virus capable of airborne transmission means that virtually everyone will be (and likely has been many times) exposed to COVID-19 particles in the environment.

But as the second row of the table makes clear, the risk of being badly sickened by the infection is not uniform across age groups. The older one is, the higher the risk that the severity of one's COVID-19 infection will result in hospitalization and ultimately, death. As the table shows, the risk of a severe COVID-19 infection (requiring hospitalization) is five times higher for someone between 65 and 74 than it is for a strapping 18–29-year-old. That risk climbs to 8 times higher for people between 75 and 85, after which it peaks at 10-fold above the average infected person. Finally, when it comes to the risk that COVID-19 will kill you, the age stratification is extreme. One's risk of death from COVID-19 infection if one is over 75 years of age is more than a full order of magnitude higher than the risk to someone between 40-49 years old.

At this point, since I'm not raging at the Ferguson modeling team or their work, you might be realizing that I'm about to say something rather different about modeling in the context of the COVID-19 pandemic, and you would be right: In this case, the modeling of disease-risk wasn't really the cause of humanity's problems with the policy response to COVID-19.

But modeling of a related sort did play a significant role in the disastrous nature of interventions that governments would pursue in respond to the actual risks posed by the virus, and in that domain, some of the modeling (by the Ferguson team) were indeed part of the problem. They provided a rationale for government's acting out of the same innate desires to control events (and profit from them politically, economically, and socially), and acting with complete disregard for what was well understood to be sane responses to the arrival of a novel respiratory virus into the human ecosystem.

Specifically, the work of Ferguson's modeling team that led to serious policy mischief was not the initial estimates of COVID-19 severity, as much as their work was about the potential for government to do anything useful about it.

In Report 9, *Impact of non-pharmaceutical interventions (NPIs) to reduce COVID-19 mortality and healthcare demand*, we see the origins of the most disastrous early government COVID-19 policies, particularly those that put "protecting our healthcare systems" above all other goals. These next two sets of charts (Figure 17 and 18) may have been the first ones to suggest that, in fact, government interventions might be useful.

As can be readily seen, this chart suggested that without interventions (such as isolation, masking, shutdowns, lockdowns, etc.) the US would see about deaths per day at the peak culminating in some 2.2 million deaths by the time COVID-19 was estimated to have run its course in August 2020. Ferguson's UK did not fare much better in this guesstimation run: Great Britain would see its COVID-19 death rate spike to 20 persons per 100,000 population, for a total of 510,000 deaths over the course of the epidemic.

Ferguson's team would go farther, however, than merely hitting the big numbers of deaths "with or without" intervention and put out these guesstimates of how things might fare under a variety of "non-pharmaceutical interventions," or NPCs.

This is perhaps the earliest origin of the 90-days to flatten the curve "flatten the curve" concept.

Figure 17. Expected Peak Mortality "No Mitigation" Scenario

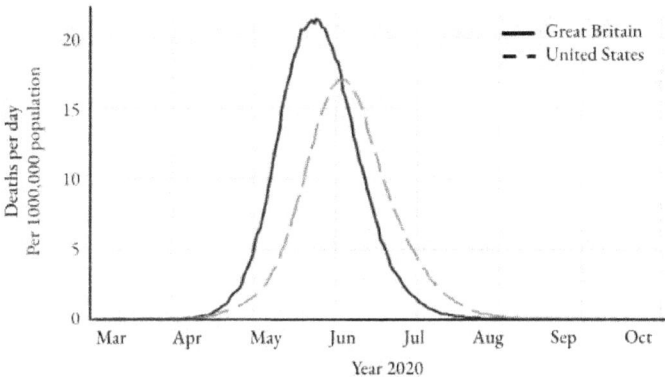

Source: Imperial College COVID-19 Response Team.

Figure 18. Case Epidemic Trajectories across the US by State

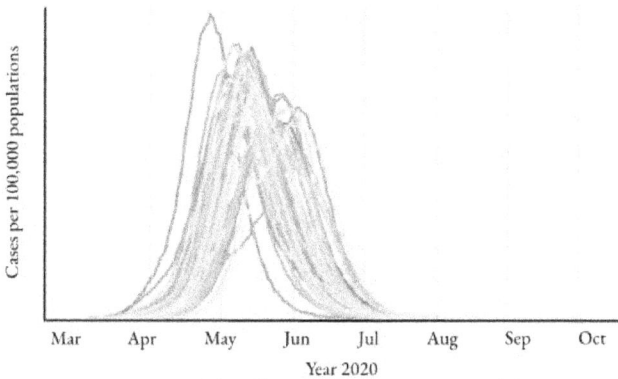

Source: Imperial College COVID-19 Response Team.

What is important to note here is that each of these guesstimates is entirely based upon assumed effectiveness of the interventions, which are simply asserted by the authors to be "plausible and largely conservative (i.e., pessimistic) assumptions about the impact of each intervention and compensatory changes in contacts (e.g. in the home) associated with reducing contact rates in specific settings outside the household." No information is given in the study indicating where these assumptions came from, or what they were based on. Table 11 summarizes the Ferguson team's assumptions about the effectiveness of the various interventions.

Figure 19. Mitigation Strategy Scenarios Critical Care (ICU) Bed Requirements.

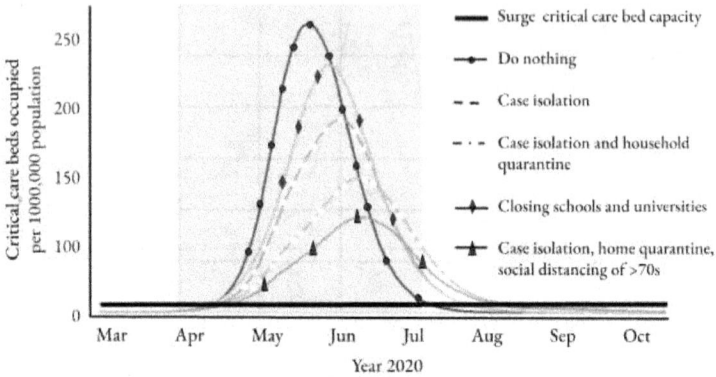

Source: Imperial College COVID-19 Response Team.

Table 11. Summary of NPI Interventions Considered

Label	Policy	Description
CI	Case isolation in the home	Symptomatic cases stay at home for 7 days, reducing non-household contacts by 75% for this period. Household contacts remain unchanged. Assume 70% of household comply with the policy.
HQ	Voluntary home quarantine	Following identification of a symptomatic case in the household, all household members remain at home for 14 days. Household contact rates double during this quarantine period, contacts in the community reduce by 75%. Assume 50% of household comply with the policy.
SDO	Social distancing of those over 70 years of age	Reduce contacts by 50% in workplaces, increase household contacts by 25% and reduce other contacts by 75%. Assume 75% compliance with policy.
SD	Social distancing of entire population	All households reduce contact outside household, school or workplace by 75%. School contact rates unchanged, workplace contact rates reduced by 25%. Household contact rates assumed to increase by 25%.
PC	Closure of schools and universities	Closure of all schools, 25% of universities remain open. Household contact rates for student families increase by 50% during closure. Contacts in the community increase by 25% during closure.

Source: Imperial College COVID-19 Response Team.

And another important point to make here is that Ferguson's framing of this exercise can be seen as somewhat political. The choice of including a "Do nothing," option (which was never, to any rational person, a reasonable expectation) loaded up the political dialogue of, "either government intervenes, or we "do nothing." Of course, human beings what they are, the "do nothing" scenario had already evaporated long before Ferguson published this chart: the second that COVID-19 emerged in China, governments were already acting to control events in a variety of ways.

But the Ferguson team wasn't done yet, in introducing new metrics that would come to dominate the handling of the COVID-19 epidemic. No, Ferguson's next modeling exercise would introduce a historical notion, as far as I've been able to determine, that the critical value which would drive virtually all policy responses to control the COVID-19 pandemic would come down to avoiding a situation where we run out of available critical-care beds anywhere around the world. There may be some historical precedent for deciding that the number of critical care beds available at a given time was some fixed value which could not be expanded, augmented, or what have you, but again, if so, I have not seen any evidence of one. As Ferguson et al. noted in the description of the table above:

> The other four NPIs (social distancing of those over 70 years, social distancing of the entire population, stopping mass gatherings and closure of schools and universities) are decisions made at the government level. For these interventions we therefore consider surveillance triggers based on testing of patients in critical care (intensive care units, ICUs). We focus on such cases as testing is most complete for the most severely ill patients. When examining mitigation strategies, we assume policies are in force for *3 months*, other than social distancing of those over the age of 70 which is assumed to remain in place for one month longer. Suppression strategies are assumed to be in place for 5 months or longer.

I consider this report from the Ferguson team to be ground zero in how the plague of CG models exploded into the midst of the COVID-19 pandemic, because this study shot straight into hypothetical estimates of how many people would die, where and when, and, more importantly, what government should do, and had to do to avoid those hypothetical deaths or to *Flatten the Curve*:

To help inform country strategies in the coming weeks, we provide here summary statistics of the potential impact of mitigation and suppression strategies in all countries across the world. These illustrate the need to act early, and the impact that failure to do so is likely to have on local health systems. It is important to note that these are not predictions of what is likely to happen; this will be determined by the action that governments and countries take in the coming weeks and the behaviour changes that occur as a result of those actions.

Table 12. Reduction in Peak ICU Bed Demand

Reproduction ratio (beds, deaths)	Trigger (cummulative ICU cases)	NPI Interventions						
		PC	CI	CI_HQ	CI_HQ_SD	CI_SD	CI_HQ_SDOL70	PC_CI_HQ_SDOL70
$R_0 = 2.2$ Peak Beds	100	23%	35%	57%	25%	39%	69%	48%
	300	22%	35%	57%	28%	43%	69%	54%
	1000	21%	35%	57%	34%	53%	69%	63%
	3000	18%	35%	57%	47%	68%	69%	75%
$R_0 = 2.2$ Total Deaths	100	3%	21%	34%	9%	15%	49%	19%
	300	3%	21%	34%	9%	17%	49%	20%
	1000	4%	21%	34%	11%	21%	49%	22%
	3000	4%	21%	34%	15%	27%	49%	24%
$R_0 = 2.4$ Peak Beds	100	14%	33%	53%	33%	53%	67%	69%
	300	14%	33%	53%	34%	57%	67%	71%
	1000	14%	33%	53%	39%	64%	67%	77%
	3000	12%	33%	53%	51%	75%	67%	81%
$R_0 = 2.4$ Total Deaths	100	2%	17%	31%	13%	20%	49%	29%
	300	2%	17%	31%	14%	23%	49%	29%
	1000	2%	17%	31%	15%	26%	50%	30%
	3000	2%	17%	31%	19%	30%	49%	32%

Note: Mitigation options for Great Britain. Relative Impact of NPI combinations applied nationally for 3 months in GB on total deaths and peak hospital ICU bed demand for different choices of cumulative ICU cases diagnosed in a country per week. Source: Ferguson et. al. 2020.

Note that the confidence suggested in the word choices above, such as the "need to act early," and the "impact of failure" imply considerably more certainty than the authors themselves explain immediately afterward, when they observe that:

There remain large uncertainties in the underlying determinants of the severity of COVID-19 infection and how these translate across settings. However, clear risk factors include age, with older people more likely to require hospitalisation and to subsequently die as a result of infection, and underlying co-morbidities including hypertension, diabetes and coronary heart disease serving to exacerbate symptoms. Both the age-profile and the distribution of relevant co-morbidities are likely to vary substantially by country, region, and economic status, as will age-specific contact patterns and social mixing. Variation in these factors between countries will have material consequences for transmission and the associated burden of disease by modifying the extent to which infection spreads to the older, more vulnerable members of society.

The key modeling representation that we see in Report 12 rapidly expanded to dominate virtually all discussion of "what we should do" about COVID-19. These are the dreaded "flatten the curve" charts showing what has to happen to prevent COVID-19 patients from overwhelming a country's critical care facilities.

Figure 20. Low Income Countries - Death Predictions

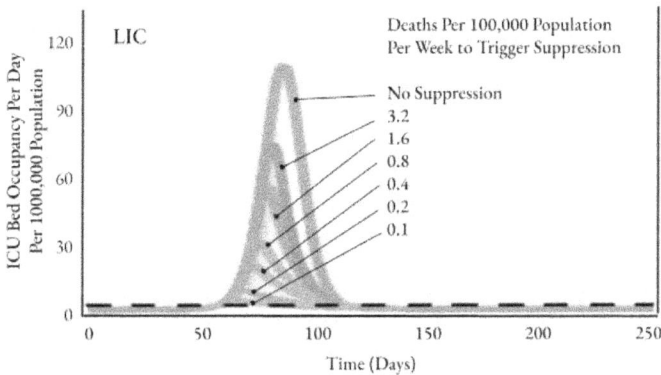

Figure Notes: Figure 20 - 27: The impact of various control strategies in representative settings. Using an age structured SEIR model along with demographies and contact patterns representative of LIC, LMIC, UMIC and HIC countries (columns left to right) the impact of different control strategies was. ICU bed occupancy per day per 100,000 population is shown in all figures. The top row shows impact of suppression (triggered at times dependent on when the rate of deaths per week increases beyond certain defined thresholds) and the bottom row shows mitigation (involving either mitigation involving general social distancing across the whole population or mitigation involving whole population social distancing as well as enhanced social distancing of the elderly).

Figure 21. Low Income Countries Strategy - Predictions

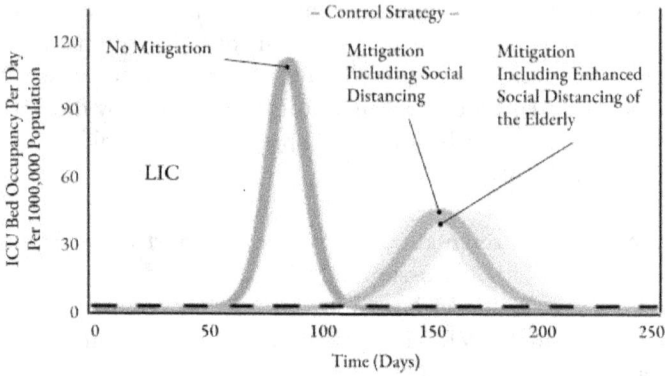

Figure 22. Low-Middle Income Countries - Death Predictions

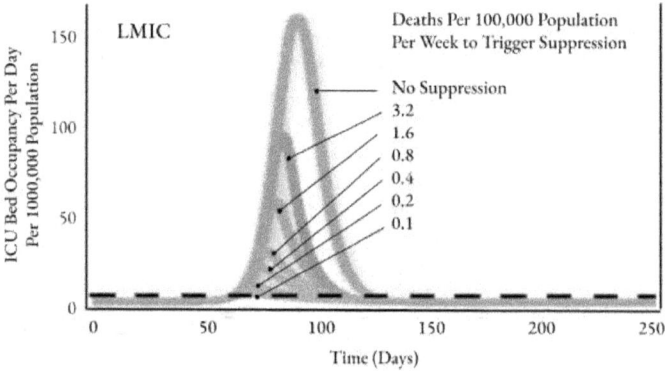

Figure 23. Low-Middle Income Countries - Control Strategy Predictions

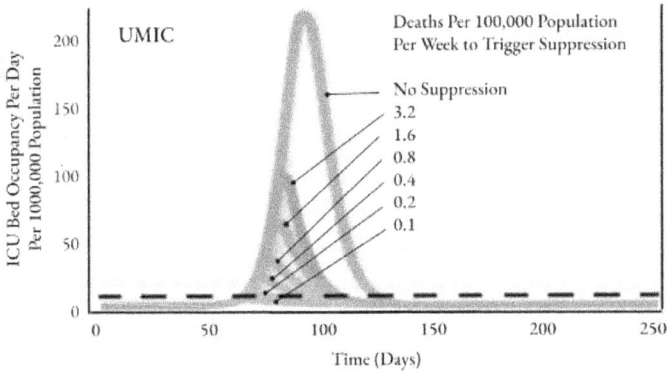

Figure 24. Upper Middle-Income Countries - Death Predictions

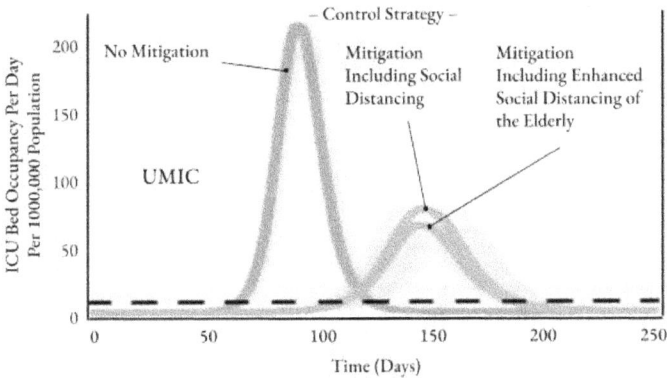

Figure 25. Upper Middle-Income Countries - Control Strategy Predictions

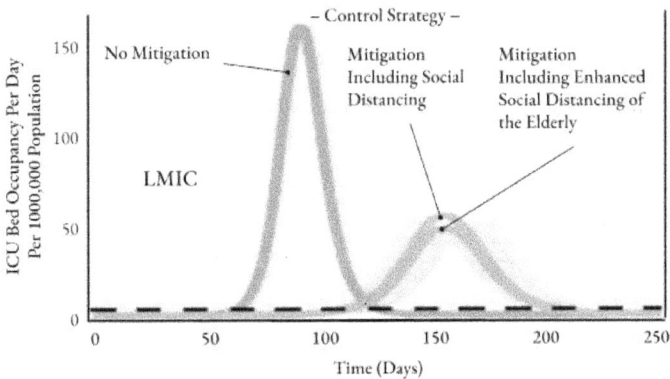

Figure 26. High Income Countries - Death Predictions

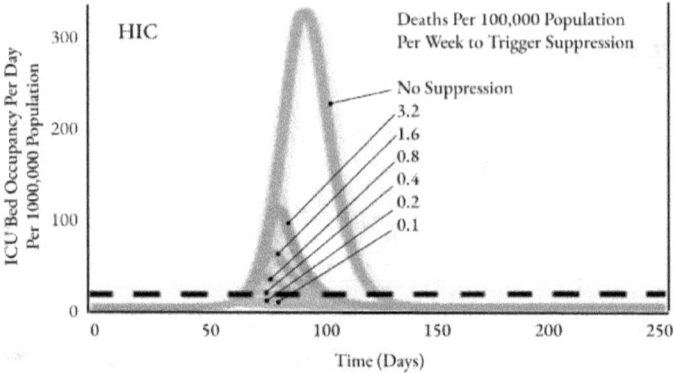

Figure 27. High Income Countries - Control Strategy Predictions

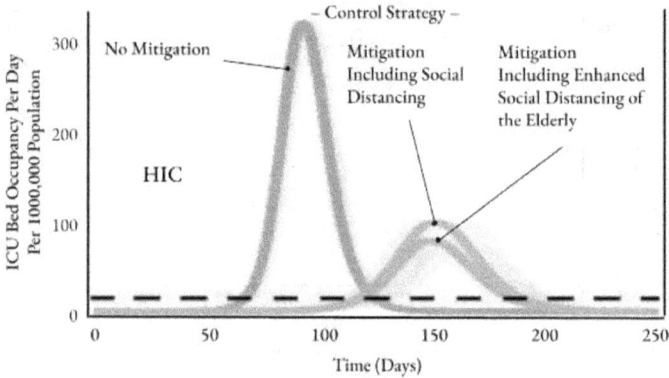

Source: Figure 20–27. Report 12, "The Global Impact of COVID-19 and strategies for mitigation and suppression.

6.2   Modeling COVID-19

Computer modeling of COVID-19 risk were not, at the end of the day, the cause of the vast panoply of horrendous public policy, rules, and regulations promulgated in dealing with COVID-19, some of which will haunt us forever.

But modeling of the potential value of COVID-19 risk-mitigation interventions did indeed play such a role, and should be a cautionary tale for the future, because they enabled panicked governments to implement intervention policies that, while completely untested, were nearly guaranteed to cause massive harm to people's lives, employment, and economies that would last many years beyond the pandemic itself. The utility of the "non-pharmaceutical" interventions, all pinned to the novel idea that society's over-arching value was the conservation of intensive care beds, were also over-estimated. Meanwhile, the damages that would be done to society by the radical changes of widespread economic sector shutdowns, exhortations to "stay home, stay safe," restrictions on occupancy in shops and restaurants, intimidating and unpleasant mask-mandates, social-distancing mandates, and all the rest were almost universally ignored. In fact, mentioning them would get you banned from most social networking in pretty short order.

7

Treatment Options for the Plague of Models

Given the way that the Federal government has been seen to handle data (particularly modeling data) that flows into its regulatory processes in the EHS arena, it will likely come as a surprise to many people to learn that the US actually has a thing called the *Federal Data Quality Act* (FDQA), but it does.

7.1 Strengthen and Expand the *Data Quality Act*

In a 2003 article for the Beckman Center for Internet and Society (Harvard), legal scholar Urs Gasser documents the largely "under the radar" development and implementation of the *Federal Data Quality Act* in 2001. As Gasser observes, the impetus for the data quality act was based on concerns of policymakers regarding the rapid expansion of computer generated (and internet transmitted) information used to make and implement public policy. Gasser explains that

> Information disseminated by Federal agencies has increased in its importance both quantitatively and qualitatively—with respect to decision-making processes within the public and private sector as a consequence of the enhanced use of digital technology in general and the Internet in particular. With this increase of the amount of information disseminated on the one hand, and the enormous expansion of the potential audience (i.e. visitors of a Federal department's website) on the other hand, the previous and, foremost, the current Administration became aware of prominent cases of the past demonstrating quality problems with regard to information collected, used and published by Federal agencies (at this point in time, of course, published by traditional means like photocopy).

That certainly was a legitimate concern at the time, and it is arguably a greater cause for concern today. But the reason most people might not know of the existence of the FDQA is that it was slipped into law somewhat sideways as a humble rider to an appropriations bill and was enacted, as Gasser observes, "without attracting public attention and was—as a so-called rider—enacted without any public debate or scrutiny."

The FDQA is something of a marvel in terms of federal rulemaking in one regard at least, because it is concise. Concise enough to include the whole thing here:

> Sec. 515. (a) In General. The Director of the Office of Management and Budget shall, by not later than September 30, 2001, and with public and Federal agency involvement, issue guidelines under sections 3504(d)(1) and 3516 of title 44, United States Code, that provide policy and procedural guidance to Federal agencies for ensuring and maximizing the quality, objectivity, utility, and integrity of information (including statistical information) disseminated by Federal agencies in fulfillment of the purposes and provisions of chapter 35 of title 44, United States Code, commonly referred to as the Paperwork Reduction Act.
>
> (b) Content of Guidelines. The guidelines under subsection (a) shall
>> (1) apply to the sharing by Federal agencies of, and access to, information disseminated by Federal agencies; and (2) require that each Federal agency to which the guidelines apply–
>> (a) issue guidelines ensuring and maximizing the quality, objectivity, utility, and integrity of information (including statistical information) disseminated by the agency, by not later than 1 year after the date of issuance of the guidelines under subsection (a);
>> (b) establish administrative mechanisms allowing affected persons to seek and obtain correction of information maintained and disseminated by the agency that does not comply with the guidelines issued under subsection (a); and
>> (c) report periodically to the Director–

(i) the number and nature of complaints received by the agency regarding the accuracy of information disseminated by the agency; and

(ii) how such complaints were handled by the agency.

[Imagine if all all-government edicts were so refreshingly concise!]

Unfortunately, from the perspective of actually ensuring the quality of data used in and disseminated by federal governmental entities, the FDQA is not only sparing in words it is sparing in teeth. The FDQA is a basically a toothless procedural mandate dumped on federal agencies which were then left entirely to their own devices in deciding how it was to be implemented. The FDQA requires federal agencies to publish statements about how they seek to maintain data quality in their particular agencies and it uses, and requires the agencies to set up a process to handle complaints of poor data quality. In addition, the federal agencies need to summarize any complaints to the Director of the Office and Management and Budget. That's about it. Agencies are supposed to tell you how they ensure what they consider to be "data quality," or "information quality," and then give you a chance to complain about their handing of some data or information if you run across it in your routine perusal of agency documents, rules, and regulations.

There are no independent regulatory bodies tasked with actually confirming whether or not any efforts are actually made to ensure data quality, nor to hold agencies responsible for failing to do so. There are not even quantitative guidelines establishing what data quality actually means. The FDQA is merely a requirement that agencies tell the public, in some unspecified way, how they view and secure data quality in the Age of the Internet.

The Office of Management and Budget (OMB), under the direction of respected risk management scholar John D. Graham, Administrator of the OMB Office of Information and Regulatory Affairs, did, in 2002, publish a guidance about how Federal agencies should implement efforts to ensure data quality. But again, this guidance simply re-stated the call for federal agencies to establish and publish their own guidance regarding what data quality or information quality was to mean in that agency and to give people a way to dispute such information with the agency. Again, the OMB guidance was much more about generalities than specifics. So, under the definitions "Quality" is an encompassing term comprising utility, objectivity, and integrity. Therefore, the guidelines sometimes refer to these four statutory terms, collectively, as "quality." Right, so that's clear then. Quality means…*quality*.

Under the OMB guidance, data "utility" doesn't get too much better treatment. Utility is defined as "data has to be useful." However, the definition of "objectivity" is fairly decent:

1. "Objectivity" includes whether disseminated information is being presented in an accurate, clear, complete, and unbiased manner. This involves whether the information is presented within a proper context. Sometimes, in disseminating certain types of information to the public, other information must also be disseminated in order to ensure an accurate, clear, complete, and unbiased presentation. Also, the agency needs to identify the sources of the disseminated information (to the extent possible, consistent with confidentiality protections) and, in a scientific or statistical context, the supporting data and models, so that the public can assess for itself whether there may be some reason to question the objectivity of the sources. Where appropriate, supporting data should have full, accurate, transparent documentation, and error sources affecting data quality should be identified and disclosed to users.

2. In addition, "objectivity" involves a focus on ensuring accurate, reliable, and unbiased information. In a scientific or statistical context, the original or supporting data shall be generated, and the analytical results shall be developed, using sound statistical and research methods.

This is actually a decent start on what ought to be required of a federal agency, that is, using and disseminating information that will be used, in many cases, to forcibly change the courses of people's lives, influence their behavioral choices, affect their economy, diminish their personal liberty and autonomy, affect the value of their properties, and perhaps place themselves and their loved ones at increased risk of sickness and death through ill-formed public policy implementation. Unfortunately, the OMB Guidance caves completely on this idea with the next three sentences:

1. If the results have been *subject to formal, independent, external peer review* [emphasis added], the information can generally be considered of acceptable objectivity.

2. In those situations, involving influential scientific or statistical information, the results must be capable of being *substantially reproduced* [emphasis added], if the original or supporting data are independently analyzed using the same models. *Reproducibility does not mean that the original or supporting data have to be capable of being replicated* [emphasis added] through new experiments, samples, or tests.

3. Making the data and models publicly available will assist in determining whether analytical results are capable of being substantially reproduced. However, these guidelines do not alter the otherwise applicable standards and procedures for determining when and how information is disclosed. *Thus, the objectivity standard does not override other compelling interests, such as privacy, trade secret, and other confidentiality protections* [emphasis added].

These three sentences make the FDQA a genuinely toothless piece of paper, putting the foxes in charge of the hen houses, the same people likely to be the ones doing the external peer review process that stands in place of a formal effort to reproduce or fully disclose data are usually the very same people that agencies such as the EPA has paid to do the research, and then paid again to serve on implementation bodies and expert review panels. The same people doing the external peer reviews of studies that are to be cited, and or weighed credibly by an agency such as the EPA, are often the very same people with a vested monetary interest in their *proprietary* models and *trade secrets*.

What is needed to address the plague of models is a vastly strengthened and expanded *Federal Data Quality Act* that would (at the very least) require that:

1. All data, information, computer models, modeling parameters, model code, and the output of all model runs (not just a sampling) must be provided to the relevant regulatory agency before any such information can be

recognized as having evidentiary reliability in an agency regulatory proceeding.

2. This information must be archived (permanently) by the regulating agency and must be made freely available to outside entities to review and or seek to replicate. In real time, well before even draft regulation has been promulgated. If those people must sign liability waivers to do so, that would be reasonable, however, charges for "information handling and processing" should not be a barrier to efforts to validate information used in government regulatory decision-making processes by people from outside of the system, that have independent standing and qualifications to do so.

3. It should be made a violation of law for agencies to fail to comply with these requirements, and provision should be made for the public to be able to sue federal agencies for compliance, accompanied by the suspension of regulatory proceedings or implementation until compliance has been achieved. There should probably be a "bounty hunter" provision in this requirement to allow for the reclamation of costs for those who find situations of violation of agencies to fulfill their data quality requirements under the law.

7.2 Restricting Model Output and Regulatory Development

Outputs of non-mechanistic, non-linear, assumption and statistically driven models should not be considered as concrete information in crafting, setting, and implementing regulations. They may serve as vague indications that regulation is worth considering, but that is as far as their utility extends.

More explicitly, specific values derived from abstract models should not be included in policy development or implementation. In the context of things, we've discussed here for example, model outputs should have had no weight in setting stringency levels for air pollutant concentrations, greenhouse gas emission levels, emissions of ozone-depleting chemicals; and so on. Abstract model outputs should not even be considered as establishing useful information on potential ranges of stringency values - they all too often wind up becoming the accepted stringency targets by regulators seeking the strictest possible regulations regardless of whatever hard data is available regarding the matter facing regulation.

If there is insufficient, empirically derived and validated data available that can be used to set regulatory thresholds, this is an indication that more research is necessary, and regulation should be deferred until such research can bring in concrete data that is likely to reflect reality, more than the imagination of computer modelers.

Eschewing the cheap and easy use of speculative model outputs in setting and implementing EHS (and other) regulations would likely result in a significant reduction in regulation across the board. To which, the author says, Amen - we have far too much regulation, based on the inappropriate use of imaginary computer modeling. We could use a lot less.

7.3 Labeling Requirements for Speculative Modeling

All discussions of modeling, in any governmental policy or regulatory consideration should be accompanied by a bold, visible warning label, that the modeling results discussed or displayed are the product of speculative modeling that may have zero correspondence with reality, or mis-represent that reality entirely. Every chart which projects outputs forward in time, based on anything other than absolutely quantified and deeply understood principles of physics as applied in the real world should also be prominently labeled as "speculation."

If governments think it appropriate to force labels about risk on consumer products such as cigarettes, alcohol, fast-food, and other things that might be harmful to the populace, they should have no objection to labeling the use of speculative model outputs scattered across their own products that pose equal prospects of causing harm such as their regulations, and regulatory analysis, and regulatory justification materials.

These labels, such as *Warning! Data used in this regulatory process are speculative and could lead to harmful outcomes* should be as prominent, and graphically compelling as labels required by governments, perhaps constituting half of all visual space, and graphic images of the harms that could befall people if and when regulations cause unintended consequences. Surely, no regulator, or supplier of modeled information to regulators would object to such labeling. After all, what is good for the modeled goose should be good for the modeled gander.

* * *

Key Take-Aways from the Plague of Models

1. *Computer models of risks to environment, health, and safety are not reality, and are not "the science."*

Computer models, and the outputs they produce are not empirical science in the normative sense of the word, and they do not produce data, or information that reliably describes reality. They are abstractions of reality, bent, folded, spindled, and mutilated (intentionally or unintentionally) into whatever pretty origami figure that the modelers want them to be. They most certainly do not produce the kind of information that any sane person would want accepted as evidence to be used in some legal proceeding against them.

2. *Accepting models as reality for use by the government in coercing the public is bad. Ghostbuster's level "bad."*

Public confusion about the fact that model outputs are not reality, nor data, nor evidence, combined with government's eager adoption of computer models as evidence for crafting regulations has unleashed a plague of coercive regulations that increasingly constrict people's lives in innumerable ways, and that have come to stifle the economic and cultural engines of Western democracies. That plague of regulations, by the way, is a large part of why the developed world economies are not "bouncing back" quickly after the Great Covid Shutdown. One can't simply start up the world's engines again, without first having an army of lawyers show that you're satisfying all the world's regulatory requirements (and are paid up on your taxes and fees!) get permissions from an infinite army of bureaucrats.

3. *The use of Computer modeling as evidence in regulatory proceedings or any coercive process should be severely restricted.*

Not only should governments be disallowed from basing regulations and public policies on speculative modeling, even their consideration of such modeling should be forced out into the open sunshine of absolute transparency to public inspection, replication, and understanding.

4. *Embrace the power of calling "humbug" on speculative computer modeling.*

Don't let people tell you that you're a "denier," or that "the science says this is so, and you must do as you're told." Because models are not science, saying so does not make you either a denier, or someone outside the realm of science. It simply is not so. When someone demands you bend your knee to some abstract model from the hallowed halls of (invariably) government science—go all Missouri Puke on them "Show me the evidence. Hard evidence, not video games. Otherwise, bugger off."

That's it. Live Long and Prosper!

Afterword

In modern times empiricism rules, and certainly we should demand exacting quantitative analysis where it is possible. Nobody wants to reject the hard, deterministic, mechanistic, empirically based science and engineering that have given us our historically unfathomably high standards of living.

But in still more modern of modern times—since the computer revolution of the 1970s—our craving for empiricism as the driver of social policy have gone astray–into chasing the pseudo-empiricism of statistical, probability-based computer modeling, and that is a problem. Our most important public matters today would benefit greatly if our political leaders and other figures of authority would stop sniffing the model glue.

As the scientific revolution accelerated in the 19th century, it was thought empiricism could unlock all the secrets of the world—and especially the human social world—and literally deliver a future utopia. Even history was thought susceptible to the discovery of scientific "laws" that would enable prediction of the future. And it did, for a while. But not without problems.

As Richard Weaver, author of the 1949 classic *Ideas Have Consequences*, anticipated our current impasse: "The theory of empiricism is plausible because it assumes that accuracy about small matters prepares the way for valid judgment about larger ones. What happens, however, is that the *judgments* are never made. The pedantic empiricist, buried in his little province of phenomena, imagines that fidelity to it exempts him from concern with larger aspects of reality—in the case of science, from consideration of whether there is reality other than matter."

And a fair-minded observer of the general scene—or the proverbial Martian dropped in for a visit—would note that the problem has worsened dramatically since Weaver: the horizon of the promises of strict empiricism and quantitative modeling has steadily narrowed, and the nearly-complete replacement of that strict empiricism with the pseudo-empiricism of computer simulation has exploded.

Accordingly, the failures of models—and governance by model—are piling up. Ambitious macroeconomic modeling was downgraded if not largely abandoned several decades ago, when it was recognized that, as John Kenneth Galbraith memorably put it, "The only function of economic forecasting is to make astrology look respectable." Intricate climate models (that Ken Green has also equated with computerized astrology) requiring massive supercomputing capacity to run have become *less* accurate as time has passed, though the models are constantly "adjusted" to hide this defect. And above all just now, much of our misguided COVID policy of the last few years (not to mention our air-pollution, climate, and ozone-hole policy of the last 20 years) was based on computer models whose flaws were apparent when they were made, though the informed critics of these models were subject to vicious personal and professional attacks.

As I say, empiricism is a necessary and valuable tool for understanding and policy making, but as COVID and climate modeling (among other examples of pseudo-empirical modeling) show, we increasingly live at a time of what can be called "policy-based evidence making," rather than the other way around. Pseudo-empiricism has displaced firm empiricism, and been taken at face value, again, without Weaver's requisite "valid judgment" applied to them.

The real lesson here is that judgment based on fundamental democratic principles should be held in at least equal measure with even the best empirical findings, and free of contamination by pseudo-empirical modeling.

Policies based on constraints on human thought and freedom won't work. As the great political scientist Edward Banfield once wrote, "It is a dangerous delusion to think that the policy scientist can successfully supplant the politician or statesman. Social problems are at bottom political; they arise from differences of opinion and interest and, except in trivial instances, are difficulties to be coped with (ignored, got around, put up with, exorcised by the arts of rhetoric, etc.) rather than puzzles to be solved. . . Would anyone maintain that in the Convention of 1787 the Founders would have reached a better result with the assistance of a staff of model builders?"

I'd go further and argue that Shakespeare offers more insight into human psychology than the top 1,000 empirical psychological studies and the top 100,000 pseudo-empirical modeling studies laid end-to-end, (which wouldn't be a bad idea, come to think of it). The point is, we shouldn't let our empiricism, nor, especially, our modeled pseudo-empiricism. make our decisions for us automatically, or as a substitute for human practical wisdom, especially as so many models today are so badly flawed, as Ken Green admirably points out in the previous pages.

Steven F. Hayward

*Steven F. Hayward is a resident scholar at UC Berkeley's Institute of Governmental Studies and a visiting lecturer at Berkeley Law. He was previously the Ronald Reagan Distinguished Visiting Professor at Pepperdine University's School of Public Policy.

Bibliography

Adam, D. (2007) UN scientists warn time is running out to tackle global warming. *The Guardian.* https://www.theguardian.com/environment/2007/may/05/climate change.climatechangeenvironment. 4 May, 2007.

Anne's rat page (n.d.). *Why Rats Can't Vomit.* ratbehavior.org/vomit.htm.

Anton, R., Barlow, S., Boskou, D. et al. (2006) Opinion of the Scientific Panel on Food Additives, Flavourings, processing Aids and Materials in contact with Food (AFC) on a request from the Commission related to a new long-term carcinogenicity study on aspartame. *EFSA Journal,* 356. https://efsa.onlinelibrary.wiley.com/doi/epdf/10.2903/j.efsa.2006.3 56.

Arrhenius, S. (1896) On the influence of carbonic acid in the air upon the temperature of the ground. *Philosophica Magazine and Journal of Science,* 5, 237–276. https://www.rsc.org/images/Arrhenius1896_tcm18-173546.pdf.

Arrow, K.J. (1970). *Social Choice and Individual Values,* 2nd edn. Yale University Press, 10 September, 1970.

Ballotpedia (2021) Information quality act. *The Administrative State: Ballotpedia.* Referenced. https://ballotpedia.org/Information_Quality_Act. 10 December, 2021.

Barker, J. (2005) Abstraction and modeling. *Beginning Java Objects.* Apress [DOI: 10.1007/978-1-4302-0036-9_1].

Boissoneault, L. (2018) The deadly Donora smog of 1948 spurred environmental protection—But have we forgotten the lesson? *Smithsonian Magazine.*

https://www.smithsonianmag.com/history/deadly-donora-smog-1948-spurred-environmental-protection-have-we-forgotten-lesson-180970533/. 26 October, 2018.

Bowden, J. (2019) Ocasio-Cortez: 'World will end in 12 years' if climate change not addressed.' https://thehill.com/policy/energy-environment/426353-ocasio-cortez-the-world-will-end-in-12-years-if-we-dont-address 22 January, 2019. Hill.

Breedinfo.ru "Mouse wallpapers HD download,". https://duckduckgo.com/?q=mouse&atb=v257-1&iar=images&iax=images&ia=images. accessed 8 December, 2021.

Brothers, W. (1993). Demolition Man. Warner Bros. Pictures: Burbank, CA, USA. https://www.imdb.com/title/tt0106697/.

Broughel, J. & Viscusi, W.K. (2021) Death by regulation: How regulations can increase mortality risk. Mercatus Center at George Mason University. https://www.mercatus.org/system/files/broughel-life-saving-regulations-wp-mercatus-v3.pdf. accessed 10 December, 2021, Vol. 2017.

Buis, A. (2020) Getting to the heart of the (particulate) matter. NASA. https://climate.nasa.gov/news/3027/getting-to-the-heart-of-the-particulate-matter/.

Bureau of Labor Statistics (2018) "Average annual expenditures on sweets, flowers, wine, jewelry and other items in 2016." *TED: The Economics Daily.* https://www.bls.gov/opub/ted/2018/average-annual-expenditures-on-sweets-flowers-wine-jewelry-and-other-items-in-2016.htm?view_full. 14 February, 2018.

Byrd, D. (2015) Today in science: Sweden goes 1st to ban aerosol sprays. *EarthSky.* https://earthsky.org/earth/this-date-in-science-sweden-goes-first-to-ban-aerosol-sprays/. 23 January, 2015.

Cappucci, M. (2018) The scent of a storm: Here's why lightning emits a smell. *The Washington Post.* https://www.washingtonpost.com/news/capital-weather-gang/wp/2018/07/18/the-scent-of-a-storm-heres-why-lightning-emits-a-smell/. 18 July, 2018.

Chappell, B. (2017) "Smog In Western U.S. Starts Out as Pollution in Asia, Researchers Say." *NPR: The two way.* https://www.npr.org/sections/thetwo-way/2017/03/03/518323094/rise-in-smog-in-western-u-s-is-blamed-on-asias-air-pollution. 3 March, 2017.

Charney et al. (1979). *Ad Hoc Study Group on Carbon Dioxide and Climate.* Climate Research Board (2021). https://www.bnl.gov/envsci/schwartz/charney_report1979.pdf.

Chen, H., Cohen, P. & Chen, S. (2010) How big is a big odds ratio? Interpreting the magnitudes of odds ratios in epidemiological studies. *Communications in Statistics – Simulation and Computation*, 39, 860–864 [DOI: 10.1080/03610911003650383].

Cordain, L., Eaton, S.B., Sebastian, A., Mann, N., Lindeberg, S., Watkins, B.A., O'Keefe, J.H. & Brand-Miller, J. (2005) Origins and evolution of the Western diet: Health implications for the 21st century. *American Journal of Clinical Nutrition*, 81, 341–354 [DOI: 10.1093/ajcn.81.2.341] [PubMed: 15699220].

Frank, R. De Gruijl et al (1993) Wavelength dependence of skin cancer induction by ultraviolet Irradiation of albino Hairless Mice. *Journal of Cancer Research*, 53, p pp. 53-60, January, 1993.

de Gruijl, F.R. & Forbes, P.D. (1995) UV-induced skin cancer in a hairless mouse model. *BioEssays: News and Reviews in Molecular, Cellular and Developmental Biology*, 17, 651–660 [DOI: 10.1002/bies.950170711] [PubMed: 7646487].

Dorigatti, I., Okell, L., Cori, A. et al. (2020). "Report 4 — Severity of. 2019 Novel Coronavirus (nCoV). Imperial College Press: London. https://www.imperial.ac.uk/mrc-global-infectious-disease-analysis/covid-19/report-4-severity-of-covid-19/.

Ferguson, N.M., Laydon, D., Gemma Nedjati-Gilani et al. (2020). "Report 9 Impact of non-pharmaceutical interventions (NPIs) to reduce COVID-19 mortality and healthcare demand. Imperial College London COVID-19 Response Team. https://www.imperial.ac.uk/media/imperial-college/medicine/mrc-gida/2020-03-16-COVID19-Report-9.pdf [DOI: 10.25561/77482] (was).

Gasser, U. (2003). "Information Quality and the Law, or, How to Catch a Difficult Horse." *SSRN: Berkman Center Research Publication No. 2003-08*. https://papers.ssrn.com/sol3/papers.cfm?abstract_id=487945.

Glutamate.com (n.d.) History of MSG. https://glutamate.com/the-history-of-msg/. 8 December, 2021.

Hicks, J. (2010) The pursuit of sweet. *Distillation*. https://www.sciencehistory.org/distillations/the-pursuit-of-sweet.

Inst. Ramazzini (n.d.) Results of study on the carcinogenicity of the artificial sweetener aspartame. Instituto Ramazzini, accessed 10 December, 2021. https://www.ramazzini.org/comunicato/results-of-study-on-the-carcinogenicity-of-the-artificial-sweetener-aspartame/.

Ioannidis, J.P.A. (2020) (2021) Infection fatality rate of COVID-19 inferred from seroprevalence data. *Bulletin of the World Health Organization*, 99, 19–33F [DOI: 10.2471/BLT.20.265892] [PubMed: 33716331]. (was). https://www.who.int/bulletin/volumes/99/1/20-265892.pdf.

Kane, J. (2017) Here's what donuts look like all around the world. *Huffpost*, December 6, 2017. https://www.huffpost.com/entry/donuts-around-world_n_7139188.

Kararli, T.T. (1995) Comparison of the gastrointestinal anatomy, physiology, and biochemistry of humans and commonly used laboratory animals. *Biopharmaceutics and Drug Disposition*, 16, 351–380 [DOI: 10.1002/bdd.2510160502] [PubMed: 8527686]. https://onlinelibrary.wiley.com/doi/pdf/10.1002/bdd.2510160502.

Konyn, C. (2020) When will polar bears go extinct? *Earth.Org.* Carol Konyn: Earth, USA.Org, 2021.

Kuhn, T.S. (1996). *The Structure of Scientific Revolutions*, 3rd edn, December 15, 1996. University of Chicago Press.

Lewis, N. (2020) COVID-19: Updated data implies that UK modelling hugely overestimates the expected death rates from infection. Climate, Etc, accessed 9 December, 2021. https://judithcurry.com/2020/03/25/covid-19-updated-data-implies-that-uk-modelling-hugely-overestimates-the-expected-death-rates-from-infection/.

Lewis, N. & Curry, J.A. (2015) The implications for climate sensitivity of AR5 forcing and heat uptake estimates. *Climate Dynamics*, 45, 1009–1023 [DOI: 10.1007/s00382-014-2342-y].

Lewis, N. & Curry, J. (2018) The impact of recent forcing and ocean heat uptake data on estimates of climate sensitivity. *Journal of Climate.* American Meteorological Society, 31, 6051–6071. https://journals.ametsoc.org/view/journals/clim/31/15/jcli-d-17-0667.1.xml [DOI: 10.1175/JCLI-D-17-0667.1].

Martinez, J. (2021). Great Smog of London *Encyclopaedia Britannica*, November 28, 2021. https://www.britannica.com/event/Great-Smog-of-London.

Masters, N. (2011). "L.A.'s Smoggy Past, in Photos." *KCET*, March 17, 2011. https://www.kcet.org/shows/lost-la/l-a-s-smoggy-past-in-photos.

Merrill, R.A. (1988) FDA's implementation of the Delaney clause: Repudiation of congressional choice or reasoned adaptation to scientific progress? *Yale Journal on Regulation*, 5, 3. https://digitalcommons.law.yale.edu/cgi/viewcontent.cgi?article=1062&context=yjreg.

Morrison, J. (2016) Air pollution goes back way further than you think. Age of Humans, *A Smithsonian Magazine Special Report*, January 11,

2016. https://www.smithsonianmag.com/science-nature/air-pollution-goes-back-way-further-you-think-180957716/.

Mosby, I. (2009) That won-ton soup headache: The Chinese restaurant syndrome, MSG and the making of American Food, 1968–1980. *Social History of Medicine*, 22, 133–151 [DOI: 10.1093/shm/hkn098]. https://academic.oup.com/shm/article-abstract/22/1/133/1627040?redirectedFrom=fulltext.

McKitrick, R. & Christy, J. (2020) Pervasive warming bias in CMIP6 tropospheric layers. *Earth and Space Science*, 7, EA001281. https://doi, e2020 [DOI: 10.1029/2020EA001281]. (was). https://agupubs.onlinelibrary.wiley.com/doi/pdfdirect/10.1029/2020EA001281.

Nagengast, B., editor (n.d.). *Air Conditioning and Refrigeration Timeline* ASHRAE. https://www.ashrae.org/about/mission-and-vision/ashrae-industry-history/air-conditioning-and-refrigeration-timeline. accessed 10 December, 2021.

Nakićenović, N. et al. (2000): 599 pp. *Special Report on Emissions Scenarios: A Special Report of Working Group III of the Intergovernmental Panel on Climate Change.* https://sedac.ciesin.columbia.edu/ddc/sres/. Cambridge University Press: Cambridge.

Nakićenović, N. & Swart, R., editors (2000). *Emissions Scenarios. A Special Report of Working Group III of the Intergovernmental Panel on Climate Change.* Cambridge University Press: Cambridge. https://www.ipcc.ch/site/assets/uploads/2018/03/emissions_scenarios-1.pdf.

Natl Cntr for Atmospheric Research/Univ. Corporation for Atmospheric Research (2021) Protecting the ozone layer is delivering vast health benefits: Montreal Protocol will spare Americans from 443 million skin cancer cases. *ScienceDaily*, accessed 9 December, 2021. https://www.sciencedaily.com/releases/2021/10/211006134930.htm.

New York Times (1948) Donora, Pennsylvania, smog disaster. https://www.rarenewspapers.com/view/566214. 31 October, 1948.

New York Times magazine (1987) (1987). *Bittersweet History of Sugar Substitutes*, 6, 24. https://www.nytimes.com/1987/03/29/magazine/the-bittersweet-history-of-sugar-substitutes.html.

N. C. State Univ. (n.d.) The Data Quality Act: A revolution in the role of science in policy making or a can of worms. Water Resources Research Institute, accessed 12 December, 2021. https://www.thecre.com/misc/20040606_worms.htm.

Oriowo, O.M., Cullen, A.P., Chou, B.R. & Jacob, G. (2001) Sivak. Action spectrum and recovery for in vitro UV-induced cataract using whole lenses. *Iovs*. https://iovs.arvojournals.org/article.aspx?articleid=2200100. October 2001.

Paddison, L. (2020) We have 10 years left to save the world, says climate expert. *Huffpost*. https://www.huffpost.com/entry/climate-change-christiana-figueres-paris-agreement_n_5e4e6e10c5b6a7bfb4c1827c. 21 February, 2020.

Pariona, A. (2019) Countries that eat the most sugar. World Facts. https://www.worldatlas.com/articles/top-sugar-consuming-nations-in-the-world.html.

Paynter, D. & Winton, M. (ND) Transient and equilibrium climate sensitivity. GFDL. https://www.gfdl.noaa.gov/transient-and-equilibrium-climate-sensitivity/. accessed 12 December, 2021.

Pitcher, H.M. & Longstreth, J.D. (1991) Melanoma mortality and exposure to ultraviolet radiation: An empirical relationship. Environment International, 17, 7–21 [DOI: 10.1016/0160-4120(91)90333-L].

Popper, K. (1985). *Popper Selections* (edited by D. Miller). Princeton University Press: Princeton, USA, March 21, 1985).

Price, J.M., Biava, C.G., Oser, B.L., Vogin, E.E., Steinfeld, J. & Ley, H.L. (1970) Bladder tumors in rats fed cyclohexylamine or high doses of a mixture of cyclamate and saccharin. *Science*, 167, 1131–1132 [DOI: 10.1126/science.167.3921.1131] [PubMed: 5411626].

Radford, T. (2004) Do trees pollute the atmosphere? *The Guardian*, May 13, 2004. https://www.theguardian.com/science/2004/may/13/thisweeksscie ncequestions3.

Rafferty, J.P. (ND) Why is the sky blue? *Encyclopaedia Britannica*. https://www.britannica.com/story/why-is-the-sky-blue.

Roser, M., Appel, C. & Ritchie, H. (2019) Human height. *Our World in Data*. https://ourworldindata.org/human-height.

Sanderson, K. (2021) We're running out of lithium for batteries – Can we use salt instead? *New Scientist*. https://www.newscientist.com/article/mg24933180-600-were-running-out-of-lithium-for-batteries-can-we-use-salt-instead/, 249, 34–39 [DOI: 10.1016/S0262-4079(21)00111-1].

Scarlett, S. (2020) Lockdown was a waste of time and could kill more than it saved, claims Nobel Laureate scientist at Stanford University. *Mailonline*. https://www.dailymail.co.uk/news/article-8351649/Lockdown-waste-time-kill-saved-claims-Nobel-laureate.html?ns_mchannel=rss&ito=1490&ns_campaign=1490.

Schroder, S. (2018) IPCC climate report gives us 10 years to save the world. Greenpeace. https://www.greenpeace.org/aotearoa/press-release/ipcc-climate-report-gives-us-10-years-to-save-the-world/. 8 October, 2018.

Sinclair, U. (1906). *The Jungle*. Project Gutenberg. January 17, 2021. https://www.gutenberg.org/files/140/140-h/140-h.htm.

Spielmann, P.J. (1989). "U.N Predicts disaster if global warming not checked. *AP News*. https://wattsupwiththat.com/wp-content/uploads/2019/06/U.N.-Predicts-Disaster-if-Global-Warming-Not-Checked.pdf. 30 June, 1989.

St Onge, P. & Campan, G. (2020) The flawed COVID-19 model that locked down Canada. MEI. https://www.iedm.org/the-flawed-covid-19-model-that-locked-down-canada/. 4 June, 2020.

Szumilas, M. (2015) Explaining odds ratios. Canadian Academy of Child and Adolescent Psychiatry, 24, 58. https://www.ncbi.nlm.nih.gov/pmc/articles/PMC2938757/.

Taubes, G. (1995) Epidemiology Faces Its Limits. *Science*, 269, 164–169. https://science.sciencemag.org/content/269/5221/164/tab-pdf [DOI: 10.1126/science.7618077] [PubMed: 7618077].

Tengs, T.O., Adams, M.E., Pliskin, J.S., Safran, D.G., Siegel, J.E., Weinstein, M.C. & Graham, J.D. (1995) Five-hundred life-saving interventions and their cost-effectiveness. *Risk Analysis*, 15, 369–390 [DOI: 10.1111/j.1539-6924.1995.tb00330.x] [PubMed: 7604170]. https://www.gwern.net/docs/statistics/decision/1995-tengs.pdf.

United Nations IPCC (1992) "FAR Climate Change: Synthesis." IPCC. https://www.ipcc.ch/report/ar1/syr/.

United Nations IPCC (1995). *SAR Climate Change 1995: Synthesis Report.* https://www.ipcc.ch/report/ar2/syr/.

United Nations IPCC (1995). *IPCC Second Assessment, Climate Change 1995 Intergovernmental Panel on Climate Change.* https://www.ipcc.ch/site/assets/uploads/2018/06/2nd-assessment-en.pdf.

United Nations IPCC (1999). *IPCC Special Report, Aviation and the Global Atmosphere, Summary for Policymakers* (edited by J. E. Penner, D. H. Lister, D. J. Griggs, D. J. Dokken & M. McFarland) Intergovernmental Panel on Climate Change (1999). https://www.ipcc.ch/site/assets/uploads/2018/03/av-en-1.pdf.

United Nations IPCC (2000). *Emissions Scenarios* (edited by N. Nakićenović & R. Swart). Cambridge University Press: Cambridge. https://www.ipcc.ch/report/emissions-scenarios/.

United Nations IPCC (2000). *IPCC Special Report: Emissions Scenarios, Summary for Policymakers.* https://www.ipcc.ch/site/assets/uploads/2018/03/sres-en.pdf.

United Nations IPCC (2001). *TAR Climate Change 2001: Synthesis Report.* https://www.ipcc.ch/report/ar3/syr/.

United Nations IPCC (2001) *TAR Climate Change 2001: The Scientific Basis.* https://www.ipcc.ch/report/ar3/wg1/.

United Nations IPCC (2007). *AR4 Climate Change 2007: Synthesis Report.* https://www.ipcc.ch/report/ar4/syr/.

United Nations IPCC (2014). *"Climate Change 2014: Synthesis Report. Contribution of Working Groups I, II and III to the Fifth Assessment Report of the Intergovernmental Panel on Climate Change."* IPCC (edited by R. K. Pachauri & L. A. Meyer). https://www.ipcc.ch/report/ar5/syr/.

United Nations IPCC (2021). *History of the IPCC.* IPCC. https://www.ipcc.ch/about/history/. accessed 13 December, 2021.

United Nations IPCC (2021). *Glasgow Climate Change Conference. The Glasgow Climate Package—Key Outcomes from COP26 United Nations Climate Change.* https://unfccc.int/. November 2021.

USA Centers for Disease Control and Prevention (2017). *"Long-term Trends in Diabetes."* CDC's Division of Diabetes Translation. https://www.cdc.gov/diabetes/statistics/slides/long_term_trends.pdf.

USA Centers for Disease Control and Prevention (n.d.). *Leading Causes of Death 1900–1998.* https://www.cdc.gov/nchs/data/dvs/lead1900_98.pdf.

USA Centers for Disease Control and Prevention (2013). *"Interpreting Results of Case-Control Studies."* CDC. Salmonella in the Caribbean, Vol. 2013.

US Environmental Protection Agency (n.d.) EPA information quality guidelines. https://www.epa.gov/quality/epa-information-quality-guidelines. Accessed 21 December, 2021.

US Environmental Protection Agency (n.d.) *The origins of EPA.* https://www.epa.gov/history/origins-epa. Accessed 12 December, 2021.

US Environmental Protection Agency (n.d.) Clean Air Act requirements and history. https://www.epa.gov/clean-air-act-overview/clean-air-act-requirements-and-history. Accessed 12 December, 2021.

US Environmental Protection Agency (n.d.). *"EPA's Statutory Obligations under the Clean Air Act."* EPA Teleconference, accessed 12 December, 2021.

US Environmental Protection Agency. "What are volatile organic compounds (VOCs)?" https://yosemite.epa.gov/sab/sabproduct.nsf/AD54D9415E5B6468852575200060D836/$File/Legal Requirements CASAC teleconference 12-19-2008.pdf. https://www.epa.gov/indoor-air-quality-iaq/what-are-volatile-organic-compounds-vocs. Accessed 12 December, 2021.

US Environmental Protection Agency (n.d.). *What Is Ozone?* Accessed 12 December, 2021. https://www.epa.gov/ozone-pollution-and-your-patients-health/what-ozone.

US Environmental Protection Agency (n.d.). *NAAQS Table* Accessed 12 December, 2021. https://www.epa.gov/criteria-air-pollutants/naaqs-table.

US Environmental Protection Agency (1979) National primary and secondary ambient air quality standards. *Federal Register*, 8202. https://tile.loc.gov/storage-services/service/ll/fedreg/fr044/fr044028/fr044028.pdf.

US Environmental Protection Agency (2008) chapters 40 CFR Parts 50 and 58. National ambient air quality standards for ozone; final rule.

In: *Federal Register*. https://www.govinfo.gov/content/pkg/FR-2008-03-27/pdf/E8-5645.pdf.

US Environmental Protection Agency (n.d.) *Timeline of particulate matter (PM) national ambient air quality standards (NAAQS).* https://www.epa.gov/pm-pollution/timeline-particulate-matter-pm-national-ambient-air-quality-standards-naaqs. Accessed 12 December, 2021.

US Environmental Protection Agency (1971). Part II Environmental Protection Agency: National primary and secondary ambient air quality standards. *Federal Register*, 36. https://www3.epa.gov/ttn/naaqs/standards/pm/previous/1971-april30-final-36fr8186.pdf. April 1971.

US Environmental Protection Agency (2015) Environmental Protection Agency: National ambient air quality standards for ozone. *Federal Register*, 80. https://www.govinfo.gov/content/pkg/FR-2015-10-26/pdf/2015-26594.pdf.

US Environmental Protection Agency (2014). *Health Risk and Exposure Assessment for Ozone, Final Report, Executive Summary* EPA (2014). https://www3.epa.gov/ttn/naaqs/standards/ozone/data/20140829 healthreasummary.pdf.

US Environmental Protection Agency (n.d.). *NAAQS Table.* "https://www.epa.gov/criteria-air-pollutants/naaqs-table, Vol. 2.

US Environmental Protection Agency (2015) Environmental Protection Agency. 40 CFR Parts 50, 51, 52, 53, and 58." *Federal Register*, 2a, 80, no. 206. https://www.govinfo.gov/content/pkg/FR-2015-10-26/pdf/2015-26594.pdf. Oct 2015.

US Environmental Protection Agency (n.d.) Particulate matter (PM) basics. U.S. Environmental Protection Agency, accessed 12 December, 2021. https://www.epa.gov/pm-pollution/particulate-matter-pm-basics.

US Environmental Protection Agency (1971). Part II: Environmental Protection Agency (1971) National ambient air Quality. *Federal*

Register, 36.
https://www3.epa.gov/ttn/naaqs/standards/pm/previous/1971-april30-final-36fr8186.pdf.

US Environmental Protection Agency (1987) Environmental Protection Agency. Revisions to the national ambient air quality standards for particulate matter. *Federal Register*, 52, 126.
https://www3.epa.gov/ttn/naaqs/standards/pm/previous/pm-1987-final-52fr24634.pdf. July 1987.

US Environmental Protection Agency (n.d.). *Stratospheric Ozone Protection: 30 Years of Progress and Achievements* EPA.
https://www.epa.gov/ozone-layer-protection/stratospheric-ozone-protection-30-years-progress-and-achievements-0. accessed 12 December, 2021.

US Environmental Protection Agency (2020) *"Updating the Atmospheric and Health Effects Framework Model: Stratospheric Ozone Protection and Human Health Benefits."* EPA, publication 430R20005.
https://www.epa.gov/sites/default/files/2020-04/documents/2020_ahef_report.pdf. May 2020.

US Environmental Protection Agency (2015). *Updating Ozone Calculations and Emissions Profiles for Use in the Atmospheric and Health Effects Framework Model* Stratospheric Protection Div. of Office of Air and Radiation & E.P.A. (2015).
https://www.epa.gov/sites/default/files/2015-11/documents/ahef_2015_update_report-final_508.pdf.

US Environmental Protection Agency (2013). Part II Environmental Protection Agency, national ambient air quality standards for particulate matter, final rule. *Federal Register*, 78.
https://www.govinfo.gov/content/pkg/FR-2013-01-15/pdf/2012-30946.pdf. January 2013.

US Environmental Protection Agency (2020) Environmental Protection Agency, review of the national ambient air quality standards for particulate matter, proposed action. *Federal Register*, 85.
https://www.govinfo.gov/content/pkg/FR-2020-04-30/pdf/2020-08143.pdf. April 2020.

US Environmental Protection Agency (n.d.). *Ozone-Depleting Substances* EPA. https://www.epa.gov/ozone-layer-protection/ozone-depleting-substances. accessed 12 December, 2021.

USA Food and Drug Agency (2019) *Part 1. The 1906 Food and Drugs Act and Its Enforcement* FDA. https://www.fda.gov/about-fda/fdas-evolving-regulatory-powers/part-i-1906-food-and-drugs-act-and-its-enforcement. accessed 12 December, 2021.

United States geologic survey (n.d.). *Office of Science Quality and Integrity.* "USGS Information Quality Guidelines." https://www.usgs.gov/about/organization/science-support/office-science-quality-and-integrity/information-quality-guidelines Accessed 12 December, 2021.

US Government Accountability Office (2006) "Information Quality Act: Expanded Oversight and Clearer Guidance by the Office of Management and Budget Could Improve Agencies' Implementation of the Act." U.S. Government Accountability Office. https://www.gao.gov/products/gao-06-765. 18 September, 2006, pp. GAO-06–GAO-765.

US Government Accountability Office (1981) *"Regulation of Cancer-Causing Food Additives—Time for a Change."* U.S. government Accountability Office, HRD-82-3. https://www.gao.gov/products/HRD-82-3. 11 December, 1981.

United States House of Representatives (1906). "The Pure Food and Drug Act: June 23, 1906." *History.* Archives: USA House of Representatives. https://history.house.gov/Historical-Highlights/1901-1950/Pure-Food-and-Drug-Act/. accessed 12 December, 2021, Art. &.

United States National Institutes of Health. *"Overweight and Obesity Statistics: Trends in Overweight and Obesity in Adults and Youth in the US."* NIH: NIDDK, accessed December 12, 2021. https://www.niddk.nih.gov/health-information/health-statistics/overweight-obesity#trends.

USA Office of the Federal Register (1936). National Archives and
Records Administration. Accessed 12 December, 2021.

USA Office of the Federal Register (2002). Part IX Office of
Management and Budget guidelines for ensuring and maximizing the
Quality, objectivity, utility, and integrity of information disseminated
by federal agencies [Notice]; Republication. *Federal Register*, 67.
https://obamawhitehouse.archives.gov/sites/default/files/omb/ass
ets/omb/fedreg/reproducible2.pdf. February 2002.

United States National Oceanic and Atmospheric Administration (n.d.)
Q2: How is ozone formed in the atmosphere? Questions, 20, 2010
Update, accessed 12 December, 2021.
https://csl.noaa.gov/assessments/ozone/2010/twentyquestions/Q2
.pdf

United States National Archives (2016). *"Executive Orders, Executive Order
12291—Federal Regulation."* https://www.archives.gov/federal-
register/codification/executive-order/12291.html accessed 12
December, 2021. National Archives.

United States National Archives (1993). "Executive Order 12866,
Regulatory Planning and Review." *Federal Register*, 58.
https://www.archives.gov/files/federal-register/executive-
orders/pdf/12866.pdf.

Vachon, D. (2005) Part 1: Doctor John Snow blames water pollution for
cholera epidemic. In: *UCLA Old News*, Vol. 16 (May and June 2005).
www.ph.ucla.edu/epi/snow/fatherofepidemiology.html, pp. 8–10.

Vought, R.T. (2019). *Memorandum for the Heads of Executive Departments and
Agencies: Improving Implementation of the Information Quality Act.*
https://www.whitehouse.gov/wp-content/uploads/2019/04/M-19-
15.pdf.

Walker, P.G.T., Wittaker, C., Watson, O. et al. (2020). Imperial College
Press: London. MRC Centre for Global Infectious Disease Analysis.
https://www.imperial.ac.uk/mrc-global-infectious-disease-
analysis/covid-19/report-12-global-impact-covid-19/.

Webster, I. (ND) "$500 in Alioth finance.
https://www.in2013dollars.com/us/inflation/1906?amount=500.
accessed 9 December, 2021, Vol. 1906 → 2021 | Inflation
Calculator." *Official Inflation Data.*

Weisse, A.B. (2012) Self-experimentation and its role in medical research.
Texas Heart Institute Journal, 39, 51–54.
https://www.ncbi.nlm.nih.gov/pmc/articles/PMC3298919/
[PubMed: 22412227].

West, S.K. PhD, Duncan, D.D. PhD, Muñoz, B. MSc, Rubin, G.S. PhD,
Fried, L.P. MD MPH, Bandeen-Roche, K. PhD & Schein, O.D. MD
MPH (1998) Sunlight exposure and risk of lens opacities in a
population-based study. JAMA, 280 [DOI: 10.1001/jama.280.8.714].

West, S.K., Longstreth, J.D., Munoz, B.E., Pitcher, H.M. & Duncan,
D.D. (2005) Model of risk of cortical cataract in the US population
with exposure to increased ultraviolet radiation due to stratospheric
ozone depletion. *American Journal of Epidemiology*, 162, 1080–1088
[DOI: 10.1093/aje/kwi329] [PubMed: 16251390].

Wildavsky, A. (1980) Richer is safer. *National Affairs*, Summer 1980.
https://www.nationalaffairs.com/public_interest/detail/richer-is-
safer.

World atlas (n.d.). *Countries That Eat. the Most Sugar.*
https://www.worldatlas.com/articles/top-sugar-consuming-nations-
in-the-world.html.

World Climate Research Program (n.d.) WCRP coupled model
intercomparison project (CMIP). WCRP. https://www.wcrp-
climate.org/wgcm-cmip. accessed 10 December, 2021.

Zanfirescu, A., Ungurianu, A., Tsatsakis, A.M., Nițulescu, G.M.,
Kouretas, D., Veskoukis, A., Tsoukalas, D., Engin, A.B., Aschner,
M. & Margină, D. (2019) A review of the alleged health hazards of
monosodium glutamate. *Comprehensive Reviews in Food Science and Food
Safety*, 18, 1111–1134 [DOI: 10.1111/1541-4337.12448] [PubMed:
31920467].

Index

Imperial College, 168, 170, 171, 172, 193, 205
infant mortality, 25
inflation, 23, 205
influenza, 25, 168
intangible models, 11
Ira Remsen, 28

J

Jacob G. Sivak, 119
Jacquie Barker, 17
James Hansen, 130
Janice D. Longstreth, 105, 117
Jean-Baptiste Fourier, 130
Jesse Hicks, 28
Jimmy Carter, 4, 23
Joe Biden, 4
Johann Baptista van Helmolt, 130
John Bailar, 117
John Bowden, 155
John Christy, 162
John D. Graham, 181
John Snow, 56, 205
John Tyndall, 130
Johns Hopkins University, 28
Jonathan Swift, 7
Joseph Black, 130
Judith Curry, 136

K

Karl Popper, 6, 92
Katharine Sanderson, 11
Kelvinator, 96
Kikunae Ikeda, 30
Kombu, 30

L

La Brea Tar Pits, 65
lactose, 26
landfills, 8
landscaping models, 15
Laura Paddison, 155
law of subtraction, 18
lead, 7, 37, 63, 134, 148, 149, 185
leukaemias, 40
liberty, 2, 94, 182
Lithium, 8, 11
Liver Problems, 42
logic models, 15
Lorraine Boissoneault, 58
lumen, 50
lymphomas, 39, 40, 116

M

Mad Cow Disease (BSE), 1
Malthusian model, 6
maltose, 26
Measles, 1
Michelangelo, 20
Mickey Mouse, 19
Minamata Bay, 56
Minamata Disease, 56
model of an owl, 20
Mononucleosis, 1
monosodium glutamate, 29, 30, 206
Montreal Protocol, 97, 98, 99, 101, 196
mouse, 19, 20, 22, 45, 47, 49, 50, 103, 109, 112, 113, 192, 193
mucosa, 49
mutant wolves of Chernobyl, 9

About the Author

KENNETH P. GREEN, D.Env.

Growing up in smoggy Los Angeles, Ken developed an interest in air pollution early, when at the tender age of 13, he collapsed with an asthma attack while running a lap around his middle-school-running track. Ken would go on from that experience to study general biology, molecular biology, and environmental science and engineering, with a goal toward remediating the environmental problems he encountered so memorably in his youth.

But over the course of his academic career, Ken observed that bad environmental, health, and safety regulations seemed to vastly outnumber good ones. Many of the highest profile environmental regulations Ken studied seemed to be grounded in shoddy science; were coercive and indifferent to individual rights; often involved cronyism and expansionist government; and, adding insult to injury, were often inefficient or entirely ineffective at remediating some actual environmental, health, or safety harm.

Ken's academic career progressed through a Bachelor of Science degree in general biology, through a Master of Science degree in molecular genetics, and then onto a doctorate in Environmental Science and Engineering at UCLA (1994). After college Ken went to work studying risk and regulation in the areas of Environmental, Health, and Safety in the United States and Canada, at a series of think tanks including the American Enterprise Institute, the Reason Foundation, the Pacific Research Institute, the Texas Public Policy Foundation, the Georgia Public Policy Foundation, the Fraser Institute (Canada), and the Frontier Centre for Public Policy Research (Canada).

Ken has published well over 800 essays and articles on public policy and regulations through a variety of think tanks, and in newspapers, technical and trade journals, and innumerable internet-based publications across North America.

Having lived in California, Texas, Virginia, British Columbia, and Alberta, Ken now lives in the Mojave Desert in Southern Nevada with his wife of 25 years by his side.

Books by the Author

Global Warming: Understanding the Debate

Berkeley Heights, NJ: Enslow Publishers, 2002.
ISBN 978-0766016910.

A textbook for middle-school students that introduces the theory of global warming and the evidence of its existence and examines possible causes and effects of the phenomenon.

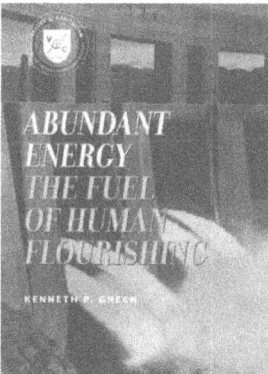

Abundant Energy: The Fuel of Human Flourishing

Washington, D.C.: AEI Press, publisher for the American Enterprise Institute, 2011.
ISBN 978-0844772042.

Abundant Energy is a concise guide to the role of energy in modern society and the ways energy policy affects life in the United States and around the world. An introduction to an array of key energy concepts, including affordability, abundance, reliability, security, independence, and environmental impacts.

www.ingramcontent.com/pod-product-compliance
Lightning Source LLC
Chambersburg PA
CBHW072124270326
41931CB00010B/1665

* 9 7 8 1 7 7 8 0 4 1 3 0 3 *